Betrayal

BETRAYAL

A Report on Violence

Toward Children in

Today's World

Edited by
Caroline Moorehead

D O U B L E D A Y

New York   London   Toronto   Sydney   Auckland

PUBLISHED BY DOUBLEDAY

a division of Bantam Doubleday Dell Publishing Group, Inc.
666 Fifth Avenue, New York, New York 10103

DOUBLEDAY and the portrayal of an anchor
with a dolphin are trademarks of Doubleday,
a division of Bantam Doubleday Dell
Publishing Group, Inc.

Library of Congress Cataloging-in-Publication Data
Betrayal: a report on violence toward children in today's world /
edited by Caroline Moorehead.—1st ed. in the United States of
America.
p.   cm.
1. Abused children.   2. Socially handicapped children.
I. Moorehead, Caroline.
HV713.B48   1990   89-28152
362.7′6—dc20   CIP
ISBN 0-385-41097-2

Printed in the United States of America

April 1990

First Edition in the United States of America

BVG

Many people helped with this book. On behalf of the authors I would like to express gratitude to the children, families, individuals and organizations who helped; unfortunately, there are too many to name.

The Anti-Slavery Society has been involved with abuse of children since the early 1970s, and this book is a contribution to the Society's program on children's rights. I am extremely grateful to Peter Davies, Peter Lowes and Maureen Alexander Sinclair for their help.

CAROLINE MOOREHEAD

Contributors

Sergei Boissier interned with the Comprehensive AIDS Family Center at the Albert Einstein College of Medicine in the Bronx, New York, and has written a novel on AIDS.

Nora Boustany is Lebanese, and a staff correspondent for the *Washington Post*. She won the George Polk Award for her coverage of Beirut.

Anne Chisholm is a British writer and free-lance journalist. Her books include a biography of Nancy Cunard and *Faces of Hiroshima*.

Andrea di Robilant is an Italian journalist, the founder of a Milan magazine called *02;* he spent the early 1980s as a roving correspondent in Latin America.

Cameron Forbes is the Southeast Asia correspondent for the *Melbourne Age* and is based in the Far East.

Isabel Hilton is the South and Central American correspondent for the *Independent,* and former China and Latin America specialist for the *Sunday Times*. She is the coauthor, with Neal Ascherson, of a book on Klaus Barbie.

Sarah Hobson is a writer and film producer whose books include *Family Web: A Story of India* and *Through Iran in Disguise.*

Caroline Moorehead is a writer and free-lance journalist. She has written on human rights for *The Times* (London) and now contributes a regular human rights column to the *Independent.* Her books include biographies of Freya Stark and Sidney Bernstein, and *Troublesome People: Enemies of War 1916–1986.*

Jonathan Randal is a roving correspondent for the *Washington Post* and has covered the Middle East for many years. He is the author of *The Tragedy of Lebanon.*

John Shaw now works for the United Nations Environment Program in Nairobi. Former correspondent for *Time* magazine and political editor of the *Sydney Morning Herald,* he has written books on Australia and the Soviet Union.

Tim Tate is a free-lance journalist and television producer who has worked for the *London Sunday Times* and, since 1982, carried out investigations for ITV's "Cook Report."

Contents

Introduction

As we move into the twenty-first century there is much to reflect upon. We look around us and see that the promises of yesterday have not come to pass. People still live in abject poverty, people are still hungry, people still struggle to survive. And among these people we see the children, always the children: their enlarged bellies, their sad eyes, their wise old faces that show the suffering, all the suffering they have endured in their short years.

They are children living in tents in the desert, in homes that have become bombed-out shells ravaged by years of war, in the streets, subway stations, rice fields. Children living in decaying orphanages, overcrowded hospitals and abandoned tenements.

During the past years I have traveled the world and seen these children, so many of them, leading lives of tremendous pain. And yet they retain their sweetness and their patience; their eyes reflect a deeper understanding, an awareness that this is not as it should be. They deserve better—a life of security and opportunity and freedom and peace of mind. Most of them have never experienced such a life, but they sense its absence. The eyes say it all.

In these pages you will find such children, and see them as I have seen them. Caroline Moorehead has gathered together the reports of abused children throughout the world: in Lebanon, where war has torn apart the fabric of their lives; in India, where they starve and beg and sleep in prison because there is simply no room for them elsewhere; in Argentina, where they have disappeared and sometimes been found again; in Great Britain, where, like their American counterparts, they are sexually abused at an alarming rate; in Brazil, where they sell their bodies but somehow manage to preserve their souls; and New York City, where they are slowly, desperately dying of AIDS.

And ironically, as we move into another century, perhaps that is what ultimately unites us as a world: the fact that, no matter how prosperous the nation, how developed, all share the plight and embarrassment of having so many suffering children. We are united by our neglect, our abuse, our absence of love. Have we forgotten about the children, and thus forsaken the next generation?

UNICEF is committed to these children; our mission is to bring their condition to the world's attention. We are determined not to forget about them, not to let them disappear into abstract political discourse. By bringing them to life in words, our hope is to keep them alive in reality.

I hope these reports will inspire people to think about the children whom in a way each of us can rescue. I hope we will learn to love not only the faces that we see and know but also the ones we will never see or know.

UNICEF is proud to support this wonderful book. Perhaps the fact that it has been written suggests that we are at last beginning to open our eyes to the plight of these beautiful children, before it is too late.

AUDREY HEPBURN

Betrayal

Preface

There are said to be three hundred and forty-one million children under sixteen today in China alone. Very roughly, they represent a quarter of the world's child population. By the year 2000 half of the world will be under twenty-five, and more than half of those under the age of sixteen. In developing countries three out of every four people will be children. There is every practical reason, therefore, in addition to the many obvious moral ones, why the needs, views and rights of children must be taken seriously. There are so very many of them.

At the beginning of the 1990s the position of children is not good. Leaving aside poverty, which accounts for most hunger, illness and death, but which afflicts adults as well, children are currently at work, at war, in prison and living on the streets; they are exploited, undereducated, bullied, malnourished, abused and without homes in every country of the world. Take twelve-year-old Zeinab Mohamed Darwish, blown up by a car bomb in Beirut in 1985, who watched her sisters burn to death and now lives in such pain from shrapnel in her brain that she can never be left alone. Or Aleandro, who has been living on the streets of São Paulo, Brazil, since he escaped from a state reformatory at the age of seven. Or Adam, sold by his destitute parents in the Philippines to a West German pedophile.

The most conservative estimate, that of the International Labor Organization (ILO), puts full-time child workers under the age of fifteen at fifty-two million (the population of the United Kingdom). The true figure is certainly three to four times as high. Child labor is cheap. Children are malleable. They have no rights and no power.

International law forbids the active participation in war of children under the age of fifteen. Yet child soldiers are to be found in Beirut, Cambodia, Ulster, Nicaragua, Iran and Peru. Two and a half thousand boy soldiers died in a single counteroffensive launched by Iran against Iraq in the spring of 1982. Children are currently caught up in fighting in some fifty countries; and along with women they make up three quarters of all the deaths and casualties of modern war.

There is a widespread and comforting assumption that children born in the civilized twentieth century are seldom treated with physical brutality. Yet in West Germany a thousand children are reported to have died last year from blows dealt them by their parents. In Britain more than seven thousand children, many of them small babies, are so badly hurt each year by their mothers and fathers that they need doctors. One British child in ten is now said to be abused sexually.

In Bangkok thirty thousand children under the age of sixteen work as prostitutes. Some are as young as six. In the United States people talk of three hundred thousand boy prostitutes alone.

Street children—those who live, work and die on the streets of the major cities—were not much heard about until the late 1970s. They are now said to number a hundred million and, unless something can be done to halt the drift, that number will have doubled by the end of the century. A very great number are to be found in Brazil, Colombia and Mexico, but twenty thousand roam the streets of New York.

No one knows just how many children are held in jail at any one time, whether for crimes they have committed or because there is nowhere else to keep a homeless and hungry child. What is known, on the other hand, is that in the six months following the imposition of the emergency powers in South Africa in June 1986, eight and a half thousand children were put in prison. While there, some were tortured.

In 1988 over twelve million people were believed to be refugees from their native lands, drifting over the borders of the African and Asian countries because of drought, famine and war. Most of them were women and children.

To take just one corner of the world: fifteen million children under five live in the countries that border on South Africa. Floods, drought, war and economic chaos have disrupted the normal distribution of food and medicine; water supplies, health centers and schools have all been destroyed. In Mozambique three hundred thousand children who should be in primary school are not, because their schools no longer exist. There and in Angola, children who should and could be alive die at the rate of one every four minutes.

These are just some statistics of child casualties. They do

not take into account all those who, caught up in civil wars, are arrested, beaten up, then killed or made to "disappear"; those who are kidnapped to be sold into prostitution or to supply the Western need for babies for adoption; those whose lives are ruined by drugs; those who are maimed by pollution and injured in industrial accidents. Their short lives are seldom recorded.

The idea of a child as a different and special category of person, with requirements essentially different from those of adults, is a modern one. In Britain, until the fourteenth century, when continuous plagues drove all fit people to work on the land, a distinction between children and adults scarcely existed at all. In medieval Europe children were regarded as adults in miniature: small, immature grown-ups who needed time—but not very much of it—in which to grow, both physically and mentally. Today childhood is still very short in developing countries, where children play a critical part in agriculture.

In the Western world it was only in the nineteenth century that a child was at last perceived as a separate kind of creature, with quite separate expectations and desires. This vision was frequently a romantic one, with much talk of innocence, weakness and a need for guidance. Control and the task of steering a child in the right direction, toward an upright adulthood, were confided to fathers. The state offered nothing in the way of protection: fathers were left to rear their children, brutally or peaceably, as they saw fit.

With industrialization, which called for an enormous, growing and, above all, compliant work force, the state began, for the first time, to interfere. As workers and "apprentices," children were separated from their parents. In Britain the intensity of child labor increased dramatically between 1780 and 1840. More and more children, "almost universally ill-looking, small, sickly, barefoot and ill-clad," as one Manchester doctor, Turner Thackrah, described them, went off to work down the mines, in the mills or as assistants to chimney sweeps—the "climbing-boys" later championed by the novelist Charles Kingsley. Parental control weakened. On the one hand, children were mercilessly exploited by employers; on the other, they were seen increasingly by reformers to be in need of moral and religious welfare.

The nineteenth century saw the beginnings of laws aimed specifically at children—the abolition of night work for children in 1802, the prohibition of children under nine from working in mills in 1819—and the setting up of a separate system of justice for the young. Criminal and vagrant children were considered to be morally depraved, and their parents deemed solely responsible. Punishment and protection were linked: the children were removed from the evil influence of home and incarcerated in special institutions.

This notion, that a child in trouble was a child in need of care, was to underpin all early thinking on children and their rights. Never was this theme better championed than by Eglantyne Jebb, a frail but exceedingly tenacious young woman born to a large Victorian family in Shropshire in 1876. At the turn of the century Eglantyne Jebb completed her degree at Oxford and took up teaching. Her brother-in-law (the Liberal Member of Parliament Charles Buxton) was interested, at that time, in the war and widespread famine in the Balkans. Through him, Eglantyne became attracted to the idea of working for the relief of starving and homeless civilians. "All wars," she was to write, "are waged against children."

As the First World War ended and the full extent of the effects of the Allied blockade on the people of Europe became known, Eglantyne Jebb joined a Fight the Famine Council, together with such figures as Ramsay MacDonald, Gilbert Murray and Leonard Woolf, to raise money for the relief of children. An early supporter of the Council was George Bernard Shaw. Attacked for being pro-German, he replied: "I have no enemies under seven." The idea that there was no such thing as an "enemy" child provided impetus for a movement for children that later became the Save the Children Fund.

In the following years Eglantyne Jebb broadened her interests. What was needed, it seemed to her, was something far more permanent to govern the lives of children, some sort of manifesto or statement that would set out a number of principles according to which children should be treated. The League of Nations had come into existence in 1919. Eglantyne Jebb spent the remaining years of her short life in Geneva, near its headquarters, lobbying for an international agreement. Her diligence paid off. A Declaration of Geneva was adopted in 1924. Written in the language of its time, and redolent of the spirit of nurturing that colored all Victorian thinking on the subject, the Declaration spoke of giving a child the means "needed for its normal development, both materially and spiritually," of feeding it when it was hungry, "reclaiming" it when it erred, and succoring it when it was orphaned.

Up until that moment, apart from some crusading work by the ILO, the only specific attention paid to children on an international scale had been to pass limited agreements on trafficking and prostitution. All other measures to control their lives had been left to national legislation. The Declaration of Geneva did not, of course, contain any policing powers nor was it binding. But its ten points did provide a guide for countries now wanted to consider their children in a new way, and who a secretariat was set up to gather information. In the next few years reports appeared in rapid succession: on blindness in children, on the juvenile courts, on adoption and illegitimacy.

In 1959, long after the League of Nations had become the United Nations, a heavily revised second document concerning children was adopted by member nations. This time it included considerably more contentious issues, like the right to a name and a nationality, as well as the right to enjoy all other rights "regardless of race, color, sex, religion, national or social origin." Like its predecessors, the UN Declaration of the Rights of the Child was neither binding nor enforceable. Many of its concerns centered around well-meaning principles—like a child's right to be loved—which are impossible to guarantee. But it did produce a number of essential rules of conduct and it did make it probable that the time would come when children's rights demanded a far stronger commitment.

1979 was the International Year of the Child. Its designation was largely the work of one man, an industrious Belgian pastor, Canon Joseph Moerman, the general secretary of the International Children's Catholic Bureau, who had once been appalled to hear a minister at a conference in Africa say of children: "As they have no right to vote, we have no interest in them." During the 1970s, observing the way in which neither International Women's Year nor International Population Year had ever made much mention of children, he suggested to the UN that a special year be allocated to them. In the event, despite a growing feeling that "international year fatigue" had gripped most member countries, there was very little actual opposition. What was more, Moerman's plan tied in very neatly with a new proposal currently doing the rounds in Geneva and New York: that of a new Convention on Children, one that would bring the 1959 Declaration of the Rights of the Child up to date and give it some sort of proper powers of enforcement. The Polish government, whose original idea this had been, hoped for a while that the Convention might be hurried through in time to crown the International Year of the Child. There was no time. Their draft elicited far more criticism than acceptance. But 1979 did see the setting up of the Working Group to discuss the Convention, and by now Poland had come up with a modified and fuller version of its first text, which has been used ever since as the basis of the Convention document.

The Poles had indeed been overhopeful. The Convention on the Rights of the Child was intended to replace the eighty-odd bits of international legislation aimed at, or including reference to, children that had trickled out in the last sixty years. It was hoped that it would update the 1959 Declaration, introduce new ideas more relevant to the 1980s and lay down guidelines for all future thinking on children and their entitlements. But it has taken almost exactly a decade to complete. The time seems impossibly long, yet the full committee has met for only one week a year, or four hundred working hours. In that extremely brief period delegates from Latin America, the Eastern bloc, Europe, Africa and Australasia have debated work and culture, nationality and discrimination, freedom of expression and privacy, prostitution, war and torture—fifty-four articles in all, and not one of them an easy subject—making it one of the longest international conventions in existence. Given that in many countries "children" were scarcely considered to exist at all, much time has been spent discussing the precise definition of a child. Is a two-year-old a child in the same way that a sixteen-year-old is? What is a satisfactory age for childhood to end? Sixteen? Eighteen? In the closing meetings the United Kingdom and the United States were still insisting on their right to be able to recruit soldiers under eighteen.

The Convention might well, in fact, have taken considerably longer. In the early 1980s very little progress of any kind was made. For all the hard work of individual organizations like the Defense of Children International, a pressure group born during 1979 to keep alive the idea that children have rights, there was very little active enthusiasm, particularly among the UN agencies whose backing was crucial. This was especially true of UNICEF, the child agency founded in 1946 to take over where the UN Relief and Rehabilitation Administration left off in bringing extra calories to the malnourished children of the postwar years and to concern itself with "child health purposes generally." UNICEF, like all UN agencies, depends upon the political will of its members. It is justifiably proud of the job it has done in reducing deaths from typhoid, measles, whooping cough and polio. But health is a safe subject, while children's rights are not.

In 1983, however, under pressure from a few members of staff inside the organization, from the executive director, James Grant, and from outside child groups, UNICEF suddenly swung around. That same year an "NGO ad hoc group on the drafting of the Convention," consisting of thirty of the more deeply involved members, threw their full energy behind the Convention. There has been no pause in the work since then. At the time this book goes to print, the Convention will have reached the last stage on its way through the UN system. The final draft is now before the General Assembly for consideration. It is expected that the Convention will be adopted on the tenth anniversary of the International Year of the Child, the thirtieth of the 1959 Declaration. Thereafter, it will be ready for ratification. And only then will it become apparent whether or not there are in fact the twenty ratifying member states needed for a quorum, plus the many others prepared to sign, ratify and prove themselves willing to accept a document concerning children far more wide-reaching and far more radical than any other that has gone before. It is widely assumed that there will be.

The Convention itself, it is agreed, is a good document. The more liberal delegates have won many of their battles over questions such as nationality, abuse, torture and imprisonment. And even if others, like age and whether life begins at birth or conception, have been glossed over, the points have nonetheless been made. Such a convention was needed because it had become obvious that the position of the child, vis-à-vis its parents and the state, needed reformulating, and also that in the modern world increasing numbers of parents are no longer able or willing to feed, house and protect their own children. The Convention reflects these issues. For the first time it has been made clear that a child has a right to have a say in its own life, and that its psychological wants are no less important than its material ones. Early agreements about children were about duties. The Convention is about rights.

Conventions are awkward and peculiar things. Viewed in some lights, they can appear futile. What has the Convention against Torture and Other Cruel, Inhuman or Degrading Treatment or Punishment, adopted on Human Rights Day, 1984, achieved when it is still widely accepted that torture is practiced in at least seventy countries? Or when it is still possible for the Deputy Prime Minister of Kuwait to announce, as he did in 1986, that *falaga*, the beating of the soles of the feet, would continue in Kuwaiti jails for as long as the security of the country required it? An ILO Convention on Child Labor was brought in during 1973. Why are an estimated seventy to one hundred million children under fourteen still at work? What enforcing powers the new Convention will possess—a Committee on the Rights of the Child to discuss reports submitted by states—will hardly intimidate those states that wish to defy them. There are, however, ambitious plans for the Convention: to put it out in language that children themselves can understand; to distribute it extremely widely; to encourage governments whose legislation is already in line to ask for what help they need in implementing it. The success of the Convention ultimately rests upon the conviction of governments and upon the drive and energy of national and international children's organizations.

The Convention matters. It matters because it sorts out all existing, confused and often contradictory legislation on children and sets out new and binding rules. It matters because it enters new areas not previously dealt with and because it has set up an unprecedented new partnership between nongovernmental organizations and UN agencies. It matters because it reiterates the most crucial point of all: that certain fundamental values are universal and inalienable, even if the world is made up of greatly differing social, economic, cultural and political realities, and even if it is currently in a state of recession and economic mayhem. And, most of all, it matters because it exists, because never again will it be possible for anyone, anywhere, to draft a law or consider a child's rights without at least some reference to the words of the Convention.

What this book set out to do was not to undermine the Convention by showing the enormity of the problems it seeks to address, but to provide a picture, some clearer images behind the bald statistics, that ordinary people can absorb. Not every "difficult circumstance," as UNICEF documents describe them, has been explored. There is, for instance, no chapter on children and drugs, and nothing about handicap. Nor is there anything about the quarter of a million children who, even in times of record harvests, die each week from the effects of prolonged malnutrition. But most of the other main issues— war, homelessness, work, imprisonment, abuse—have been covered. The writers are not specialists but reporters who went to see for themselves what each one of these states actually means to a child who experiences it. They looked for real children, not statistics. The locations—street children in Brazil, refugee children in Somalia—are often fortuitous. The entire book could possibly have been written in any one of a number of single countries. But that would have been to defeat its aim, which was to show that children are losing out everywhere, in every continent and every country, and that what they suffer from is seldom solely a product of underdevelopment.

This book is not for experts. It is for people who want to know what it is like to be a child in the modern world.

CAROLINE MOOREHEAD

1

Street Children

in Brazil

Andrea di Robilant

"Come with me," he said. The rain had stopped and a warm October sun shone over Cathedral Square in São Paulo. Aleandro stepped out of the church portal that had sheltered us during the storm. Below, the square glistened and filled with possibilities. Fruit vendors opened their carts and laid out mangoes and oranges. Evangelical preachers summoned small crowds of believers. Shoeshine boys, palm readers and jugglers set out their paraphernalia. Prostitutes came back one by one and lined up against the granite wall of the cathedral.

Aleandro slapped his crinkled feet in the puddles and took an occasional sniff of "Cosacola" glue from a plastic bag which he kept under his shirt sleeve to avoid being caught by the police. He was twelve years old and had grown up in FEBEM (Fundacão Educacional pelo Bem Estar do Menor), the state reformatory. He had escaped at the age of seven and had lived on the square ever since. He did not know who his parents were and whether he had any brothers or sisters. "But I have my friends here on the square," he said. As the potency of the glue waned, the sniffs became more frequent until he brazenly yanked the bag from under his shirt sleeve and buried his face in it.

We reached the entrance of the subway station. Three girls staggered up to him, sniffing on their own glue bags. There was a woman in the ladies' room, they said, and she was wearing a Champion wristwatch. Champions were the rage in São Paulo—large billboards advertising them were visible all over town. The information jolted Aleandro out of his stupor and the four children scrambled into the ladies' room. A shriek resonated in the subway station and within seconds they came rushing out. Aleandro shook his head. "I didn't grab it right," he said, "and the woman was screaming her head off. I'm no good at stealing when I take glue. Better to wander around the square and enjoy the show."

A group of children had gathered at the edge of the fountain. They swapped stories and took sniffs of Cosacola, swaying gently in the late afternoon glow. The incident concerning the woman in the ladies' room was already making the rounds. Aleandro joined in, smiling at his own ineptitude. He repeated the story several times over. The children laughed and stuffed their faces in glue bags. When the laughter died down, they took off their ragged clothes and jumped in the brown water of the fountain. Aleandro came out shivering, pressing his arms against his skinny chest. He took his plastic bag and carefully picked out the clumps of hardened glue. Then he lay down on the pavement, which was filthy but still warm from the sun. One by one the other children stepped out of the fountain and stretched on the ground. Their shiny wet bodies were all lined up now, like strange amphibian creatures resting in the stillness of dusk.

A crowd of onlookers stared at them with that fascination that sets in at the sight of wild animals. Since the return of a democratic regime in 1985, street children have become another attraction on the square. During the dictatorship any pretext was sufficient to round them up, beat them and lock them up in FEBEM. There seemed to be a maniacal determination on the part of the authorities to "clean the place up." And the public generally went along with it. A social worker told me how he had gone to lay a wreath where a child had been clubbed to death after stealing a necklace, and was nearly assaulted by the crowd himself.

The civilian government has been far more sensitive. It has inaugurated a relief center for street children two blocks away from Cathedral Square and opened several shelters in the neighborhood. The military police are decidedly less violent in handling the children now and the public, in turn, has become more tolerant of them. Paulo Collen, a former street child who has written an autobiography *(Mais Que a Realidade,* Cortez Editora, 1987) felt that the days of persecution were over and threw his book-launching party right in the middle of the square. He told me: "We gave out bags of popcorn to the kids. They were all there. It was like coming home."

The new regime has made it possible to confront the problem of the street children, but it is a long way from solving it. On the contrary, the number of children living in the streets of São Paulo has never grown so fast. When Governor Orestes Quercia took office in 1987 he established a special secretariat for minors. Its first task was to work out how extensive the problem was. It would have been impossible to count the actual number of children living on the street, so the secretariat decided to estimate the total number of "needy minors"—extremely deprived children who either lived on the street or who lived in such appalling conditions that they were inexorably bound for it. The estimate included all children coming from families of six or more, living on an income of one or two minimum wages (the minimum monthly wage in Brazil hovers around the equivalent of forty-five dollars and is one of the lowest in the world). The final figure was startling: eight million children in the state of São Paulo, out of a population of thirty-two million.

At the beginning of this century São Paulo, then only the fourteenth largest city in Brazil, was a quiet rural center with a population of one hundred thousand. After the crash of 1929 the price of coffee collapsed and the basis of the local economy crumbled. The wealthy *paulista* landowners shifted their resources to industry. What followed was a massive, convulsive development that transformed São Paulo into the most prosperous Brazilian city. The rapid industrialization generated large-scale migrations from the countryside that continue today. São Paulo now has a population of fifteen million and the highest rate of population growth in the world. Economic development, though, was not accompanied by adequate workers' legislation, and the most basic welfare, health and educational needs of the immigrants have never been provided for. Skyscrapers have proliferated as the shanty towns, known as *favelas*, have spread farther and farther around the city.

Predictably, the situation worsened when the *milagro* (the Brazilian economic miracle) came to an end. After the oil shocks of the 1970s, the military regime extended economic growth through massive borrowing on the petrodollar market. But their bluff was called in 1982, when the Latin American debt crisis exploded. Since then the economy has grown in fits and starts and purchasing power has collapsed as inflation has spiraled to three-digit figures. For millions of *paulistas*, living conditions that were already precarious have become untenable.

In the *favelas* the girls are sent out to scrounge for food around the marketplaces while the boys improvise odd jobs (windshield-wiping, shoe-shining, carrying groceries at the supermarkets) to bring home some extra money. School accounts for only three hours a day and in any case attendance is erratic. Social workers say that there is a recurrent pattern in *favela* families. The father starts drinking because he cannot support his wife and children and eventually abandons the household. The mother, left with a shackful of hungry children, takes in another man who, in turn, cannot support his new family. Tensions set in and beatings become systematic. The drift toward street life becomes a liberation from hell. Desperate mothers will not stop their children because they too believe that life will be more bearable for them on the street.

When a child leaves home, Cathedral Square is where he heads for. Set in the old financial district, the square is surrounded by grayish, run-down buildings. The cathedral is the dominating presence; next to it is the oppressive Ministry of Justice. Then there are food stores, drugstores, greasy lunchbars and cheap hotels. In the center of the square a plaza has been built on five levels around a grandiose system of interconnecting fountains and basins. Here and there modern sculptures by Brazilian artists liven up the slabs of concrete. Jacarandas, paulownias and weeping willows provide some shade. Flower beds are filled with tiger lilies and bougainvillea. A frieze of *coroas de Jesus Cristo*, a thorny evergreen with bright red flowers, runs around the fountain.

The new plaza was intended to clean up the neighborhood, but after its inauguration in 1979 it immediately attracted those whom it was meant to keep away: hoboes, bag ladies, petty thieves, small-time dealers in stolen goods and the swelling ranks of street children. Today some two hundred children live on the square on a permanent basis, but its importance as a symbolic homeland resonates throughout the street-child population of São Paulo.

In other large cities in Latin America life among street children tends to be fairly regimented and hierarchical. On Cathedral Square there are no organized gangs, no recognized leaders—simply children together by solidarity and real friendship. In a sense, they have recreated a big family in which the older boys and girls often act out parental roles and show their affection for the younger ones with hugs and kisses. Paulo Collen, the street child turned author, lived for a while in a shelter he built in the ruins of a collapsed building. He brought cardboard boxes and blankets and stored the place with food. "It was like a real house. Many children came to live there. Fifteen, maybe twenty. It was known as 'Collen's shelter' but no one was more important than the others. Each kid spoke for himself and we shared everything. We shared the food and we shared the money we made stealing. On Cathedral Square we invented socialism."

Collen's view is excessively romantic. The economic system on the square is based on theft, not socialism. It is also strictly dependent on "street fathers," the paltry dealers who hang around the square reading the papers, smoking cigarettes and recycling the flotsam of stolen goods that comes their way. The system works because it provides the children with a basic supply of food and glue. If Aleandro had not bungled his assault on the woman in the ladies' room, he would have sold her Champion wristwatch to one of the "street fathers" for four hundred cruzados (seventy-five cents) and kept his share, one hundred cruzados. And this, he said, is how he would have spent them: a ham *sanduichi* (twenty cruzados), a Coca-Cola (ten cruzados), a small can of Cosacola glue—enough to fill five plastic bags (forty cruzados). The rest he would have blown on the videogames at the local "Fliperama."

17

At first the life of street children seduces one like an adventure story, but it soon reveals itself as a deadening routine shrouded in a haze of glue-induced contentment. A typical day on Cathedral Square begins with coffee and bread, courtesy of Dona Caterina Lombardí Frantauzzi. A widow in her mid-fifties, Dona Caterina gets up at five to prepare her canisters of coffee. It takes her an hour to drive from her exclusive neighborhood to Cathedral Square and every day she rushes, in her flame-red Fiat Uno, onto the plaza at eight o'clock. "Four years ago," she said to me one morning, "I came here to Xerox some papers. A kid was caught stealing a necklace and the crowd wanted to kill him. It was terrifying and I felt helpless. I resolved to do something for these children and the very next morning I brought them coffee and bread. I haven't missed a day, rain or shine."

After breakfast the children take a swim in the fountain, which also serves as a communal toilet and as a washbowl. If the sun is shining they set their rags out to dry on the hedges of bougainvillea. The rest of the day they sniff glue and look out for easy snatches. Wristwatches, portable radios and necklaces are favorites because the "street fathers" pay instant cash. But the children go for lesser spoils as well: a slice of pizza, a bag of groceries, a pack of cigarettes. I saw a child steal a pair of shoes off a man who was napping under a weeping willow.

Stealing is a sport as well as a necessity. And part of the sport is to stay clear of the military policemen who stand at strategic points in the square. The children use several daytime shelters (behind thorny bushes or in secret nooks in the subway station) as hideouts and storage places. While the older children are out stealing, the younger ones collect good money on their noontime begging sweeps in the lunchbars. It is not uncommon to see scruffy children walking out of one of these places puffing on a cigarette butt and clutching a wad of cruzados.

By afternoon the glue has stultified their brains and they walk around like zombies, staring at the jugglers and preachers, clowns and fortunetellers. When the square empties at nightfall the children huddle together in their three favorite spots: by the grating of the subway air vent, on the steps of the Ministry of Justice and in the huge doorway of the cathedral. When there is a little money left over and the night is cold, a group of children will take a room in one of the seedy little hotels where the prostitutes bring their daytime clients.

The children start having sexual intercourse when they are very young, sometimes as early as eight or nine years old. They are riddled with venereal diseases. I met Katia in the small colonial Church of the Good Death, just off Cathedral Square. It was peaceful and cool inside and Katia was curled up on a side pew. She was a ten-year-old mulatto with pockmarks and a black growth on her left cheek. She had escaped from FEBEM at the age of seven to come and live on the square. Two years later she started having intercourse regularly, first with the boys, then with older men for small amounts of money. She contracted syphilis and gonorrhea. The pus irritated the skin around her vagina and she developed a bad infection. Now the wound had become very painful. "I cannot pee," she said. "It burns and burns." She turned to the wall to hide the tears that were streaming down her face.

Eventually the older girls told Katia to go and see José Nelson de Freitas, a social worker at Perola Byington, the local hospital. José Nelson persuaded her to stay. She was washed and scrubbed and treated with antibiotics. When I visited her in the hospital, she was in the television room, wearing clean pajamas with red and blue animal prints. José Nelson had managed to keep her in the hospital for three days. "Three days without glue," Katia said. "Tomorrow I'm leaving this place." The next day she was in fact dismissed because she had made a nuisance of herself by eating other children's food, being noisy and wandering into the operating room.

Some say that street children prefer to sniff glue rather than smoke marijuana because it deadens the pangs of hunger whereas grass gives them the "munchies." But food is always available on Cathedral Square. If the children do not have money to buy it, they can have a hot meal at one of the shelters. They prefer glue because it is their means of identity. Those who do not sniff are considered *laranjas* (street novices). For the youngest ones, glue sniffing is an initiation rite that makes them feel part of the group.

But glue is far more debilitating than marijuana. The toxic chemicals attack the neurons, congest the respiratory system and damage the liver. It is not physically addictive, but the children quickly develop a psychological dependence on it. The law prohibits the sale of glue to minors and several hardware stores around the square have been fined. Increasingly, the children rely on "street fathers" for their daily supply.

Father Batista, the auxiliary vicar at the cathedral, told me that the consumption of glue on the square had practically doubled in the two months before my visit. "The government decided to hand out free milk tickets to all needy minors. But the street children couldn't receive them because they have no fixed domicile. So I was asked to give them the tickets. And what do you think they do with them? They trade them for glue, of course. Five milk tickets for one bag of glue. I say: what's the point of thinking up elephantine schemes that don't work? If we want to help these kids we must think like the ants that we are."

Father Batista is a tall black priest in his late thirties. He knows all the children on the square and has been a pioneer in starting projects aimed at drawing them back to society. In 1983, when the military were still in power and the Church was one of the few institutions trying to draw attention to the street children, Father Batista rented a space on Cathedral Square and started a shoeshine cooperative for the children.

Membership entitles them to have two hot meals a day, to keep their toolboxes safely in the cooperative and to buy brushes, rags and polish at a fifty per cent discount. In exchange they must agree to charge their clients a fixed rate and carry an official membership card.

These are minimal requirements, yet Father Batista has been only partially successful. He has attracted poor children sent out to work by their parents, but not those who actually live on the street. Some have joined the cooperative momentarily: taken a few meals, spent a few hours on the shoeshine beat and then dropped out. As Father Batista sees it, the children wrestle with two antagonistic forces: the well-meaning spirit behind projects like the shoeshine cooperative and the corrupting spirit of the "street fathers." He told me: "It is tempting to join the co-op and buy one's material at fifty percent discount. But it is more tempting to steal a watch, buy the polish and have plenty left for food and glue. So you see, it is a struggle."

Pressure from the others also inhibits children from joining the cooperative. Its members have a "family" and a "home"—some of them even go to school. These children work on Cathedral Square, but they do not belong there. They are outsiders. If a street child joins the cooperative he is branded a *xepeiro,* which means someone who is corrupted by food.

The best-known *xepeiro* on Cathedral Square is an overweight thirteen-year-old who regularly piles up his plate at the cooperative mess. His name is Moises and, on a hot afternoon, his big black belly can be seen drifting happily under the fountain spray. But most of the time he is hard at work, flicking his shoeshine brush high in the air and telling funny stories to his steady clientele.

Moises, who did not admit to me that he lived for three years on the square with the others, has done very well as a *xepeiro.* He takes an average of three thousand cruzados a month, which is more than the minimum wage. Like the other cooperative members, he keeps a certain distance between himself and the street children, of whom he has a very low opinion. "I learned the hard way," he said to me one day as he polished off a plate of rice and beans at the cooperative mess. "I learned to wax, to polish, to tint, to shine. These other guys are hopeless. They'll put black polish on brown shoes and then soak them in the wrong tint. They just don't have a head for it. Too little brain and too much glue. It's not even worth trying to help them. They don't want a job. They don't even want a home. The street is their thing. Sure, sometimes they'll come to the co-op and say they want to be like me: work, make some legitimate dough. But if the work is slack or the money isn't too good on the first day, they just sell their shoeshine box and go back to stealing and sniffing glue."

Despite the frustrations that come from trying to improve the life of street children, Father Batista continues to develop new projects. Next on his list is a shelter for pregnant girls. Pregnancies are increasing so fast that social workers speak of the coming Cathedral Square generation. To provide immediate assistance, the Perola Byington Hospital agreed in May 1987 to make its maternity ward available to pregnant street girls.

No one came for over a month. Finally, on a cold morning in June, twelve-year-old Teresa wandered barefoot into the hospital carrying a stinking bundle in her arms. She asked the doctors what was wrong with her child. They unwrapped the bundle and found a tiny, decomposing corpse. The baby was a month old: she had died of infections around her anus and her vagina. The acid of urine and feces had corroded the flesh to such an extent that the bones stuck out. José Nelson de Freitas covered his face as he told me the story. "She had never changed those filthy wrappings. Never once cleaned the child. She thought the baby was a doll! When we told her it was dead she sobbed and had nervous convulsions. We calmed her down with sedatives. Four hours later she slipped out of the hospital and went back to the square."

After a few weeks, fifteen-year-old Neuza shuffled into Perola Byington just as she was entering labor. She had already had one baby on the street and taken him to FEBEM. Her second child was born in the hospital, but he was very weak and would clearly not survive if Neuza took him away. José Nelson took her to see the crèche. "I showed her the healthy babies and told her how important it was that she stay in the hospital until her child got stronger. She didn't say anything. She stayed the night, and the following morning she was gone with the baby."

During the first six months of the project a total of eleven pregnant girls went to see José Nelson. Nine of them had advanced cases of syphilis and were likely to transmit the disease to their babies. But not one of them was willing to stay at the hospital to be properly treated with antibiotics.

The crust of suspicion that surrounds the world of street children is hard to break through, even with the best of intentions. Reinaldo Bulgarelli, a twenty-six-year-old social worker, spoke to me in his cramped little office on Cathedral Square: "These children have run away from hellish situations. They have formed a new family here on the square but there is a lingering fear in them that we will take them back to where they came from. They don't want to leave traces behind them and so they give us false names and make up their life stories over and over."

To circumvent these fears, Bulgarelli and his friends decided to provide the children with a shelter where they could come as a group and not be required to join any activity. Rules would be kept to a minimum: no glue, no weapons, no stolen goods on the premises. In July 1985, shortly after the return of democracy, they were able to secure a space: a former prison that was rotting away near a São Paulo freeway.

Bulgarelli drove me out to the Vila Maria project one night in his battered Volkswagen. After half an hour we reached a dilapidated bunker: a small *favela*—not more than twenty cardboard shacks—spread out from its northern flank. "That shanty town you see there is our main threat," Bulgarelli said. "The *favela* gangs persecute the children who come to the shelter and sometimes storm Vila Maria to steal clothes and food. They are armed with knives and guns. The street children are terrified of them. Just the other day a kid was ambushed and stabbed to death as he tried to get back into Vila Maria. Now the children are bused from Cathedral Square, for reasons of precaution as well as convenience."

Inside the bunker the view was desolate: a muddy courtyard surrounded by dingy cells, broken doors, smashed windows, heaps of garbage mixed with feces, a pungent smell of urine. A sinister drumbeat came from the *favela* and one felt that the place was under siege. Bulgarelli assured me that a pleasanter place would have made the children suspicious and kept them away. He showed me a makeshift classroom, a couple of workshops and even a small library with a few tattered paperbacks lying on the shelves. But the facilities were little used because most of the children who came to spend the night at Vila Maria went back to Cathedral Square during the day. Why was Bulgarelli devoting all this time to these children for a pitiful government salary? He burst out laughing. "Because I'm crazy," he yelled.

At nine o'clock the bus turned at great speed into the bunker and the front gate was quickly shut to prevent lightning incursions. A dozen scruffy children tumbled out and went through a body check before scattering in the yard. They were glad to find Bulgarelli, whom they had nicknamed "Giraffe" on account of his height. The older boys gave him serious handshakes, the girls kissed him, the little ones clung to his legs or dangled from his long neck.

With the arrival of the children the bunker came alive. In the yard a loudspeaker spewed out the scratchy notes of a Brazilian samba. The girls danced. The boys kicked a ball around. The television room filled with smooching couples.

Aleandro, whom I had not seen since the day he tried to steal the Champion wristwatch, invited Giraffe and me to the mess hall and we sat down to a meal of rice, beans and stewed beef with onions.

At the table a shy twelve-year-old girl stood out from the rest of the children. Rosemary was clean and properly dressed, as if she had washed and changed for supper. She had two personal items that also stood out: a Portuguese translation of a Barbara Cartland romantic novel and a pale blue plastic case crammed with lipstick, powder, skin moisturizers, toothpaste and a great number of loose Q-tips.

She ate with perfect manners, determined to keep up standards in the face of misfortune. Her mother had died giving birth to her and her father had recently drunk himself to death. She found refuge at Vila Maria, where she had been for just over a week. "I don't plan to stay here long," she said. "Friends are waiting for me outside."

When I finished my food Aleandro poked me in the ribs and pointed to my plate. "They say you are a *xepeiro*," he said. The children laughed and shouted, "*Xepeiro! xepeiro!*"

"Please forgive them," Rosemary said. "They have no manners." A tear rolled down her cheek. Aleandro snatched her case and the mess hall turned into a circus. The children yelled and danced, sticking Q-tips up their noses, squirting toothpaste around and powdering their faces. Rosemary asked me if she could be excused. Silence fell and she left the room clutching her empty tray and her book in heartbreaking loneliness.

After dinner the children disappeared into their cells or into the television room. John Lennon's song "Imagine" played quietly in the courtyard. A boy and a pregnant girl danced cheek to cheek in the glow of a flickering neon light. "Tonight all is quiet," Bulgarelli said. "There is a good feeling about this place. It is a pity there are not more children. Most of them still feel freer on the street. It's a false freedom, though. The road from Cathedral Square leads only to FEBEM, where there is no freedom."

In fact it is a prison where homeless children are thrown in with juvenile delinquents and young murderers. During the military regime it became a violent, extremely repressive institution—a symbol of the period. That reputation is hard to lose and the one fear that the children always admit to is of being taken back to the reformatory. Yet many FEBEM officials now recognize the need for radical changes in the way the children are treated there. And they welcome visitors (Princess Anne was there on an official tour a few weeks before my visit) as an opportunity to show the outside world that even FEBEM is catching up with the times.

The reformatory is set on thirty hectares of public land in a run-down neighborhood fifteen minutes away from Cathedral Square. The main building houses administrative offices while the prison units, which hold a total of two thousand six hundred inmates, are scattered around the estate like an archipelago. When the military were in power, there was practically no communication between the units. The children were never let out and the grounds slowly turned to wasteland. There was little communication with the central office as well. FEBEM presidents came and went through the revolving door of political appointments so that each unit was run like an independent fief by its director.

I was taken around by José Braga, an energetic fifty-one-year-old warden who had been at FEBEM for eleven years and had put himself squarely in the camp of the reformers. He said that the most urgent task was to open up all the prison units that had been closed during the dictatorship and let the children out on the estate. The process had been accelerated in view of Princess Anne's visit but was still far from complete. The difference between the units was startling. In the more liberal ones the children had sunny rooms, learned a trade in the workshops, played sports and even organized theater shows. In the closed units they slept in gloomy cells, were not allowed to speak during meals and spent day after day in a crowded courtyard surrounded by walls so high the sun never shone over them. Braga said that the slowness of change was due to the resistance of old-fashioned wardens. "The personnel at FEBEM was formed during the dictatorship. It relied on violence to maintain discipline. The higher the wall enclosing their unit, the safer it felt."

Braga also wanted to make constructive use of the land within the FEBEM perimeter that had gone to waste. He took me to his favorite project, a vegetable garden where several children were hoeing the earth and setting up stakes. We walked through patches of cabbages, tomatoes, lettuces, beets, carrots, chives, onions and zucchini. Braga was very proud. He picked a zucchini flower and said: "We stuff them with cheese and anchovies and fry them in batter. Delicious."

The children who work in the vegetable garden earn half the minimum wage. The money is kept for them on deposit until they leave FEBEM. If children escape from FEBEM, as most of them try to do, they obviously forsake their earnings and Braga hopes that this new regime will be a small inducement to stay. "Of course the temptation will always be strong as we will never persuade them that life in FEBEM is better than life on Cathedral Square. But we must convince them that it is at least as good."

Braga said that he planned to start a fish farm on the same basis as the vegetable garden; and now that the prison units were gradually opening up he hoped to activate fully the car-repair, carpentry and glass-blowing workshops that had been underused for years. "A child who leaves FEBEM—because his time is up or because he runs away—eventually ends up here again. The transition to society is impossible because they do not have the tools to survive out there without becoming criminals. Now we want to break that cycle. For our survival as well: as it is, the system is congested and explosive."

The tour ended with an eerie sight: over a hundred rusty, metal cribs stacked in a huge pile. "It is very sad," Braga said. "You can't imagine how many destitute mothers bring their babies here to FEBEM because they can't afford to feed them. So they grow up here and go through the cycle, starting out in those metal cribs there and ending up as criminals."

Paulo Collen started out in one of those cribs and became a writer. His mother was a prostitute from out of town and when Collen was born she left him with Dona Antonia, a cleaning woman who lived in a *favela*. But Dona Antonia had too much on her hands and after a few days she took the baby to FEBEM. Collen grew up in the reformatory where he learned to read and write. At eleven he ran away, but he was caught after a couple of weeks and locked up again. Twice he tried to kill himself: first with a splinter of glass, then with a razor blade. He was transferred to a psychiatric asylum and kept there heavily sedated. After a few months he was sent back to FEBEM. He escaped a second time and went to live on Cathedral Square, where he was known as a *laranja*, a street novice, because he was not much of a glue sniffer. Otherwise his life on the square followed the usual routine: stealing, begging, shining shoes, wiping windshields, splashing in the fountain.

The turning point came in November 1985, when the city inaugurated Escola Oficina, a government-run center for street children just off Cathedral Square. In the meantime Bulgarelli and his friends had started the Vila Maria project. So Collen started a new life. During the day he took reading and writing courses at the Escola Oficina; in the late evening he took the bus out to Vila Maria and spent the night in the bunker. He progressed rapidly. Soon he was writing essays and reading the long novels of Jorge Amado, his favorite author. The social workers at Escola Oficina encouraged him to write a book about his life as a street child.

I met Collen in a back room of his publisher's at the time

that the book was coming out. A mischievous seventeen-year-old with fair skin, curly blond hair and eyes like a weasel's, he sauntered into the room two hours late for his appointment. He grinned. "Street children have no notion of time," he said. "Here, have some popcorn." Collen could not sit still in his chair. "Ever been on a plane? Scary, eh? Tonight is my first time. I'm flying out to the northeast. For the promo tour. They want to show me around. Coming attraction: poor street child becomes author. It makes them feel good." Again he grinned and helped himself to more popcorn.

In the last chapter of his book Collen has a few good words for the social workers at Escola Oficina, for Father Batista and for Dona Caterina. But the words of gratitude have a perfunctory ring. When I asked him about his feelings toward them, he answered with contrived anger. "The truth is I can't stand their goddamn charity. Do you really think they'll make better people of us by handing out coffee and shoeshine boxes? Street children are a political problem, with roots deeper than those of the Brazilian foreign debt."

Collen paused and shoved some more popcorn into his mouth. "I have read Karl Marx, you know. The problem lies in the system. I say the children of Cathedral Square want to know why they are taken away and locked up in FEBEM, when the rulers of this country steal much more yet go about freely and call each other 'excellencies.'" He brought the empty bag of popcorn to his lips and let the crumbs slide into his mouth. "Have you written all this down?" he asked. Slowly, he repeated his last sentence. Then he picked up the notebook, went through the sentence himself and flashed a big smile.

Collen was a celebrity. His book was being reviewed in the major papers and his picture was in the magazines. Though he enjoyed the publicity, he was also wary of it. He was not the first street child to find himself suddenly thrown into the limelight. It had happened once before and that story had a tragic epilogue a few weeks before I met Collen.

In the early 1980s the Argentine director Hector Babenco made a movie about Brazilian street children. It was called *Pixote*, after the boy chosen for the lead role. The movie was an international success and won many awards. For months Pixote, the street child turned actor, was caught in a glittering whirlwind. When the lights dimmed he tried to follow courses at several acting schools but had trouble adapting to formal training. He dropped out and drifted back to street life as the money earned with the movie evaporated. Nothing was heard of him until the spring of 1987, when his name again made headlines around the world. Suspected of armed robbery, he was tracked down by a squad of military policemen and killed in a shoot-out.

"Pixote was used by society," Collen said. "People feel less guilty when kids like Pixote and myself become celebrities. But Pixote was a fool. He got all caught up in his success. He thought of himself as an artist, as some kind of special person, just because he acted in one movie. I'm not going to fall for that. I don't think I'm Jorge Amado just because I've written a book. I'm not going back to the street. Do you hear?"

There are thought to be some hundred million children living on the streets of the world's cities today. They live not as children, but adrift on the margins of the adult world, surviving by scavenging, stealing and finding random, transient jobs. If nothing is done their number could double within a generation.

The phenomenon is not a new one. In the Middle Ages, after the failure of the Children's Crusade in 1212, bands of children roamed the countryside before being sold into slavery in Italy and southern France. During the Industrial Revolution and the early days of the Russian Revolution, homeless and destitute children took to the streets and begged. What is remarkable today is not so much that these children still exist, but the speed at which their number is increasing and the little that is being done about them. One reason for this neglect is simply that as a coherent, recognizable group they do not

*exist. In some countries they are the "dropouts," the "juvenile delin-
quents," the "child workers"; in others, latchkey children and orphans. The nicknames for them—scugnizzo in Italy (from spinning
top),* moineaux *(sparrows) in Zaire,* moustiques *(mosquitoes) in
the Cameroons—give some insight into how they are viewed by those
in authority.*

*By the year 2000, for the first time, people living in cities will
exceed those living in the countryside. If the present trends continue
there will be four hundred and thirty cities with over a million inhabitants. The population of these cities is becoming younger. Within
the next ten years half the world's population will be under twenty-
five. Projections for the year 2020 in Latin America put the number
of urban children at three hundred million, a third of whom will be
very poor.*

*Street children are born of the failures of development and over-
whelming social pressures. They are there as a result of the migration
from the countryside into the cities, of poverty, of unemployment, of
broken families and the growth of vast urban conglomerations now
decaying and bursting under the weight of people. There are no rural
street children.*

*There are few places in the world where people living in poverty in
the countryside do not believe that the future of their children lies in
the cities. Cities promise education, high earnings, a more varied life.
Modern transport has made it easier to get to them. Most new arrivals, however, have difficulty finding anywhere to live and end up in
slums. They search for work which cannot be found. Families dis-
integrate under the strain. Children are left to fend for themselves.*

*No government has given much thought to the problem, and there is
no realistic prospect of the labor market being able to absorb these
children. Yet, in order to survive, street children must work: they stay
alive by foraging and bartering; selling postcards and shining shoes;
carrying shopping bags and singing on buses; guarding and washing
cars. When they wake in the morning—on a park bench, in a gutter,
on a building site—they have no idea where the next meal is going to
come from.*

Only the toughest children survive: violence, on the street, is en-

demic. Street children, who are invariably small and undernourished, have to contend with stabbings, beatings, car accidents and the constant fear of prison. The consumption of drugs by street children is universal—from sniffing glue and cleaning fluid to injecting heroin. In Latin America children have become prime targets for drug dealers, who use them as couriers and for pimps—prostitution is now as common among boys as among girls. In one large Latin American city the officially licensed radio station not long ago broadcast a suggestion that citizens should take matters into their own hands and put an end to the children who are infesting their streets. The result, for a while, was that an average of two street children were found dead every day.

The youngest age at which a child seems to be able to survive on the street is five, if a member of a gang, or six or seven if alone. There are more boys than girls among street children, largely because girls are more valuable at home, where they can look after younger children. When gangs form they can be very highly structured. In Bogotá, between the ages of five and ten, children are said to set themselves up in gangs they call gallada, *with a leader in charge, usually the oldest and toughest boy, who is often armed. Gang members are extremely loyal to one another.*

The countries with the highest number of street children tend, paradoxically, not to be the poorest but those with middle-income societies like Brazil, Colombia and Mexico. In Africa the phenomenon is more recent. In industrialized countries street children most often take the form of runaways: twenty thousand are said to roam the streets of New York.

Until the International Year of the Child in 1979 very little thought was given internationally to street children. When delegates met at the convention they found that programs existed for virtually every branch of life that affects children—but not street children. Since then UNICEF has been running projects, and a new organization, dealing with nothing but street children and made up of a number of nongovernmental organizations, was founded in New York in 1987 with the name Childhope. Its intentions are excellent; its possibilities minimal. It is the scale of the problem that is so daunting, the sheer numbers in this uncounted, ragged, struggling, uneducated, vulnerable and ever growing army of stray children.

C.M.

2

Children at Work

in Italy

Caroline Moorehead

Naples

When Tonino was seven a judge of the Neapolitan juvenile court ordered that he be put to live with the caretaker of a block of flats who had asked to foster him. The caretaker's children were long since grown up and the elderly couple soon became very fond of their new small son. In their house he ate well, went to school and acquired a padded blue and red anorak and a shiny knapsack of his own. It was all very different from home, where his father was in a mental hospital, his mother was a prostitute and her new lover traded in marijuana and cocaine. None of them cared much for him and he was often hungry.

Last year, when Tonino was eleven, his mother petitioned the courts to have her son returned to her. The caretaker was too old to be able to apply for formal adoption—Italian law lays down that parents must be no more than forty years and no less than eighteen years older than the child they wish to adopt—and in any case now that Tonino was nearing a more useful earning age his mother wanted him back. Tonino found himself once again in the two rooms in one of the city's more battered areas, near Piazza Garibaldi and the central station. His mother still shows him few signs of affection, evidently preferring the child born while he was away and whom he looks after during her long absences from home. Describing his family to me, Tonino listed an older brother, two sisters and this new child. "Is she your new stepfather's?" "I don't know," said Tonino. "But she is your mother's?" "I'm not sure."

So erratic is Tonino's attendance at Pisacane Secondary School, just near the cathedral, which he began in October, that his teachers have written out a special pass for him which allows him to enter school at any time, since they know that his hours are linked to those of the smaller child whose nursery school timetable is very different. Rafaela Civela, his first teacher, asked the class one day how many beds there were in each child's bedroom. "Five," replied Tonino. And occupants? "Seven." Rafaela expressed surprise. "Surely not seven . . . more people than beds?" "No, no, of course not, I made a mistake, five," answered Tonino, turning very pink. Later she thought how insensitive her question had been.

Under Rafaela's warm but severe eye Tonino has gradually relaxed. She brings him sandwiches to eat for lunch and listens to the stories of home that he tells her and that he cannot bear his friends to know. Not even she, however, can make him part with his knapsack. He prefers to sit hunched over his desk, with the leather and plastic bag a hump on his back, for it contains everything he possesses. He is a still, compact boy, with heavy brown hair and the unassuming air of a very small dormouse.

On Sundays Tonino takes a tray of plastic toys and sells them along the Via Toledo, carved out of the surrounding city chaos in 1536 by a Don Pedro of Toledo who lined it with convents and *palazzi*. Today the Via Toledo is Naples's finest shopping street, the visible window for the city's flourishing black economy. It is one of the very few parts of the city where the buildings are still in good repair. All the big names have shops along the Toledo, and much of the work that goes into the bags, shoes, belts and suitcases on sale is done in workshops in the roads leading steeply down to it, where, by contrast, all is peeling, cracked and musty, with many of the handsome *palazzi* now derelict and dangerous to live in. The money Tonino earns, a few dollars, goes directly to his mother.

Every week or so he helps his grandfather unload vegetables and set up a stall in a piazza near the city outskirts. He minds neither of these jobs. What he does mind is collecting the packets of marijuana for his mother's lover from a middleman in the Piazza Garibaldi, often preferring the beating he knows will come to the terrors of avoiding the police. Rafaela sometimes wonders whether he would not in fact be better off if the police did pick him up. Too young to be prosecuted—Italian law stipulates fourteen as the youngest age for a conviction—Tonino, with his mother's record, would wind up in one of the province's two hundred or so institutions for children. Rafaela has often deliberated whether she should go further and tip off the police to the child's activities. But then she remembers the violence of these institutions and reasons that, now, he at least enjoys occasional contact with his foster parents, and the company of herself and other teachers. Tonino talks readily about his life, at least to adults. He says that he wants to become a plumber when he grows up. The caretaker's oldest son is a plumber.

No one knows precisely how many children are at work in Naples. Statistics, in a place in which no attempt is made to keep figures either of school attendance or of numbers of children registered, and in which school inspectors do not exist, are plentiful and much quoted but seldom trusted. From time to time a child's death while at work sends the topic back onto the front pages of *Il Mattino,* Naples's morning paper, but then the sense of outrage dies away, submerged by other tragedies, other accidents. The bleakness of Tonino's life is not usual, for Neapolitans, like most Italians, show great love for their children; but the work that he does is. It does not take newspaper scandals to alert a visitor to the city to the fact that, everywhere, children are at work. They bring you coffee and wait at your table; they sell you ham and vegetables and soft drinks; they clean your windshield and polish your shoes; they mend your car tires and offer you black-market cigarettes. Out of sight, they are also putting together your bags and suitcases and cutting out the paper flowers that are one of Naples's most popular tourist gifts. Nearly all of them are boys; the girls work, but at home with their mothers or in the workshops.

As many as one in four children may be working in Naples today and earning as little as three dollars a week for a seven-hour day. This would mean a work force of some fifteen thousand children under the age of fourteen. Why there are so many working children in Naples is a subject of widespread fascination about which everyone has views. Professor Amato Lamberti is a sociologist at the university, an affable man in a canary-yellow sweater. He speaks of a divided Naples, a city of two completely different societies, coexisting alongside one another; one obeying the rules of any conven-

tional European urban middle-class society, the other, anar-
chic, uncontrollable, violent and predatory. It is in this latter
section, he says, within a black economy that employs as
much as half the population, that child labor flourishes, as it
always has done. It is neither growing nor diminishing. For
the traditionally poor of the city, school is not now, nor has it
ever been, a viable or interesting alternative to work. Only
among the real workers, away from the confusing and different values that generations of bourgeois teachers have tried to
impose on uncomprehending pupils, will children learn
where their futures really lie. Children, he says, mature fast
in the south; their parents do not believe that they need
school for very long.

If Naples has always been an exploiter of child workers, the
city has also consistently demonstrated concern about them.
Surveys, studies, discussion papers, the allocation of small
amounts of money to alleviate the darker sides of child employment are referred to in its earliest recorded documents.
A city that has the densest population of any Italian town—
some say of any European town—with 10,533 people per
square kilometer, as compared to Rome's 1,845, it has been a
pioneer in crusading experiments, few of which have touched
the lives of more than a very small number of children. Most
of the people who instigated them started out full of hope but
have ended up confused.

The best known of these crusading figures is Padre Borelli,
a spirited former priest in his sixties with tufted white hair,
who affects the slightly wry and weary air of a man who has
traveled this road many times and who still walks as if a
soutane were swishing around his legs. Padre Borelli has his
headquarters in the Casa dello Scugnizzo ("House of the
Street Urchin"), a new concrete and glass building put up in
the 1970s with international money, on the site of the disused
church that Borelli used in the 1950s as a refuge for street
children.

Even today, in touch with international conferences and international money, Borelli has remained close to his former parishioners. He welcomes visitors. "I was a street child myself," he will tell those who climb the steep road that leads to Piazza Martedei. "I started work for a barber at the age of eight. Then I worked for a jeweler's. Then I cut leather for shoes. Then I became a barber again." At eighteen Borelli entered a seminary and on taking orders his first act was to acquire an ambulance abandoned by the Allies after their occupation of the city. He turned it into a traveling church in which he toured the poorer quarters of the city, the districts with the sweatshops and the big factories, and the slums around the edges of the port. When he was given the use of an abandoned church in his own parish he opened it as a refuge for the boys he saw sleeping in the streets, so that they had somewhere to spend the night, and, later, as a little money came in, somewhere to spend the days and to eat. At the end of the 1960s Borelli toured Italy and Europe to raise money for a new building.

"It took me ten years to understand that, for these children, conventional schooling is a myth and a delusion. In my first days here I used to think: give these boys a proper education and they'll be fine. And so they got a proper education. But then what happened to them? They went back onto the streets. Some found work in the black economy. Others found nothing at all. I realized that I had to involve myself more deeply, try and understand something about their families and their expectations." Borelli then moved to live on the edge of the city, in a shanty town, among the really poor. Seven years later he came back to the Casa dello Scugnizzo, believing that he had begun to understand the process whereby a Neapolitan child avoids school in order to work. Now he broadened out his concerns to encompass not just abandoned and working children but the elderly, prostitutes, anyone he felt to be particularly vulnerable.

"My advantage with these children," he explains, in his

sunny and efficient-looking office full of filing cabinets and functional school furniture, "is that I come from their world. I know that they can't survive here without learning how to deal with violence. I teach them tricks. But what disorients me now is that I no longer have any faith in what I used to believe. I do not know what is right for them. I don't know which values are important. I have no ideas about the future."

I asked Padre Borelli if he would introduce me to some of the children in his neighborhood who worked. I said that I did not feel that it was right to approach children without some guarantee for them that I was not after anything. Borelli smiled but refused. He said he would only do so if I stayed several weeks in the Piazza Martedei, something I could not do. "I would prefer it if you simply went up to the children you saw working. They'll talk to you. For me, it's not just like making a pizza: pouf, and it's done. I would have to live with the consequences of your visit. But don't think that they'll be frightened of you. You should be frightened of them. You are their natural prey."

Other idealists have followed Padre Borelli down this path. Inner Naples, with a population of some 1.2 million, is a place in which the cause of the children binds people together, and all those who work in the field know of each other's efforts. Introductions come quickly; there is no referring back to higher bureaucratic levels. Several people had told me about Giovanni Laino, a former architect in his late twenties. He is a long, thin man with the unexpectedly deep laugh and full black beard of an older, rounder man, and an extreme tenderness of manner toward the children of his neighborhood. Eight years ago Laino came to the Quartiere degli Spagnoli, one of the earliest inhabited quarters of the city, a district of parallel streets with now decaying *palazzi* which are so narrowly separated one from the other that in some lights they appear to meet at the top. The Spanish

Quarter is where the leather workers live. Once congregated in large factories in the suburbs, the leather business today relies on hundreds of small workshops, uncontrolled and uninspected, where Italy's foremost fashion houses farm out their piecework. The leather business is a large employer of children.

Feeling more drawn to the possibility of doing some good for the poorer inhabitants of this district than furthering his architectural career, Laino set up house with three like-minded friends, each of whom was in the process of discarding a career to do the same thing. They rented a flat a bit farther north—near the national museum, on the very edge of the Quartiere degli Spagnoli—and one room in the center of the district, a vaulted basement which they covered with posters about peace and filled with clean pine furniture. Though not a religious community themselves, many of their closest links are with some of the Catholic associations whose work resembles theirs. By the entrance door there is a galley-like kitchen which is intended to be kept open at all times for those who want to come and talk. Most afternoons there are constant visitors: a transvestite, an addict, a teenager on remand. While they talk they sit at the table stitching buckles for a workshop.

To finance their voluntary work Maria, a former civil servant, is a secretary in a technical school; Giovanni, an art teacher; and Anna, once a biologist, runs a small factory. Lina, her identical twin sister—both of them are women in their late forties with straight, graying hair cut severely short, and round glasses—is searching for a part-time job. In the afternoons she is a visitor at Naples's main women's prison. Anna is the only one of the four to have merged both sides of her life. Some years ago, having herself worked in a leather workshop to win acceptance by the neighborhood, she decided to challenge the usual pattern of middlemen who collect money from each transaction between firm and workshop. She set up business on her own, as a cooperative venture that would employ some of those least able to find work; ex-prisoners, the handicapped and a number of the transvestites who live in the district. Knowing of the playwright Eduardo de Filippo's past involvement with the poor children of Naples, she wrote to ask for help. De Filippo replied that he had no money to offer, but was there anything else that he could do? Yes, replied Anna, he could speak to the head of Valentino, one of Naples's largest fashion firms, and ask him to deal directly with her, without going through the usual middlemen. A few months later a contract was signed. Today Anna's workshop makes bags for Valentino.

It is one of the paradoxes of Neapolitan life that, while blaming its excesses, few people feel unambivalently opposed to child labor. A teacher called Fernanda Testa wrote a book, published last year, about working children in Naples. In it she noted that, far from regarding work as bad, most Neapolitans reported that for them it represented links with a better past and provided children with a sense of identity which school failed to give them. In the same way that a judge of the juvenile court will happily accept his coffee every morning from a small boy he knows should legally be at school, Anna herself is an employer of two children. If they did not work for her, she reasons, they would still not be at school; they would be on the streets.

Gianni, a thin, awkward boy who looks much younger than his age, is fourteen. He is the fourth in a family of seven children; at nine he was already making bags in a workshop. That was part time, after a morning in elementary school. At eleven he simply decided not to enroll himself for secondary school and, though he regards life as a maker of bags with some apathy, it is, he says, far preferable to school. In any case he is now skilled at his job, as he explains with some pride: he can glue, cut and trim the leather and complete the borders. For five working days, from nine till two and three till seven, Anna pays him forty dollars. Half goes to his mother; the rest on gas for the motorcycle he inherited from an older brother and on the snacks he buys from a nearby bar. On Saturdays and Sundays he sleeps late and goes out riding on his motorbicycle; in the summer he goes to swim off the rocks that divide the grand hotels of the esplanade from the sea. His father is dead, his mother a caretaker at a nursery school. In his family all the children work in the bag business, from a sister of thirteen to a brother of twenty-one.

The afternoon I was in Anna's room, Gianni arrived with Alberto, a twelve-year-old as fly and slippery as a small animal, whose restlessness was both endearing and infectious. The consuming passion of Alberto's life is football, and in particular the fortunes of his hero Maradona, Naples' star player. Alberto is a grocer's boy. His father, also a grocer, would have preferred to see him still in school. For his five-day week, nine till three and four till eight-thirty, Alberto earns forty-three dollars, with overtime at Christmas, a present of champagne and cake at Easter and fifteen days' paid holiday in the summer. His employer is a *padrone*, a boss of the old school, a man who sees Alberto as his apprentice, to train and to keep straight. Last summer he took the boy on his family holiday, driving around the resorts of central Italy. Not long ago, pushed by Anna, Alberto went to talk to the headmaster of the nearby secondary school. There is a chance that he may now go to school in the mornings, reducing his job to part time. Would he like this? Alberto looks sheepishly at Anna and grins. "Not really. It's boring." What of the future? "I'm going to be a footballer." He wanted to know what the English thought of Maradona: were they very envious?

Anna and Giovanni know most of the working children in their neighborhood, at least by sight. They know that the fifty or so illegal workshops employ at least a couple of children each, that their pay rarely exceeds forty dollars a week, and that life for some of these children is extremely tough, particularly where the workshops are overcrowded and dusty and the employers exacting. Though the toxic content of the glue has been greatly reduced, in the aftermath of a scandal that saw one hundred and fifty children permanently disabled and four workshops closed down, health and safety are still regarded with scant interest. People say, laughing, that at least no one any longer has to keep the traditional caged canary whose death used to be an indication that the fumes from the glue had reached a dangerous level.

Like Professor Lamberti, however, they see reason for the work, and find it hard to conceive of a new order of things for the poorer children of the city. "Years ago," explains Giovanni, "the working children in this quarter were younger and more exploited. Now literacy is perceived by parents to be important; most are kept at school at least until the end of elementary school at eleven. After that it's not so much economic necessity that drives the children to work as the fact that parents want them to learn about work, and that they are terrified that with nothing to do the boys will get drawn into drugs and the Camorra [the mafia of Naples]. The girls they simply keep at home to help their mothers."

And is this right for the children? Both Anna and Giovanni pause. "No," says Giovanni. "But what is to be put in its place? A child ought to have basic rights: to live decently, to be born equal, to have some kind of schooling. But in Naples we are a long way from that. Reform, as I see it, should take the form of specifying a minimum age at which a child can work, the types of work which are appropriate for children, and possibly even insisting that there are only certain jobs that a child may do outside his family. There is talk now of experimenting with paid schooling, though where that money will come from I have no idea." "How can you expect mothers to send their children of thirteen and fourteen to school," asks Anna, "when all that means is a morning, or an afternoon, and nothing for the rest of the day? There are no parks here, no football pitches, no swimming pools, no open spaces. The neighborhood has become full of drugs. The Camorra are using small children today to carry out their crimes. In comparison, a full working day looks safe."

Not long before, in the streets of the Quartiere degli Spagnoli, a ten-year-old boy, acting for a Camorra family, fired three shots into the forehead of a Christian Democrat called Alfonso Brunitto. Being under age, he was not charged. A thirteen-year-old called Gigetto has described to police that he charges five hundred thousand lire (three hundred and fifty dollars) for a killing. Two years ago fifty cases of murder committed by children came before the courts in a single twelve-month period. Neapolitans refer to what is happening as *micro delinquenza*.

The unsung heroes of the war against exploited working children are some of Naples's younger teachers. Italian schools have been *in crisi*, a state of crisis, for as long as most of them can remember. Now, as in the 1950s, 1960s and 1970s, there are too many children for too few schools, so that the city's secondary schools invariably operate a shift system. Classes are crowded and money for equipment so scarce that no extracurricular activities are ever possible. And no records are kept of the numbers of children in the city, so that no one can tell at any one moment how many have not bothered to turn up for school at all. None of these facts is surprising in a city in which lawlessness and disorder have been woven into daily life; in which cars do not stop for red lights and one-way signs have lost all meaning; in which the city police wear jeans and T-shirts since the administration has run out of money with which to buy them uniforms; in which the mayor himself declared not long ago, "How can we possibly close down the black economy? It would be like closing down Fiat in Turin."

In the spring of 1988 a conference on truancy was organized by Diamare Secondary School, near the old port. It is a rough, busy area, with all the transitoriness of port life. The idea was to bring together all those teachers from the city who shared a common conviction that the *crisi* had reached a point of no return, that and if the system were not to collapse altogether, more would have to be done to make schools attractive and desirable to children. Geppino Fiorenza is a school psychologist, a rare figure in Naples, and one of the founders of a new League for the Rights of Children. He took me to the conference, telling me on the way of his own interest in the subject. "In 1975 Naples voted in a left-wing administration. They gave a little money toward a plan for providing after-school activities for children. A group of us used it to open a center in a disused building that happened to have the immense good fortune to possess a large garden. Here, in the afternoons, largely with the help of volunteers and a number of young men who opted for the social work that Italy permits in lieu of military service, we arranged plays, ran sports, made puppets and put on street carnivals. One hundred and fifty children became regular attenders. In 1980 the city administration was taken over by the Christian Democrats. They withdrew the money and the scheme collapsed. Now I go to conferences and hear teachers speak of the desperate need for after-school projects, like theater, sport, puppets and carnivals. I feel despair."

The Scuola Diamare is a long, modern, one-story building in glass and concrete, with generous, wide corridors. It was built in the 1960s. To a foreign eye it looks bald and gloomy: there are neither posters nor school art. In the main assembly hall, during the conference, teachers rose, one after the other, to speak of their particular sense of *crisi*, of the alienation of their pupils and the irrelevance of the curriculum; Professor Lamberti expounded his theory about a dual and divided society and administrators in suits from the city council came and listened and said nothing.

Next morning the headmaster, Franco di Vaio, introduced me to three of his working pupils. A fourth, a girl, could not be found. A friend appeared to say that she was at work in a hairdressing salon, and Di Vaio offered to send a caretaker in a taxi to collect her. He seemed more worried by not being able to produce her than by the fact that she was, yet again, missing school. The three boys who knocked and came in together were all thirteen: two bar boys and one garage mechanic. They had drawn, sleepy faces and slightly truculent manners. All three worked in the afternoons and evenings, after school, and each said that the choice to work had been his own, encouraged by a mother who preferred the idea of work to seven or eight hours on the streets.

Paolo was a serious, neatly dressed boy. At the age of eleven he had exchanged a job making leather dog collars in a workshop for one in a bar, where he was now allowed to operate the cappuccino machine. He said that he had first looked for work simply because he was so miserably bored at home, where his mother fussed interminably about the dangers of street life. Paolo is one of nine children and plans to return to the leather business when he leaves school the year after next. He says it is more fun than a bar, where he finds the cappuccino machine too hot in the summer, and in any case it brings in more money. Half his salary of forty-three dollars a week goes to his mother; tips and the rest go to playing the computer games in Naples' new futuristic game park and to the alternative football pools, for, as with everything else, Naples runs a dual pools system, the legal and the illegal coexisting in harmony.

When he inherited the school a few years ago Di Vaio found a state of almost complete anarchy: children turned up for their lessons randomly, many of the boys were belligerent to the point of violence, and failure rates—children repeating classes again and again—ran at over thirty percent a year. Only one child in the school had a father with a degree; the rest were laborers, shop assistants, sailors or unemployed. His first written report to his staff was bleak. "For those children who say they work because they don't want to be alone," he wrote, "because they need money, because they want to belong to a group they can identify with and which gives them security—what can we offer that is better?"

Di Vaio comes from the same background as his pupils. "As a child I spoke this strange archaic dialect of Naples. I thought that by now it must surely have vanished. But when I came to this school and heard the children speak I realized that there were still two worlds here, and that in one of them children still spoke a different language and lived by different rules. Furthermore, the education system does nothing to make things easy for me. I need teachers who are alive to the problems these children suffer from, who react sympathetically and move gently. However, I can't choose my own teachers. The ones who come to this school, in the heart of the city, tend to be those nearing retirement, who have worked their way up the educational hierarchy over the years, starting out in the far corners of Campania and moving their way toward the center as they progressed up the ladder. They want a quiet life, not a battle of wills. Few of them feel much sympathy for these children, some of whom are so wary and so aggressive when they come to us that, if in passing them you should happen to brush against them, they rear back and yell out obscenities."

Di Vaio himself has moved with caution, playing the city administration with a subtlety born of long years of practice. He has brought in two young teachers, both of them interested less in the curriculum than in the challenge of capturing the attention of these wild and suspicious children, on the pretext that his school has an above average number of children with handicaps. He has used these teachers to start up workshops in puppet making and theater, and some of the more untamable children have been transferred entirely to their care.

Over the last two years the figures for absenteeism at Di Vaio's school have dropped, from thirty per cent in the first year to fifteen per cent and then eleven per cent. When a child on his books fails to come to school he telephones his house; then he sends one of his four caretakers to investigate; then he sends a teacher; then he calls on the services of one of the city's small band of social workers. As a last resort, when all else has failed repeatedly, he reports the matter to the police. "But that is a policy of desperation. The courts move like snails. By the time a case of truancy reaches a magistrate, the child has probably long since turned fifteen. If he hasn't, the parents are fined fifty thousand lire. The child attends for a few weeks; then he disappears."

Di Vaio is very clear about what he is trying to do: he wants to turn his school, against formidable odds, into a place his pupils will find desirable and their parents see as a real alternative to work. He is a short, balding, agitated man whose eyes gleam with passion from behind his round glasses, and he has a heavy growth of black beard. His manner with visitors is courteous; with his pupils solicitous. Before I left his school he said that he had something he wanted to show me. Remembering other schools, other dreams of fanatical teachers, I thought with resignation of a new science lab, a special display of pottery. He led me down the wide corridors, loitering children scattering like rabbits into doorways as we approached, and into an immense, deserted back hall. With a theatrical sweep he pointed before him. There, piled up one upon another, chipped, legless and twisted, were several hundred broken tables and chairs. "That's what I mean when I say that I have no money in this school. I can't even get these mended. I have to rely on the occasional good will of some of my more practical teachers."

As I left he asked me about education in England. Was it like this? How did teachers feel? Was absenteeism high? He wanted to come and see for himself, but laughed at the sheer impossibility of such a notion. His final gesture was to hand me a piece of paper he had sent his secretary to photocopy. It was one page from a report on absent pupils, prepared not long before by one of his teachers.

Di Clemente, Anna. 10/11/87. I spoke to her sister: Anna does not want to come to school. Her mother was not at home.

23/11/87. I spoke to her mother. Her own mother had died eight days before. Anna is very depressed and does not want to come to school.

D'Ambrosio, Salvatore. 10/11/87. Salvatore will not be coming to school again because he has found work as a mechanic. He says he may attend some night classes.

23/11/87. I spoke to his grandmother. Salvatore is working and will not be returning to school.

Zappa, Francesca. 10/11/87. I spoke to her sister. She said, very aggressively, that she was about to get married and that Francesca was to take her place at home working with their mother. There was no question at all of her coming to school again.

23/11/87. I spoke again to the sister, who merely repeated what she had said before.

Paolella, Roberto. 23/11/87. He doesn't want to come to school, because he and his brother are selling things from a stall.

These four children were all thirteen.

Officially, Italian children cannot leave school before they complete the third year of secondary school, or before they reach their fifteenth birthday. By definition, all work is forbidden to them until then. These laws are some of the most progressive in Europe. They have been evaded for so long in Naples, however, that they have ceased to have any meaning. Of the many people who spoke to me about children, only one knew exactly what the law said; the others spoke vaguely of twelve and thirteen as the school-leaving age and were not at all certain what the law said about work. Alongside these confusions goes a marked degree of defensiveness: Naples has been criticized for its backwardness for so long that

Neapolitans have become uneasy in the face of prying foreigners.

Between the old town, behind the port of Naples, and the postwar villas of Posillipo lies the Rivera di Chiaia, a broad street separated from the sea by a park. In one of the *palazzi* facing the water Mirella Barracco, until four years ago a lecturer in literature at Naples University, has started a foundation aimed at restoring pride in the decaying buildings of the city center. She is an energetic, enthusiastic woman in her early fifties, with bushy black hair. She was surprised and disbelieving when I told her that I had been talking to children pasting up bags in small workshops. "It's much better than it used to be, even twenty years ago. At least ninety per cent of twelve-year-old children go to school. Leatherwork? No. You must have got that wrong. Women do it, not children. For one thing, children could never be made to sit still for long enough. When they work, they work outside, in the fresh air, selling cigarettes or wiping windshields. There's no Dickens story here, not now, probably not even since the nineteenth century. In any case, a twelve-year-old Neapolitan child is just not the same as a twelve-year-old English one."

Others would not agree with her. Geppino Fiorenza's League for the Rights of Children was set up in 1986 and it has been collecting statistics ever since. Its chairman, Boris Ulianich, is a senator in the Rome parliament and much involved in local politics, having settled in Posillipo, in a modern flat overlooking the bay, over twenty years ago. His statistics tell him that well over ten thousand Neapolitan children under thirteen are avoiding school and that ninety per cent do so because they work. Ulianich is a northerner from the border with Yugoslavia, a tall, imposing, elegantly dressed man who regards Naples's many contradictions with a calm eye. "You have to remember that every child you see at work, whatever he is doing, is behaving illegally. You have to start from there. Then you have to take in the fact that last year, for these ten thousand or so totally illegal jobs, there were only four hundred *denuncie* [prosecutions brought by the police]. In most of these cases, against employers as well as parents, nothing happened at all. A few finished up by paying fines of fifty thousand lire. Good will is now no longer enough. We need a new mentality. As I see it, we are almost wholly impotent. We see, we know, but what do we do?"

All over the city there are men and women gathering statistics on the lives of Neapolitan children. Out of Geppino Fiorenza's play scheme grew the idea for a small library in which to collect relevant documents, and funds just allow for a part-time librarian and a small rented room. Farther around the bay, in a new Naples of modern blocks, is the city of Naples's Center of Research. They too lay aside a large room and five researchers to collate figures about children. Even the Industrialists' Federation, in a fine baroque *palazzo* in Piazza dei Martiri, has its own child-watcher.

Dr. Cesarino was once a journalist. For the last twenty years he has been employed to run the Federation's information department. He is a slight, precise, retiring man in a pale English tweed jacket. His desk is in the corner of a splendid wood-lined office looking out over a wall covered in wisteria. "I have been here so long that I have had time to make a special study of the black economy," Dr. Cesarino explained. He had a tidy blue file, full of cuttings which went back to 1972, waiting for me. What does he do with all these records, these newspaper cuttings and official reports? He looked surprised. "It's my special subject." What conclusions has he reached, over the years? "That the situation is static. Stable. That there will be no change until someone comes up with an answer." What sort of answer? We might have gone on forever. Instead, to my surprise, he handed me his file to take away and read. "Remember. Look after it. These are precious bits of paper."

At seven-fifty on the night of November 23, 1980, Naples was hit by an earthquake. All over the city the electricity failed.

For ten minutes the shocks continued, growing weaker. When it was all over, when those trapped inside buildings had been dug out, when the electricity was restored and the city officials had a chance to assess the damage, they found chaos. Some of the enormous baroque *palazzi* had weathered the experience astonishingly well. Others, already fragile through years of neglect, had now become totally unsafe. In ten minutes thousands of Naples's poorer families, already living seven or eight to a room, had been made homeless. Schools and hotels were commandeered as temporary homes. (Not all that temporary, as it has turned out. The occupation of a number of secondary schools to this day by destitute families has significantly added to the *crisi* in the school system.)

Today Naples is a city of building sites. In the narrow streets scaffolding, looking like skeins of string in the pale light, holds together the fabric of the crumbling *palazzi*. A boom in building is taking place, egged on by speculators in the Camorra, and with it a growth in small building firms. Like the leather workshops, these are frequent employers of children.

Between November 1987 and the end of March 1988 nine people working for the building trade were killed in accidents. Three of them were children: a twelve-year-old, a thirteen-year-old and a fourteen-year-old. "We know what is going on," says Stanislau Nocera, the secretary of one of the unions dealing with building employees. "When we walk around we see dozens of children at work on these sites, carrying buckets, mixing cement, handling dangerous implements. But we're not a police force. There's nothing we can do. We are by no means representative of the whole industry. Where the union is present, we naturally prohibit child workers. But the very nature of the work—ill organized, precarious, full of subcontracting—is against us. Children drift into this kind of work because they can't find anything else, and employers take them on because they are cheap. Most parents hate it. Here in the south it's a very complicated subject: vast firms on the one hand and extreme backwardness on the other." Above Signor Nocera's desk, in an untidy room full of desks and hard wooden chairs, was a portrait of Berlinguer, the dead Communist leader, in a raincoat, windswept and full of optimism, apparently caught by the photographer at a moment of elation.

My last visit in Naples was to Pisacane Secondary School, where Rafaela Civela, Tonino's teacher, had agreed to introduce me to a group of her pupils who combine work with school. It took me some time to find. Though the street was empty in the early afternoon, no building along the Via del Duomo, a wide street sloping up toward the cathedral in the direction of Piazza Garibaldi, looked like a school. There were bookshops and bars, dry goods shops, grocers and shoeshops, solid eighteenth-century buildings and several churches, but nothing that remotely resembled a school. I was about to give up when I saw, high up on the façade of one of the more battered buildings, a small sign saying "Scuola Pisacane." Far below, a door cut into the vast original wooden entrance stood open, the top floors now occupied by the school. There was no playground; the courtyard had a scuffed, dirty air.

At Pisacane the children walk up the six flights; the teachers travel by lift, an open cage, its painted surfaces covered with graffiti. On the sixth floor Rafaela and a friend, a young mathematics teacher, were waiting. In her windowless classroom twenty-four boys and one girl, all between the ages of eleven and fourteen, were jostling and ragging, as light and quick as birds, and very cheerful.

Maria is a tall, sturdy girl of twelve with the neat hairstyle and sensible skirt of a far older woman. She has an air of domesticity and reliability. She works for her father as his secretary in a firm selling furniture to offices. Her hours are fixed—two o'clock until seven every day—but not her pay.

Her father gives her between twenty-five and forty dollars a week, depending on what she needs. Were her mathematics better, she says, she would certainly think of staying on at school after fifteen for further training.

Only one other child, a lanky, uncoordinated fourteen-year-old boy with a thin, sharp face, who loads bottles in a liquor warehouse and has been doing so since the age of nine, spoke of more schooling after fifteen. The others talked only of freedom and of their jobs. There was Livio, twelve, who sells videos; Pietro, thirteen, who glues bags; Arturo, nearly thirteen, who works for an uncle in the upholstery business; and Mario, just twelve, who started work a month ago in a butcher's shop. Their stories, after a while, began to sound the same: big families, overcrowded homes, parents fearful of the Camorra and drugs, a desire to be like other, richer boys and have smart clothes and the money to drift around the games arcade on Sundays. The world they described was a tricky, abrasive one. Gianni, who has been making paper flowers since before his eleventh birthday, said that his father was in the hospital in a coma. Two weeks previously, coming upon two men in the process of breaking into his car, he had fought back. One of the men slashed at his head with a knife.

Speaking of their work, the boys conjured up a tough, exacting existence, not one of abuse, but not one that most people associate with childhood either: they work long hours for little pay and there is no room for mindless ragging or loitering, casual games, football stickers or sports. Knowing and independent, they hardly seemed to be children any more.

It was, as Giovanni Laino had explained on my first day, an area of immense complexity. On the surface much has clearly altered since the days when large factories in the city openly exploited their child workers. But it may be a change for the worse, for now the children work not where they can be seen, but hidden away in the hundreds of small workshops that have taken their place. Driven underground, the problem may now be more intractable. For many of the children of Naples in the early 1990s, work is simply the natural order of things.

It was not all that long ago that child work was regarded as natural, a part of learning, a necessary component of growing up. Indeed, in many areas of the world the work of children is still seen as a logical ingredient in family life and a rehearsal for adulthood. Viewed this way, work becomes exploitative only when this process of learning ceases to take place within the family or in the form of an apprenticeship, when children are separated from adults and forced to do work similar to theirs and often alongside them. Children washing their parents' cars for pocket money in Western Europe cannot be compared with those working forty-hour weeks on tea plantations in Southeast Asia.

Estimates of how many children work throughout the world vary widely. The International Labor Organization in Geneva, which has been concerned with regulating child work since the end of the First World War, puts the number at fifty-two million. The Anti-Slavery Society in London, which has published a lengthy series of reports on child labor, suggests one hundred million; while the United Nations Subcommission on the Prevention of Discrimination and Protection of Minorities believes the true figure to be closer to a hundred and fifty million. With such vast discrepancies the question of an accurate number becomes meaningless. What is perfectly clear, however, is that all over the world, in every country, children are at work. Furthermore, in the early 1990s there is virtually no occupation that they are not engaged in. There are child domestic workers in Peru and Kenya, boy shepherds in central Italy, children on farms in South Africa, in agriculture in the United States, in factories in India, in workshops in Singapore, in shops and restaurants in Britain and in carpet factories in Morocco. The highest numbers are to be found in agriculture, small industry workshops, retail shops, restaurants, street trade and domestic service.

Some kinds of work are by their very nature exploitative, particularly when they endanger the lives and health of children—as, for instance, in the drug trade. They are exploitative when they use children as cheap substitutes for adults and when they deprive children of an education and a childhood. Exploitation exists in industrialized as well as in Third World countries. It exists because of poverty, because in many countries children are unprotected, malleable and powerless, and because consumers and producers alike benefit from the cheapness of child labor. For children the major hazards of illegal and unregulated work lie in retarded growth, malnutrition, accidents, environmental pollution, separation from their families and restricted education. What concerns people is not the fact that children work, but that, being defenseless, they are exploited when they do so, by being paid little or nothing, and by being made to work long hours in unsafe and unhealthy conditions.

In most people's minds the concept of slavery is linked with the history of the plantations. What is often not known is that the labor force on many present-day plantations lives and works in conditions that closely resemble those recorded in the eighteenth and nineteenth centuries. There are children working on plantations in India where it is common to find ten-year-olds working forty-hour weeks for half the adult wage on tea estates; in Brazil, where children form half the work force on sugar-cane plantations; and in Malaysia, where children as young as six work on the palm-oil plantations. These children are frequently undernourished, uneducated and, as they are still growing, particularly vulnerable to pesticides and herbicides.

The simplest way to approach the question of whether children can work has always been held to be one of establishing a minimum age for different types of work. Age, therefore, has been the cornerstone of the many conventions and declarations passed in the last sixty-five years. The most recent and most respected of them is the 1973 ILO Minimum Age Convention (No. 138), which prohibits any employment whatsoever under the age of twelve, and any work which "prejudices the schooling and development of children under fifteen."

Only twenty-eight countries have ratified the Convention, though many others have passed laws of their own along similar lines, laws which are often humane and radical—but unenforced and unenforceable. Where the work of children is illegal—as it virtually always is

—there is a conspiracy of silence between employer, child and parent. Those Third World countries which have not ratified the Convention cite social and economic conditions in their countries as the reasons for refusing to do so.

In any case, the irony of all this legislation which prohibits child labor and provides compulsory schooling is that it does not stop children from working. Where adults cannot bring home enough money, children will work, often in conditions far more exploitative than the factories or mines from which they have been excluded. The sad truth is that, without the money earned by their children, many families would be very short of food. And while it is reasonably easy to exclude children from industry, it is far harder to oust them from the illegal workshops into which they find their way instead.

In the long run the elimination of child labor can only be achieved with the elimination of poverty. No law, however liberal, will make much difference. Or, as a United Nations rapporteur put it not long ago, what is needed is a "broader, more systematic, more aggressive and more probing awareness of the vast gap between good intentions and the sordid reality."

C.M.

3

Children of War

in Lebanon

Jonathan Randal and Nora Boustany

Learning in childhood is like chiseling on stone

Lebanese proverb

The proverb's ancient folk wisdom implies that a child's first steps in education require great effort, but, once mastered, remain indelible and unchanged for life. The stern injunction now resounds in Lebanon with terrible unintended mockery. Since 1975 that tiny, atomized country has pioneered new forms of savagery, even in a century saturated with examples of innovative inhumanity. And it is the children who, by every reasonable yardstick, are paying the dearest price for Lebanon's kaleidoscopic war—that baffling conflict, with its constantly changing allies and enemies, which has no discernible turning point or foreseeable end.

Lebanese children's drawings, those Rosetta stones to even a traumatized child's innermost thoughts, tell the mindless tale. A cursory glance unfolds more than a decade's permutation of massacre, siege, invasion, uprooting, car bombing, disrupted education, hostage taking, torture, drug addiction and —more recently, because of the devaluation of a once proud and gold-backed currency—economic collapse, with its attendant evils of malnutrition and disease.

A young Christian girl draws a sun, flowers, birds and ordinary cottages—an apparently idyllic scene until the eye comes to rest on a tiny figure squeezed into the upper right-hand corner. Who, the child is asked, is that? "It's me, looking for my house," replies the girl, who has yet to come to grips with being driven out of her native village years earlier.

Her drawing is benign compared to other, more graphic ones: children trapped in burning buildings; militiamen laughing as they bayonet, shoot or take hostage hapless civilian victims; artillery, tanks, fighter bombers or helicopters firing into crowds. They provide a sample harvest of horror recorded by these young, Levantine, latter-day disciples of Hieronymus Bosch.

Despite the near fanatical political indoctrination so rampant in Lebanon, in a small but surprising number of children's drawings the perpetrators of violence, if they are identified at all, are simply described as "the enemy." The labels of the many confusing, opportunistic, often momentary alliances of the past and present are not used. So dehumanized has the violence become that these child artists have given up trying to assign responsibility for their plight by identifying the forces responsible for it.

That simplifying clarity is common to children in all the seventeen officially recognized religious communities which, in this complicated country, range from Jews and Druze to both Shia and Sunni Muslims and thirteen Christian sects, as well as the Palestinians. Whether the work of Christian refugees from the Muslim-dominated south in the early 1980s or Palestinian children whose fathers, uncles and elder brothers were killed by Christian militiamen in the first stages of the conflict, their drawings show little variation. The overwhelming knowledge exhibited in the children's drawings is all the more extraordinary in its defiance of often successful efforts to perpetuate the isolation of these communities, which seethe with ancestral hatred and can easily be exploited by local warlords and their foreign influences.

Studies, conducted by mental health specialists, of the effect on children of earlier wars this century have shed enough light on the lingering legacy of trauma to discourage optimism and encourage caution when predicting the repercussions of this conflict on them. Indeed, studies undertaken in Lebanon in recent years stress the tentative nature of their findings in a land without a reliable census, other basic statistics, or sufficient psychologists or social workers. Are there 2.5, 2.3 or 2.4 million residents? How many hundreds of thousands have fled abroad? Is the death toll since 1975 a hundred thousand? And the number of orphans seventy-three thousand? No one knows.

The data that do exist are frequently partial and indicate a high incidence of every imaginable disorder due to the trauma of unending violence. Childhood is dead, just another victim of an atomized society without ideals or working institutions, be they courts, prisons and reform schools, or adequate water supply and garbage collection. Kidnapping, violent death and frequent forced changes of domicile due to neighborhood fighting compete with a surge of psychosomatic illness in as many as eighty percent of those interviewed. Constantly recurring effects are irritability, bedwetting, nightmares, beatings, anxiety, screaming, kicking and general rebelliousness.

A UNICEF report conducted with the American University of Beirut suggests that, since 1975, ninety percent of Lebanon's residents have been displaced at least once. In West Beirut, in 1986, seventy percent of those interviewed reported fighting in their neighborhood in the previous six months, and half were unable to find a safe place during bouts of combat. Forty percent lost a member of their extended family, 14.5 percent had a child or husband killed, 16.1 percent a child or husband imprisoned or kidnapped.

A Beirut University College study of children aged between three and nine suggests that eighty-one percent of those polled report increased fear and anxiety, sixty-two percent suffer from hyperactivity, forty-eight percent from nervous tics, a similar percent from distractibility, twenty-seven percent still use baby talk, fifteen percent report bedwetting, sixty-two percent indulge in shouting and screaming, thirty-five percent in hitting and kicking, thirty-five percent suffer from withdrawal and thirty percent from nightmares. So ingrained has violence become that, in the UNICEF-AUB study, mothers rate marital difficulties as more upsetting than fighting in the neighborhood.

Despite their statistical lacunae, the studies all bear the same message: the single most damaging aspect of the Lebanese conflict is its longevity. Other conflicts, even in the Middle East, taper off, sometimes stop. In Lebanon no end is in sight. Violence in its most Hobbesian form has been the law of the land for so long that it is the only norm reliably remembered by anyone under twenty-five today, and that covers more than half the population.

Nor can much be expected from the adults who proved unwilling or unable to prevent the breakdown of law and order, much less to mend their fractured society. More than five years ago, when a solution to the strife still seemed possible, questions were asked at a conference organized by Radda Barnen, the Swedish branch of Save the Children:

> What does it mean for a child to lose his childhood, to become a responsible adult at age eight or ten, to lose faith forever in his parents' ability to protect him, to lose family members temporarily or for good without understanding why? What does it mean for a child not to learn any other method of solving a conflict than killing?

The questions still await adequate response. And with every passing day the children's plight is made more depressing by the mass exodus for safer and saner shores of the once substantial, pace-setting elite who made Lebanon's residents among the most educated and resourceful Arabs, and Beirut the intellectual and educational capital of the Arab world. For education and the pursuit of excellence were hallmarks of a Lebanon that had prospered despite a dearth of natural resources. Now widespread cheating, and failure for the last five years even to agree on where to administer the *baccalauréat*, have prevented the implementation of that once prized, final, secondary school examination.

Distraught teachers who have rarely managed an uninterrupted school year since 1975 recognize their own irritability and the disobedience and general unruliness that are as much part of the classroom as of the rest of Lebanese society. Even in Beirut's Western-oriented, private educational institutions, which, decade after decade, produced many of the brightest —and often trilingual—students in the Middle East, the remaining faculty members soldier on without illusions.

"The students have known nothing but war and are terribly cynical and totally alienated," said Jean Makdessi, dean of humanities at Beirut University College. "The kind of stuff we teach them is in total contradiction of their own experience. Their intellectual capacity is vastly diminished. They don't have language skills, not just in English, but in French or their mother tongue, Arabic. You give them something to read and they go home and find that there's no electricity because of power cuts. There are no museums, no visiting foreign musicians, theater or dance groups. Few have traveled—even to the other side of Beirut. The cosmopolitan, widely traveled and experienced group of yore is no longer there. The young don't believe anything anybody says."

She recalls that she once "made the mistake of asking students in English composition to write about something awful that had happened to them. It was all hair-raising and made me realize that they had seen the most appalling things—not just one bad experience but an unending list of horror stories.

"In what context can you put Descartes and Socrates? What's missing is the real sense of an intellectual experience. In fact, they have become the enemies of the intellectual experience."

So intent, she said, are many students to get a degree, seen as a ticket to a job abroad despite their "pathetically bad language skills," that they forge certificates to gain entry and then cheat once in. To be caught cheating in an exam does not seem much of a crime to them next to killing or blowing up a hospital.

Even those members of the elite who left Lebanon years ago but now return for occasional vacations have second thoughts about trying to maintain their roots. Two concerned teenage Druze brothers, Sari, eighteen, and Tamer, sixteen, remember their own close calls with disaster before the family moved abroad in 1982. Five years later they returned for the first time and questioned their motives for spending their holidays in Beirut. "When I am abroad," Tamer said, "I always regard myself as Lebanese, but when I return here I realize I am no longer. There's so little to identify with. I don't think I'll ever come back to live because every time I return it's more depressing." "I've seen so many people come back and try to change things in Lebanon and fail," his brother said. "If I ever had a son I don't think I would want him to go through what we as a family have gone through."

They and the students at BUC are still part of a privileged minority and know it. They can still come and go. So, too, can the Lebanese émigrés who work in the Gulf or Western Europe and return to visit relatives or to partake of the inexpensive medical and dental services available for those with hard currency. Such mobility is a luxury no longer within the grasp of even the once well-off Lebanese whose now depleted savings had paid for trips abroad to wait out the violent paroxysms of earlier crises. These years of upheaval have had a leveling effect on everyone, aside from a handful of war profiteers and militia leaders.

Yet the Palestinians, unloved outcasts from their own country, arguably have suffered more—or at least more often—at the hands of more numerous, and changing, foes. They are in Palestinian refugee camps and in Beirut; they have been besieged and fought over by Lebanese Christians and Shiites, Israelis, Syrians and even fellow Palestinians at one time or another. School is, therefore, an increasingly distant memory for a community which long worshiped education as a stepping-stone for self-improvement. Taking its place is the survival course dispensed in the camps.

"You notice the effect of the war when you watch the children's games," recalls Susan Wighton, a community health worker from Glasgow who spent seven months in 1987 working in Chatila and Bourj el-Brajneh camps, which were then under siege from the Shiite militia called Amal. After months undergoing shelling it took the arrival of five-year-old Marko, who had returned from his home in Germany to visit his grandmother in Bourj el-Brajneh, to make her realize how the years of violence had left their mark on everyday life. "Marko sat by the water fountain and pretended he was driving a car with a little girl sitting next to him while others the same age were building a tomb with cardboard boxes and stones." Other children used matchsticks to simulate planes or devised automatic weapons from broken tennis rackets salvaged from the garbage.

In a game played all over Lebanon children as young as three or four act out the harrowing experience of negotiating the checkpoints which delineate the territory of the often warring militias. In the front lines of Bourj el-Brajneh, under siege in 1987, Nora Boustany watched a Palestinian boy named Ihab issue realistic orders to other children at an imaginary checkpoint. So used was the boy to having fellow Palestinians pushed around that he barked: "You Palestinians, all to one side. You Lebanese can all go in."

As the game evolves, children give their stuffed animals *noms de guerre* and devise ruses to outsmart those playing the role of soldiers at the checkpoint. In real life, girls no longer just play with dolls but carry out military functions as couriers and food and medicine carriers. Even in the camp equivalent of playing house, girls say: "My brother has gone out on guard duty." As their drawings testify, little girls all over the country routinely see themselves as front-line nurses and stretcher-bearers tending the dead and wounded. For both girls and boys in all communities, a favorite game throughout Lebanon is a chillingly realistic version of evacuating the wounded. Holding imaginary walkie-talkies to their ears, children excitedly mime mayhem, shouting, "There are wounded, we cannot get them out. Help."

But such concern with the incapacitated is far from universal. In the camps children display a peculiar savagery to other children, to anything that moves, cats, other living objects. "They half kill each other," Wighton observes. "Killing is just a normal part of life. When something happens, their eyes glaze over. There is no surface reaction whatsoever. But there is a lot of behavioral disturbance: inability to sleep, hypochondria, numbness, not just toward violence but toward life in general. Some children stop playing."

Ahmad, who was seven in Bourj el-Brajneh in 1987, lost an

arm two years earlier and remains completely withdrawn, refusing to eat or play. Wighton said he would "grab small kittens and smash their heads with stones. I've told him off, but it doesn't register. He even did it to my cat and I am supposed to be his friend." At four, Thaer, whose name means "rebellious" in Arabic, clung to Nora Boustany when she visited him in kindergarten in the besieged camps in 1987. Without blinking his beautiful blue eyes Thaer, who had lost his mother in the fighting, said, "I want to strangle you and get a knife and kill you."

From the relative safety of another camp called Mar Elias, five-year-old Mohamed Selim Abdel Mooti said that during the siege of nearby Sabra and Chatila he "wanted to get an iron wire and tie it around him and pull it until he was strangled." Who, he was asked, was his intended victim? "Amal" (the Shiite militia then conducting the siege), he replied. "And then put him inside the grave so that my family would all come and cry over him day after day."

If anything, children actually involved in violence seem outwardly calmer. As a five-year-old, Munir Ali Hajj survived the Christian militia massacre of hundreds of Palestinians in Sabra and Chatila in September 1982 by hiding in a pigeon cage with his friend, Mohamed Mamdouh. "The militiamen brought out the sofa from Mohamed's house and the drinks from the shop they'd looted and started drinking," he said. "When the women came they would shoot them or bring them over and rape them, then hack their bodies with red-tipped hatchets with *Mukafaha* [struggle] inscribed on them. They blew up cars, stole jewelry from the women's necks, hands and arms. We saw death with our own eyes. Militiamen told those Palestinians hiding inside the camp to give up and be saved, but when they did they were put up against the wall and shot."

"When I remember what happened I think of how we were afraid," Mohamed said. He insisted that he would recognize the killers if he saw them again, recalling watching the murders of his eight-year-old friend, Ali Mohamed Abdel Rahman, Ali's parents and another young friend, Khalil Mohameddein. Khalil "was riding his bike, they called to him, he didn't respond so they shot him twice in the head."

Encountered at random in 1987, Munir, Mohamed and their other barefoot, grimy-fingernailed, battle-hardened friends struck Boustany as so many teenage generals—quintessential survivors. Recounting his years as a front-line combatant, Munir, who has lost two brothers and a sister in the fighting over the years, said he wanted to finish school, but only so he could take "advanced military training to learn how to operate heavy weapons." Like veterans of other conflicts before them, the children loved telling war stories and were proud to show off their battle scars. One stripped off his shirt to point out to Boustany a scar on his stomach; another peeled off his trousers to show a long cicatrice on his thigh.

One sixteen-year-old named Nasser Walid Okkar said: "I was sitting behind a wall at a barricade in Chatila with an M-16 when a tank came by with the picture of Hafez Assad, the Syrian President, plastered on it. I started shooting and men from Fatah joined in, destroying the tank with a shell. I was badly hit: my insides, my legs and hips. After I was operated on they just put me in a house. There was no real hospital."

Another time, Nasser went on, "two of us were positioned on a first floor with Amal men downstairs on the ground floor. We felt it was all over for us and thought we could at least take four or five of them with a grenade.

"One of our men was lying dead downstairs already and my friend and I thought we were going to die too," he said. "Since we had plenty of weapons and ammunition we started shooting and they left, but we had no radio to tell our people we were still alive." Finally, Palestinian fighters, thinking them dead, approached, and "we called out a secret password, so they came and we eventually recaptured the building."

He first said he had no ambition other than defending the

camp. Then he changed his mind: "I want to lead a suicide mission against the army of Saad Haddad" (the late leader of the Israeli-supported militia in south Lebanon; many Palestinians in Beirut mistakenly hold him responsible for the 1982 Sabra and Chatila massacres).

"Children are the most adaptable creatures," Wighton said. "But what has happened in the camps they will never forget. Conscious memory starts at the age of two. Some kids are mute because they have seen horrific things: people killed in front of them. Muteness disappears later like hysterical blindness."

Ramadan Afrisi, eleven years old when Nora Boustany interviewed him during a five-month siege of the camps in 1987, remembers eating cats to survive. Matter-of-factly, he recalls the death of his friend, Wassim Shehadeh, wounded by a shell when he ventured outside the shelter to play near the water tank. Wassim was one of five children killed and twenty-five wounded on one day in the camp. "He was hit by a rocket and we were in Haifa hospital when they brought in the wounded," Ramadan recalls. "I saw him. They say he died immediately. I got very sad and cried. We stopped playing there for a while. But now we play there again."

In 1987 Boustany interviewed two teenage girls who braved gunfire to smuggle in desperately needed medical supplies to the besieged camps. It was a time when a food-laden Palestinian woman waiting at a notoriously hostile militia checkpoint known as the "passage of death" remarked: "Every mouthful that enters the camp is washed with blood." The girls, Mirvet Ahmad Lubani, thirteen, and Hanadi Abu Laban, twelve, negotiated exposed sand dunes and a high wall with gauze, antibiotics, injections and blood bags. The girls said they were not afraid when they were being shot at. "We just kept reciting a verse of the Koran," Hanadi recalled, "that says: 'He erected a wall before their hands and behind them.' We thought if God loved us He would keep us alive, and if not, He would let us die."

Why would children, or anyone, expose themselves to such an obvious danger by playing exactly where a friend had been mortally wounded or volunteer repeatedly for such a dangerous mission? Anita Lindqvist, a Swedish clinical child psychologist who has worked in Beirut, supplies an answer: "In psychological terms, people's behavior in stressed situations is contradictory. They lose the awareness of danger and do not protect themselves properly, for example, in the case of shelling."

Children's willingness to deal directly with the war's dangers, in drawings or in everyday life, reflects their highly developed gift for adaptation. For Professor Leila Chikhani-Nacouz, a Lebanese child psychosociologist who has studied children's drawings, "Their reality is the war while adults sublimate. Thus, a child's willingness to draw war scenes constitutes a personal defense. But too much adaptation creates a violent, aggressive scale of values. A child's fascination with war implies a grave danger for its metaphysical and moral development."

In other words these children have become trapped in a savage state in which they are forced to survive. Day after day, year after year, they lose respect for fathers who hang around the house without work or who are routinely humiliated in front of their families by teenagers manning checkpoints. Who is to protect these children from their own aggressive tendencies and fantasies in a world without meaningful constraints?

Sylvie is so obsessive about her two children's safety that she often keeps them out of school, claiming that "it's too dangerous." In a society where small children routinely distinguish between the different dangers represented by light and heavy weapons, she rushes hers to a shelter at the slightest untoward development which she monitors on a constantly turned-on radio. Her husband insists on taking the children for walks but, once back home, Sylvie resumes the cycle destined to keep the children dependent on her.

Even less overprotected children do not study as much as they used to since they feel that, in any case, there are no jobs waiting for them if they do work hard. The various militias' press, radio and television propaganda harps on themes designed to activate the most primitive fears. The aim is to overcome the accumulated resentment against the militiamen, who are increasingly seen as the thugs that they are, and to substitute resigned acceptance: "If the gunmen leave, what will happen to us?"

A batch of ninety-five Christmas cards drawn in 1985 by seven- to twelve-year-old Christian schoolchildren provides frightening corroboration for such a pessimistic view. All but twelve cards bear some symbol of war, with blood as the most frequently recurring theme, followed by shelling and light arms. Death, massacre, fire, explosions and various forms of bombardment abound in the drawings. The most frequently used colors, in descending order, are brown, dark red, dark blue, purple, black and gray, which, according to Professor Nacouz, represent respectively regression, violence, rigidity, uneasiness, anguish and opposition. Other drawings use barely any color, reflecting a kind of desert of the mind and spirit. In theme and coloring these drawings are basically interchangeable with others executed by Palestinian child survivors of a Christian militia massacre in the Tel Zaater refugee camp in 1976.

Like Bruno Bettelheim and other psychologists who have studied children under wartime stress, Professor Nacouz recognizes that drawings or violent play are merely the tools that children use to cope with the reality they do not understand. Professor Nacouz also argues that the war has not created mental illness, but rather helped crystallize already existing emotional disturbance. Yet her case history of a young girl named Mireille is a cautionary tale.

The daughter of a Christian family displaced from their home by the fighting, Mireille stammers and idolizes her militiaman brother who was killed in one of Lebanon's innumerable half-forgotten "little wars." Her family and teachers insist she is "sweet and dutiful," but a glance at one of her drawings is enough to discount the view. In one corner a dead man and a Lebanese flag lean on a sandbag; in the other is a burning house. Nothing at all adorns the rest of the page. Professor Nacouz describes Mireille as "boiling and full of passion." Mireille is determined to join the Christian militia to avenge her brother. She routinely speaks of herself as "he," suggesting that she has taken his place and does not recognize her female identity. Applying Mireille's case to other Lebanese children, Professor Nacouz asked: "What kind of lover, wife or mother will Mireille make?" More generally, what kind of parents, in an eventual postwar period, will today's children make, with their legacy of bereavement, trauma, anguish and physical and emotional handicaps?

Throughout Lebanon the fighting is skewing many other traditional relationships. With many men forced to seek hard-currency-producing jobs abroad or too exposed to militia violence to risk leaving home, women have come into their own, even among those Muslims traditionally jealous of women working outside the home. With many parents at their wits' end, psychologists report an increasing number of families turning to them for help in handling disturbed children—a departure from normal practice. But skilled therapists and psychologists, who were never a large group, are leaving the country in despair, like other members of liberal professions.

The violence is also sorely testing the traditional cement of the three-generation extended Arab family. With its decline, divorce is reaching what sociologists describe as "shocking rates." Especially hard hit are young couples, some still teenagers, who hoped wartime marriage would serve as a bulwark against the prevailing anarchy and violence. Doctors report a growing number of complaints concerning impotence and frigidity which they blame on a suppression of desire due to stress. Incest seems to be increasing. So, too, is child-beating, which was culturally acceptable even before 1975.

Prostitution, once a near monopoly of Egyptians, Syrians and other foreigners in Beirut, now affects ever younger women of all Lebanese communities which traditionally demanded that their women remain virgin until marriage. According to one study, nearly twenty percent of two thousand mothers polled said they resort to end-of-month prostitution to feed their families. For Professor Nacouz, "Mental health is no longer the top priority. The economic collapse is. I know a mother of four so desperately poor she feeds two children one day and the other two the next. I assure you there are thousands of such cases."

Instant gratification is the order of the day. Gambling flourishes as never before. With clerical benediction, young Shiite Muslim girls, barely past puberty, contract "pleasure marriages" for short periods of time so that their offspring will not be considered illegitimate. Young Christian girls live openly with their men friends without benefit of clergy. There is a flourishing business throughout the country in resewing the hymen of young women who are no longer virgins, to satisfy formal demands for blood on the wedding-bed sheets.

In Lebanon, where illegitimate children were traditionally cared for by members of the mother's extended family, newborn babies are now found abandoned in cemeteries or garbage dumps. Teenage mothers give birth in clinics and hospitals, then disappear quickly, leaving their babies behind.

Cigarettes, alcohol and pharmaceutical drugs are readily available and readily abused by young and old. The use of narcotics, from locally produced hashish and heroin to imported cocaine, is so widespread that the Lebanese automatically assume that the various militias derive a substantial part of their income from the home market. Only one hospital deals with addicts, but many of them either don't have the money to pay for treatment or refuse its care because it is a psychiatric hospital in a country which still views admission of emotional disturbance as taboo.

In 1987 a survey of a thousand secondary school and university students conducted by Benoit Soukar suggested that there are two hundred and forty thousand Lebanese addicts —roughly ten percent of the population—including three thousand children aged between ten and twelve. It is widely believed that between seventy-five and ninety percent of the crack militia units thrown into battle in crisis periods are hard-drug addicts, and many of them are teenagers. One psychologist said: "Their leaders know all about it but cannot do without them. So, in reality, the leaders are encouraging their addiction."

Judged against such a background, despite its other manifest drawbacks, life in the Palestinian camps prevents most families from being split up, at least those not slaughtered along the way. That is the other side of the coin of living in a ghetto. And family separation, as was first noted in studies of London children evacuated to the countryside or to North America in the Second World War, proved to have more damaging long-term effects on children than did the most punishing of German air raids which the move sought to avoid.

Social scientists who have studied children think that the Palestinian camp children show more self-confidence than other children in Lebanon, thanks to their greater sense of sticking together and the need to survive in hostile surroundings. The camp children, for example, ape adults in organizing themselves into the various factions that make up the Palestine Liberation Organization.

Whatever comfort such clinging to clan may produce, Elie Nassif, a part-time psychologist with experience in both sides of the divided city, is convinced that the unbroken cycle of violence provides a dangerous model for troublemakers young and old, who can hide within their community no matter what their misdeeds and those of their adversaries.

Consider the case of Zeinab Mohamed Darwish, interviewed by Boustany in 1987 when she was a pretty, tall, slim, eleven-year-old. She had been left for dead in a 1985 car bomb explosion that was widely believed to have been executed at CIA instigation to avenge the deaths of more than two hundred and fifty American diplomats and Marines two years earlier. The intended victim, who survived, was Sheikh Mohamed Hossein Fadlallah, an influential Shiite cleric, considered close to the pro-Iranian radicals of Hezbollah and held responsible for the anti-American terrorism. Instead, the car bomb explosion in the teeming southern suburb of Bir al Abed killed eighty Lebanese and wounded two hundred and sixteen others. Many of the victims were children returning from prayers in a nearby mosque. Zeinab recalls watching two of her nine sisters burn to death in the explosion in front of her eyes. A third died later of wounds. Zeinab herself remembers screaming: "No, I swear it wasn't me. Go see the man who did it." Psychologists interpret her protestation of innocence as reflecting a desire not to alienate adults who, for her, symbolize protection.

Zeinab passed out and rescue workers assumed she was dead. They dumped her, along with other victims, in an ambulance. The drive to the hospital morgue was so bumpy that she awoke screaming, with corpses above and below her. Two weeks later she began complaining of headaches. Doctors found shrapnel in her brain and deemed her inoperable. The pain remains so excruciating that, without constant medication, she bangs her head on the floor. She cannot be left alone in the one room she shares with her parents and her five surviving siblings for fear she will swallow her tongue. Her brother-in-law tends her, carefully coaching her responses for visitors. Gently he asks her who was responsible for the car bombing. "In the name of God, the compassionate, the merciful," she quotes from the Koran, "the Americans."

For Zeinab and the countless other victims in Lebanon, specialists confess that surprisingly little is known about the long-term effects of catastrophes on the development of children who survive, especially in the Third World. Studies of Israeli children born during the 1967 Arab-Israeli conflict show a higher incidence of emotional disturbance and behavioral problems than was found with children born two years later. And that war lasted only six days and was won hands down by Israel. A 1977 study of Vietnamese children, forced to leave their village five years earlier because of the war there, came to similar conclusions.

Nevertheless, the fate of the children that the Lebanese violence has spawned remains unclear. Two studies by reputable American psychologists point in opposite directions. Rona Fields, a clinical psychologist from Alexandria, Virginia, and a specialist on terrorism, studied eight-year-old Palestinian boys enrolled in the *ashbal* or PLO clubs who survived the Sabra and Chatila massacres in September 1982. She discovered that they had been antagonistic toward the instructors who forced basic military training on them before the Israeli army entered West Beirut and let loose the Lebanese Christian militiamen on the camps.

"After the massacre," in which hundreds of civilians were killed, she noted, "the boys felt grief and resentment. Psychologically, they somehow felt responsible for what had happened and felt the only way they could make amends was by taking the place of the person who had been killed." They were left "with a monomaniacal obsession with revenge," she said, and noted that "many of these children had become recruits for terrorist units within the Palestinian movement."

Over the years a pattern of the terrorist personality emerged from her research: "In their fantasy stories terrible things happen to children and there is nobody, including their father or mother, who can help. In the stories of healthy children the same sort of predicaments almost always end up with a happy rescue. But these children fixate on an infantile sense of impotent rage."

Based on the still unfolding suffering in Lebanon since 1975, the chilling assessment certainly would seem to provide a reasonable—if fearful—indication of what lies ahead, and not just for the Palestinians. Yet Nina Murray, a child psychologist at Harvard University who has worked with disturbed children in Northern Ireland and Beirut, has suggested that a less frightening outcome may be likely. In studying Jewish survivors of Hitler's extermination camps she discovered that almost all were now well-adjusted adults. "They do have occasional symptoms, such as flashbacks and nightmares," Dr. Murray noted. "But they are generally stable, productive and compassionate people who are not cynical or pessimistic, but optimistic despite what they have lived through."

Buoyed by hopes of a similarly optimistic outcome, some Lebanese, against all reasonable odds, refuse to give up on their country. Rafic Hariri, a Sunni Muslim who left Lebanon virtually penniless in the 1960s and made a colossal fortune in construction in Saudi Arabia, has invested at least two hundred and fifty million dollars in educating Lebanese in the past decade. He spent a hundred and fifty million dollars building a medical school and other university departments in Kfar Falous outside his hometown of Sidon. Christian militiamen sacked the site in the wake of the Israeli invasion of 1982. Undaunted, Hariri started sending Lebanese boys and girls of all communities to the United States, France and other Western European countries. In the periods 1985–86 and 1986–87, the bill came to a hundred million dollars for educating eleven thousand Lebanese children in everything from surgery to repairing air conditioners.

Hariri is wise enough to know that some will fritter away their chance, that many others will find no jobs in Lebanon's ruined economy. Meanwhile he doggedly finds work for his scholars in the Arab world. He knows that many will probably never choose to live again in Lebanon. But he says he can wait for the day when "Lebanon will no longer be hijacked by militiamen." In a way, the longer his scholars stay away the better. "Can you imagine that they will go back to Lebanon and fight with each other?" he says incredulously of his scholars. His secret hope is that they will form a kind of informal alumni association whose shared experience will provide the foundation for a new Lebanese nationalism.

The story of Alain would also seem to justify some cautious hope, at least since he left Beirut. The violence he was born into in 1979 so upset Alain that, from the time he first spoke, he never talked to friends except in the third person and through his parents.

In October 1983 he was living in a West Beirut apartment house opposite the Drakkar building when pro-Iranian Shiite Muslims blew up the multistory headquarters of the French contingent of the ill-fated multinational force sent to Beirut after the Sabra and Chatila massacres the year before. Alain, his mother and her brother were covered with blood from wounds inflicted by flying glass from the explosion next door. Alain stopped talking about war. He kept telling his mother he wanted to crawl back into her belly.

Alain and his family are lucky: they all hold French passports. His mother, who, like many others, for years had sworn not to leave Lebanon, moved to Paris with Alain. Attending a French school was hard at first, especially dealing with French children. Alain made few friends at the beginning and still avoids violent classmates. He still has nightmares. Initially his teachers thought he was deaf because he did not always answer them and even now he does not talk easily with many adults. But Alain has always been at the top of his class. He does not speak Arabic any more although he still understands a bit. But he is militantly proud of being Lebanese, as he tells anyone within earshot—not a tactic calculated to win him many friends among the French, for whom Lebanon is synonymous with terrorism and mindless violence.

When the killing finally does stop, how old will Alain and Hariri's scholars be? Will he and they want to go back to help pick up the pieces in Lebanon? Will they and others of their generation, who seem to have got out in time, be allowed back to participate in that arduous task with the others who were not so fortunate? One can only hope so.

As civil wars multiply and armed conflict continues in many of the developing countries, paramilitary forces and guerrilla movements are increasingly recruiting children as soldiers. The phenomenon of child combatants, which Europe experienced at the end of the Second World War, now seems to be recurring, particularly in Asia, Africa and Latin America. The Quakers' UN office in Geneva currently has a list of twenty countries in which children between the ages of ten and eighteen are reported to be involved in military training. As the numbers of child soldiers rise, so their ages decrease.

In some places, and contrary to their own national conscription laws, the army has been seizing young boys and forcing them to fight; anti-government guerrillas are known to kidnap children for the same ends. In countries with liberation wars, the children from poor families are the first to be conscripted before being used as mine detectors, as messengers in enemy territory, as secret carriers of ammunition and as part of assault troops. In Cambodia and Vietnam children have been fighting since the early 1970s. There have been reports of child soldiers in Ethiopia and Uganda, El Salvador, Colombia and Honduras.

Following the Iranian counteroffensive against Iraq of March 1982, it became known that children as young as ten were being sent to the front to be used as human mine detectors. A figure of two and a half thousand was given for the number of children who died during the six weeks after the counteroffensive was launched. Boy recruits are mostly from the villages. Some have left school at ten to enter a religious and military class where they are taught that sacrifice and martyrdom for Islam is the ultimate objective of their lives. The literature they are given to read glorifies war and the lives of the martyrs. Pictures of boys who have died in the war are hung on the walls. Parental permission is no longer necessary in order to volunteer. Under this pressure, boys are urged to enroll in groups called bassidjis; *they are given guns and shirts with their names on the back, and are granted the Imam's permission to enter paradise. Some also get a key with which to enter. At the height of the fighting, it has been estimated that nine out of ten of the boy soldiers die.*

In Mozambique, eighty-four thousand children are said to have lost their lives because of the war and its consequences. The Washington Post *reported on January 5, 1988, that the government had opened a center in Maputo for thirty-five returned children guerrillas, where they were taught games and introduced to other children, in order to "change them back into children."*

Current international law prohibits the participation in hostilities of children under the age of fifteen and urges that, when recruiting fifteen- to eighteen-year-olds, the older children should be recruited first. The Geneva Convention and additional protocols provide for further safeguards for children and civilians during wars. However, responsibility for implementing them lies with each state, and states can seldom control the activities of combatants within their borders and still less those of opposition forces. The result is that children are rarely protected. An extreme example of this is where miniature mines are designed as toys and left for children to find. Despite the fact that torture has been outlawed repeatedly in international legislation, children are also known to have been tortured in recent times in Iraq, Afghanistan and Colombia in order to extract information about their parents.

It is not only on the battlefield that children experience war. Civilian losses in times of war have grown steeply. In the First World War only five percent of casualties were civilian. By the Second World War this had risen to fifty percent. Since then the figure has reached eighty and ninety percent. Of the estimated twenty million people who have died in armed conflicts since 1945, the majority are women and children. In Cambodia, under Pol Pot, a million people are believed to have been massacred.

It was during and after the Second World War that doctors and psychologists first began to study the effects of war on children. What they found was that acute anxiety frequently follows violence, that children caught up in wars feel grief, depression and extreme pessimism about the future, that they can become very aggressive and that in the end many will adapt to war in a negative and dangerous way. After twenty-two years of war in Namibia, children who have never known anything else now accept as normal a situation the rest of the world would regard as unacceptable. Constant exposure to a singularly brutal war is producing children who readily turn to delinquency and alcoholism and show signs of what has been described as "emotional blunting." During the 1968 riots in Belfast there was a notable increase in mental illness and psychological disorders among children. Their immediate reaction was hysteria, with young children unable to stop crying. Insomnia, bed-wetting and a general emotional imbalance followed. Further research has shown that fear of war is widespread among children and that fear of nuclear war is one of the greatest terrors that children experience. Of all categories, it is the younger girl who most fears that she will never live to see adulthood.

The idea of creating a "zone of peace" dates back to the eleventh century, when the Church designated a "truce of God," and soldiers were threatened with ex-communication if they did not refrain from fighting during several days each week. In modern times the credit for making children into a "neutral, conflict-free zone in human relations" goes to the Red Cross and the Red Crescent, who have suggested that during times of conflict children should be protected, as should all services related to them and all access to them. This idea found expression in El Salvador when, in the spring of 1985, fighting stopped for three days to allow three thousand health workers to vaccinate two hundred and fifty thousand children against polio, measles, diphtheria, tetanus and whooping cough. In Uganda, when government troops lost control of the southwest and children there were cut off *from health programs, UNICEF managed to get agreement to set up an air corridor along which to ferry vaccines and essential drugs. Those, at least, got through.*

C.M.

4

Children in Prison

in India

Anne Chisholm

If a child is a national asset, it is the duty of the state to look after the child with a view to ensuring full development of its personality. That is why all the statutes dealing with children provide that a child shall not be kept in gaol. Even apart from this statutory prescription it is elementary that a gaol is hardly a place where a child should be kept. . . . It is a matter of regret that despite statutory provisions and frequent exhortations by social scientists, there are still a large number of children in different gaols in the country.

Indian Supreme Court, 1986

In India, as in every other country in the world, the law is clear: children should never, for any reason, in any circumstances, be kept in prison. But India, in common with most other countries in the world, has found the law very hard to implement. Although it is virtually impossible to get accurate figures for a problem that is not supposed to exist, it has been estimated that, in 1987, out of some thirty-four thousand children held in various institutions, over a thousand were in jail. The problem is acknowledged and it is a sensitive issue. Meanwhile, many of India's other problems are on an infinitely bigger scale: there are more than four million homeless people in India; the child labor force is over thirty million.

The gap between principle and practice, between what the law says and what actually happens, exists everywhere; but in India, where all social problems are magnified, it is an enormous gulf. At the end of 1986 a new Juvenile Justice Act was passed, so that for the first time there is now a unified law relating to children applicable in all states. Local variations in age limits were removed by the act: now all boys under seventeen and all girls under nineteen are considered juveniles in legal terms. Children are now supposed to be held only in observation homes, not police stations or jails, before being brought before specially constituted juvenile courts or boards. During 1987, under pressure from the central government, the Supreme Court and the press, the states began attempts to turn the new provisions into reality.

I went to India hoping to discover what it is like to confront the problem there, both from the children's point of view and from that of the professionals concerned: social workers, lawyers, magistrates, administrators. I visited two cities: Calcutta in West Bengal and Patna in Bihar.

"It is the easiest thing in the world," writes Geoffrey Moorhouse in his classic study of Calcutta, "to come close to despair in Calcutta. Every statistic that you tear out of the place reeks of doom. Every half mile can produce something that is guaranteed to turn a newcomer's stomach with fear or disgust or a sense of hopelessness."

Although there has always been a dark side to Calcutta (Kipling called it the "city of dreadful night"), a hundred years ago it was the proudest city of the British Empire, renowned for its riches and cultural life. In the late twentieth century, however, the city's name has become synonymous with urban nightmare, and it is almost inevitable to assume on arrival in Calcutta that the plight of the casualties of modern Indian society—the poor, the homeless, the children in trouble with the law—would not only be the worst in all India but probably the worst in the world.

At first, every glimpse of Calcutta street life confirms the newcomer's worst fears. Between the airport and the city center are shanty towns of unimaginable squalor where adults and children, as well as pigs, dogs and vultures, pick through vast mounds of refuse. Once into the back streets, there in close-up is the teeming spectacle of Calcutta's poor. Four million people, a third of the city's population, live in slum areas. One million live on the streets, under shelters made of brushwood, rags, sheets of plastic, or just in the open. In central Calcutta you can peer into knee-high tentlike structures in the gutter and see a whole family in rags, with two or three small children huddled together, and perhaps a naked baby lying on a newspaper.

Then there are the beggars. Many of them are children and if they are able-bodied they rush up and push their small hands into your face or pull on your sleeve and wail for money. Often a child of seven or eight will be carrying a tiny baby. If they are crippled or sick they thrust their stumps at you or point to their sores or running eyes. Sometimes they lie motionless on the hot pavement. One boy I walked past every day was about ten years old; he had no arms and his legs were thin and twisted. Everyone, including kindly, concerned local residents, tells you not to give these children money as they are organized by crooks who exploit and train them to a lifetime of beggary. Each time I walked past the armless boy I wondered if his arms were missing from birth or if someone had mutilated him to make him more pathetic and more profitable.

Against this background the whole matter of imprisoned children can begin to appear in a new light. It was not long before I heard people say that at least children in prison were likely to be fed; at least they were not sleeping in the gutter. No one I met tried to justify holding children in prison, but several pointed out that there could be worse predicaments. But I found, after a few days had passed and the first shock of exposure to Calcutta's poverty had faded, that I, like most Western visitors, began to notice the other side of the coin. For all the desperate squalor and deprivation, there are also unmistakable signs of vitality, energy and hope among even the very poor. The people do not seem apathetic or defeated. In the slums, on the streets, they work, cook, wash and play. They all, including the children, laugh and smile a lot. Unless a child was being starved, abused or tortured, it seemed to me dangerous to regard imprisonment as an improvement on street life.

In fact, as I soon discovered, over the last eighteen months or so the Marxist government of West Bengal has made great efforts to tackle the problem of "jail children," as they are called. Early in 1986 a series of embarrassing newspaper stories had appeared, pointing out that, of the thousand or so children officially acknowledged to be in Indian jails, four hundred and ninety were in West Bengal. Some reports were quite specific. In February 1986 the juvenile court magistrate in Salt Lake, Calcutta, summoned a police officer to appear, "to show cause why he did not produce Rabi Das, a four-year-old boy, in the juvenile court," but had sent him instead to the ordinary court, whence he was "sent to Howrah jail for custody, much to his reluctance." In April 1986 the Prime Minister, Rajiv Gandhi, made a personal request to the West Bengal government asking that "the process of shifting the children should be expedited." National attention was being focused on West Bengal. The authorities were even more embarrassed when, in July 1986, the Supreme Court in Delhi directed them "to transfer to a children's home two minor girls lodged in the Jalpaiguri district jail." One was eight and had been there eighteen months; the other was ten and had been there a year. "Neither," said the report, "was charged with any offense."

In July 1987, after the passage of the Juvenile Justice Act, the West Bengal government voted to implement the act immediately and to fund and establish children's homes as alternatives to jail. Since then some progress has been made.

Mrs. Aloka Mitra is a senior social worker in her late forties. She took up social work after ten years at home in Calcutta bringing up two children. Her husband is a successful businessman, and she comes from a progressive Bengali family. She is a slender, fine-featured woman with apparently inexhaustible energy and a gentle, humorous manner that belies a steely practical commitment to what she believes are the real interests of the people she is trying to help. She is one of the key figures on the Women's Coordinating Council, the most influential and well-organized voluntary body doing social work in West Bengal. When I met her she had just been picked by Rajiv Gandhi for a new national advisory body on women's problems.

Mrs. Mitra thoroughly understands the prison and welfare systems of Calcutta; she is especially concerned with women and children, and has a natural suspicion of outsiders who arrive looking for sensational stories and instant solutions. While agreeing that, in principle, no child should ever be kept in jail, she points out that sometimes there is no alternative: "The only reason that children are kept temporarily in jail is that there is no other accommodation for them. Say the police pick up a lost child; they then produce the child before a magistrate; the child is sent to a reception center but the place is full up. What then? It is quite a dilemma. You certainly can't leave the child in the lockup at the police station. So the child goes to a jail, usually the women's section, where a special area has been set aside for children; they are not put in with criminals."

Mrs. Mitra said that the conditions in the prisons she visits regularly are good: "These children are more protected inside the jails than outside. They never complain; they are well fed and very well looked after. They are visited regularly by lady social welfare officers and social workers; we as social workers go in and out of the jails all the time. We run classes inside the jails." She explained that, in addition to lost or destitute children, there are other categories of children who inevitably spend time in jails: infants and children up to the age of two or three who cannot be separated from their mothers, and older children, usually girls of fourteen or fifteen, who come to the police to ask for protection from sexual exploitation. There is also the problem of the children of illegal immigrants to West Bengal, who stream across from Bangladesh in thousands and set up camp all around Calcutta. From time to time the authorities launch a campaign to deport large numbers of them; in the process whole families very often end up in prison.

It was clear that Mrs. Mitra, whose approach to the subject of children and prison was sympathetic and at the same time pragmatic, felt that the recent publicity and wave of pressure to get all children out of West Bengal's prisons overnight had not been altogether a good thing. "The problem was there weren't enough homes," she said. "It would have been easy just to let them out—but to what? I felt that they were more likely to be victimized outside the jail."

I was anxious to see some of Calcutta's children's homes. Mrs. Mitra took me first to a well-known establishment where she has worked for many years and of which she is now chairman: the All Bengal Women's Union Children's Welfare Home. This home is part of an impressive network of welfare organizations that has grown up since 1932, when the first voluntary women's organization was founded in Calcutta to campaign against "immoral traffic in women and children." Initially, a residential home for three "rescued women" was founded. Now, as well as the home for children, it includes an adult home, a primary school, a working women's hostel, an elderly women's home and a training and production center. The All Bengal is respected and prestigious, the showpiece of Calcutta's voluntary welfare establishment. When a distinguished visitor comes to the city (such as Princess Anne in her capacity as president of Save the Children Fund), the All Bengal is on the agenda.

Housed in a large, shabby compound of gray buildings near the center of Calcutta, the children's home at first seems bleak and dingy. Comforts and decorations are few; the children sleep in large bare dormitories, eat on the floor (as is Hindu custom) in cavernous, dark halls, and play outside in a scrubby courtyard overlooked by tall buildings. But when I arrived with Mrs. Mitra on an unannounced visit, it was immediately apparent that the atmosphere in the home was warm and the morale high. The children were evidently delighted to see Mrs. Mitra and clustered around her. We went into several classrooms where children were studying or working at drawings or sewing; the school is famous for crafts and needlework.

The emphasis at All Bengal is on rehabilitation and education. "I regard it as a boarding school," Mrs. Mitra said firmly. "I don't like to call it a home for orphans and destitute girls." The aim is that the girls should eventually be reintegrated with their communities, either through a job or through marriage. This is why the home is not redecorated or equipped with many toys or books, although well-wishers often offer such things: the staff feel the children should not grow up in more comfort than they will find outside. The priority is to restore the children's self-respect and encourage their confidence and natural abilities; and the school performs well in public examinations, in music and sporting competitions. Mrs. Mitra is proud of the considerable number of girls who have moved on from All Bengal to train as nurses. Her pleasure in the success stories she told me and in the smiling, energetic little girls who came up to talk to us was striking.

But not all of them are smiling. While I was there Mrs. Mitra was told the latest development in the story of an orphan girl of thirteen who had been so maltreated by her employers that she tried to commit suicide. The hospital authorities had contacted All Bengal and the people in charge of the home had applied to be her legal guardians; that day they had heard that the application had succeeded.

Some of the children need long-term psychiatric help, and a psychiatrist is available once a week or more often if required. The home has a number of physically and mentally handicapped girls who receive special education and training where possible. While we were talking a slow, heavy girl of about fourteen came up to us. She bent to touch Mrs. Mitra's feet in the traditional sign of respect, and then leaned her head against her shoulder. She was evidently emotionally disturbed, and Mrs. Mitra spoke to her very gently before sending her away. "She is one of our slow learners," said Mrs. Mitra. "She came to us from prison, about four years ago. We think she was sexually assaulted there."

In the Salt Lake area of Calcutta is another residential home watched over by Mrs. Mitra, the Child Care Home. This home, I learned, was opened in 1985 and has been used as one of the main alternatives to jail after the initiative by the central and state governments in 1986. There was therefore a high proportion of children there who had come from jail, some of them after several years. At the time of my visit the home could accommodate up to fifty girls, up to the age of eighteen. The intention was to expand to a capacity of one hundred.

The Child Care Home is a forbidding-looking place. It is bare and dingy and is badly in need of a coat of paint and some new mosquito netting. On the ground floor are offices, a big room where meetings are held, a dining hall with a dark kitchen area off it; upstairs are dormitories, furnished only with wooden beds. From the roof there is a view over what looks like normal village life; the rows of small uniform houses were built by the Lutheran World Service, a religious aid organization that also helped to build the Child Care Home, which otherwise is funded by the state with additional help from charities. The home is run by an elderly male superintendent and three young house mothers; the girls go out to school, and to the market, and to learn dancing and singing. Soon after I arrived a crowd of small girls in blue and white check cotton dresses came back from school and raced in to see Mrs. Mitra. She seemed to know all about each one of them, spotted which of them had a slight cold or looked tired, and discussed the need for vitamin supplements with the superintendent. None of the girls had any known relatives. The Child Care Home had been appointed their legal guardian by the courts.

One of the girls stayed behind to talk to us. She was about eight, slender and pretty, with a long neck, pigtails tied with red ribbons and a dazzling smile. Her nickname was Baby. Mrs. Mitra asked her how she had found herself in jail, and translated her answers for me. Baby did not seem reluctant to answer but gazed trustingly at Mrs. Mitra and spoke without hesitation.

"She was on a bus with her mother," said Mrs. Mitra, "and her mother got off the bus to get some water. She got off and never came back, and Baby was left in the bus. Someone took her from the bus and she went to court next day, and then she was sent to Presidency jail." How long was she there? "She's not sure. Quite a long time." What happened to her in the jail? Could she remember what she did all day? "She was not really studying, but singing, playing games, playing with toys." What did she feel when she moved from the jail to the Child Care Home? "She says it's quite different here and she likes it better. She especially likes dancing and going to school." What would she like to do when she grows up? "She wants to do housework," said Mrs. Mitra, laughing. "And also be a dancing teacher."

Baby's friend Barnali came up to talk to us as well. She too had landed up in jail after getting lost. Children often get lost in Calcutta. The city is crowded and confused and the train and bus stations are full of poor families who have come to make their fortunes in the city but are totally unused to such chaos: it is only too easy to become separated from a small child. "I was on a train, going with my mother to my uncle's house. My mother went to get some food and the train started. A big boy found me and took me to his home. Then the police came." Had she spent a long time in jail? She looked a little wary. "Not too long," she said.

It was not easy to talk to the girls about their previous lives. It was not that they were reluctant to answer; on the contrary, they often seemed to be rattling off a prepared story, as if they had learned what was expected of them. A volunteer I met later, who had spent some weeks getting to know them, found the same. She had observed a group of new arrivals, five girls aged between six and eight, all of whom had been together in jail. All told much the same story, of getting lost on the way to visit a relative; all of them seemed wary of adults and clung together in a group for security. "My feeling was that they mistrusted pretty well everybody outside their group," said the volunteer. She also deduced from their drawings and games that they were all afraid of men, and drew her own conclusions.

Before I left I looked through the ledgers in which the Child Care Home listed the bare facts about each child on admission. Small photographs showed a series of anxious, scowling, panic-stricken faces. None of the children I saw that afternoon still looked like that. "Well, they have their ups and downs emotionally," said Mrs. Mitra. "But we notice that when they come here they all have that same expression. Then after a while they change, and become individuals."

In India, as elsewhere, the law works slowly and is expensive. Given that children in trouble with the law or the police are predominantly from the poorest and least educated sections of society, I wondered what kind of legal representation they or their families managed to find, and how, if at all, their plight came to be recognized and dealt with by the legal system. If the way to improve the lot of vulnerable children is to close the gap between principle and practice, and to implement the laws and regulations pertaining to children's rights, then surely among the legal profession in India there should be people working toward that aim.

Through one of India's most distinguished human rights lawyers, Dr. Subrata Roy Chowdury, I visited the High Court in Calcutta to talk to a High Court judge, Mr. Justice Dilip Basu. At first I looked for him in the old High Court building, an elaborate, pinnacled red and white Gothic pile copied from the town hall at Ypres in Belgium in 1872. It contains a warren of corridors, galleries and ancient, inadequate lifts, and is thronged by lawyers in black gowns, white ties and wigs who surge through the halls and into the courtrooms. I eventually found Mr. Basu with three pupils in a quiet room in the modern annex.

"Since the early 1980s," he told me, "there has been an important new development here: Public Interest Litigation, known as PIL. With cases where children are concerned, when young boys or girls are being kept in jail, one problem is money; the other is access to the courts. In 1979," he went on, "a woman wrote a letter to the *Times of India* complaining of an inordinate delay in dealing with her case. This letter was treated as a 'writ petition,' and on the basis of her letter alone her case was dealt with in ten days. Now, since then, anyone can introduce a letter petition."

Later that evening I went to visit a controversial young lawyer, Shib Sankar Chakraborty. For four years he has specialized in cases concerning the sexual exploitation and victimization of women and children whom he considers to have been unjustly imprisoned. Not only does he welcome and secure press exposure for these cases, but he also writes a column about his work for a popular Bengali women's magazine. Mr. Chakraborty is a slim, tense young man with sharp eyes and a sudden brilliant smile. His office, where he is available most evenings for his clients, is one of a cluster of small wooden shacks opening onto a pavement in a Calcutta suburb close to Alipore jail. Inside, the tiny room is partitioned into a waiting area and a cubicle where he sits at a rickety table covered with papers.

"Since 1984," he said, "I have been fighting against the illegal detention of young girls in jail. It is my opinion that girls are more vulnerable than boys, and need more physical protection." He came across the case that awoke his interest almost by accident, when a prison warder came to him for legal advice. The warder told him about a girl of sixteen, a rape victim, who had been sent to jail for "safe custody." The man who raped her was given bail after fifteen days, and two years later the case against him was dropped. The girl spent four years in jail and her family did not know where she was. "I thought this must be a single bad example," said Mr. Chakraborty, his voice rising angrily. "Then I was told of twenty-five similar cases in the same jail, and eventually I came to know of three hundred and forty innocent girls behind bars."

Since then he has worked with passionate dedication to get these girls out of prison and reunited with their families or placed in homes. His tactics, which have included going on hunger strike outside the government building in Calcutta, have not made him popular with the rest of the legal profession or the authorities. He told me that a requisition order had been placed on his office, to force him farther out of the city and away from the jail itself, and said that he had been physically attacked on several occasions. "But my only offense is to say to the authorities: what right have you got to put children behind bars? You cannot curtail the rights of Indian women and children."

Through his efforts and publicity, and pressure from the

Supreme Court, the situation has improved since 1985, but Mr. Chakraborty does not feel that his crusade is over. He is indignant about conditions in some of the government-run homes, and describes the case of a teenage girl who recently left a home seven months pregnant. "She was molested by one of the staff: a government employee. The government is ashamed of conditions in these homes. We need to keep checking on what happens there." Recently he has been involved in a complicated case about a woman prison warder who has been trying to take custody of a girl in her care, claiming falsely to be related to her. He believes that the warder is involved in a prostitution racket.

Mr. Chakraborty struck me as fearless, almost fanatical in his determination to free the girls he regards as victims of corruption, cruelty and ignorance. He lives on almost nothing, subsidizes cases with his journalism and charges only for expenses. He once spent a year living on the pavement in a Calcutta slum to get closer to the people he represents. He resists all suggestions that he might join forces with government projects or social workers. "We have a saying in Bengal," he told me. "A hired soldier cannot win a battle. I don't need money. What I believe, I must do." He knows and respects Mrs. Mitra, but her way of tackling problems is not for him. "She is trying to get change by compromise. I am trying to get change by fighting."

There is only one juvenile court in Calcutta; even more astonishingly, it is the only juvenile court in the whole of West Bengal. Since 1979 the court has been housed a half hour's drive from the city center, in the area called Salt Lake where a huge new sports stadium and expensive-looking modern villas have been built alongside squatters' huts and half-finished housing developments. My contact, a lawyer who attends the court regularly, explained that I could not make a formal visit or interview any of the officials, but he was prepared to take me there and help me with general inquiries.

The court premises consist of the ground floor of a bare concrete building with unpainted walls, naked light bulbs, minimal furnishings and a general air of poverty and neglect. Two clerks, two policemen and a woman magistrate were present. The whole place was quiet, almost somnolent; I had been anticipating a crowded scene full of incident and drama. A teenage boy with a hangdog expression was waiting behind bars in the lockup at the end of the corridor. His case had been dealt with that morning and he was about to be taken to a remand home.

Like most juvenile offenders who reach the court, the boy had been accused of theft. Such offenses are committed mainly by boys aged between nine and fourteen; frequently the thefts are prompted by desperate poverty or hunger. Often the younger children are organized and directed by older boys or adults; the court sometimes delays sentencing the youngsters to give the police a chance to investigate. The usual penalties imposed in such cases are a fine, often paid by the parents, or two or three months' detention in a reform school. Such boys are not sent to jail, but there are not enough establishments available to separate the younger children from the older teenagers. Often the same boys reappear time after time and it may become clear that their parents or older brothers are organizing them. However, when they are released from detention there is no system for getting them any further training, let alone a job, so they tend to drift back into petty crime.

The juvenile court also handles destitute, lost and abandoned children. That morning the magistrate had dealt with two abandoned newborn babies whom she had transferred from the hospital to a children's home. While I was there a large policeman arrived, holding by the hand a small, composed boy of four or five who had been found lost in the street. Without delay the magistrate summoned the court into session and sat the little boy beside her at a large wooden table on a platform looking down on several rows of wooden chairs, a clerk and three spectators. The boy knew his name —Singh—but not his address. A screw in his pocket led the magistrate to speculate that he might be a mechanic's son. She also found a few coins in his pocket, which turned out to have been given him by a policeman to buy sweets. He was sent to a girls' remand home while efforts were made to find his family.

The juvenile court was understaffed, and some of those working there felt that no one was interested in their work or their problems. "Important lawyers do not often come here," said my lawyer friend ruefully on our way back to the city. In the recent past a series of complaints about conditions at the court surfaced in the newspapers, concerning broken telephones and inadequate facilities for the care of hungry or sick children. The place seemed oddly stagnant, a backwater. It was impossible to believe that there was not more work to be done there, in dealing with the multifarious needs of Calcutta's huge population of children in trouble. The system, such as it was, could not be working, or else it was so congested as to be unworkable. In theory the court was the vital link between children in trouble and the institutions supposed to be catering to their needs. In practice, the children did not reach the court, and the institutions either did not function properly or did not exist. In the rest of the state of West Bengal children still appear at ordinary courts which are temporarily designated for juveniles. Eight more juvenile courts staffed by specially trained officers have been promised, but no one seemed to know when, where or how they would materialize.

I left Calcutta feeling that, although the problem of children who find themselves in prison is a long way from being a thing of the past, at least it is on the agenda and the focus for concern and dedicated effort. I was warned that the situation in Bihar was different.

The state of Bihar borders West Bengal to the north and east and is usually described as one of the most backward and depressed parts of India. Of the population of around seventy million (it is the second most populous state, after Uttar Pradesh) most are employed as agricultural laborers, and many are still caught up in the infamous bonded labor system which in effect makes them serfs. To the rest of India, Bihar is often a source of scandal and embarrassment. The local politicians, administrators and police are regarded as profoundly corrupt, ruthless and often violent. When I was there the newspapers reported that a gang of policemen had rampaged through a remote village, raping the women and beating up the men. The Bihar government's immediate reaction was to support the police.

The legal system of Bihar is equally suspect. In the early 1980s a man was found in a Bihar jail awaiting trial for being on a train without a ticket. He had been held for thirty years. He is now free, thanks to a civil liberties action group, but insane. Around the same time an inquiry unearthed four boys aged about eighteen who had been in prison, untried, since they were ten. The Supreme Court ordered them to be freed, saying: "This is one more instance of the callousness and indifference of our judicial system. People are easily forgotten."

I flew to Patna, the state capital, on a fine spring afternoon. After Calcutta the city seemed small and manageable; it contains about half a million people and straggles along the southern bank of the Ganges. Before I left London I had been told about Sanhat Sinha, who was said to be closer to the problem of children in prison in India than anyone and to run a project for them from Patna. I located him in a small block of flats down a side road away from the city center.

Sanhat Sinha is a calm and scholarly-looking man of about forty. "In Bihar," he told me, "an ordinance was passed by the state government in 1970, based on the 1960 Children's Act, but nothing at all was done. In 1979 the Indian Supreme

98

Court reprimanded the Bihar government for not implementing the Children's Act and in 1980 the Bihar Children's Act was passed. But still nothing was done till 1982, when it was meant to come into immediate effect all over Bihar. The authorities were supposed to frame rules to implement the law, but again nothing happened. There were none of the required institutions or homes, like children's boards, juvenile courts, children's homes or special schools—they didn't exist."

In 1985 Sanhat Sinha and a small team of social scientists at the University of Bombay arrived in Patna to set up the Project for the Protection of Children's Rights. He comes from Bihar and was eager to tackle the problem while knowing it would not be easy. "We met everybody, in government, the prison service, the legal profession, and everybody blamed each other," he said wryly. "The welfare department blamed the politicians for failing to provide funds. The jails and remand homes blamed the shortage of qualified staff. There was no juvenile court in the whole state of Bihar—and there still isn't. In 1985 magistrates were ordered by the Patna High Court to constitute children's courts and children's boards. But still today we find children's cases coming up in ordinary courts."

In 1986, after waiting six months for the necessary permissions, Sinha and his team of researchers visited eight remand homes in Bihar and three prisons. The report he gave me, distilling months of research and interviews with a hundred children, stated that they had found forty-four boys between the ages of ten and sixteen in prison. Most of the boys were aged between fourteen and sixteen, and more than seventy percent were illiterate. About half of the children came from large families (of between six and ten), and the same proportion came from very poor families living on three hundred rupees (about twenty dollars) or less a month.

The team reported that forty-three percent of the children had been involved in "major offenses" such as murder, robbery or rape; fifty-seven percent were accused of theft, "destroying public property" or "street quarreling." But seventy-five percent of the boys aged fourteen or under had been involved only in lesser offenses; and, in the team's view, a significant number of those accused and convicted of more serious offenses had been "falsely implicated." "It is needless to say," the report added, "that in such an environment the children are consistently exposed to interaction with hardened criminals. The integrity of the child is constantly under threat."

"Our first priority," said Sanhat Sinha, "was that no child should be kept in jail. Early in 1987 we had a meeting with the Inspector General of Prisons. First he told us that there were no children in prison in Bihar. Then, when we disagreed, he said there were only six children in jail. I doubted whether that number was correct; we had visited only three, out of at least a hundred jails in the state. After that we found that children were being transferred from prison to remand homes. But there are still many problems. Often the remand homes are in a remote place, and the policeman who has to escort the child does not want to go there; so he falsifies the child's age. Sometimes there is a genuine doubt about the age of the child, so the prison doctor is consulted, whose expertise I doubt. But it is true that now most children in trouble with the law are being kept in remand homes, which have been designated (i.e., renamed) as observation centers." "How many remand homes are there in Bihar?" I asked. "On paper, there are twenty-four, but in fact only sixteen are functioning." "And what are they like?" "Worse than the jails," he said, without hesitation.

Sinha, like some of the people I had met in Calcutta, was in a painful predicament. Once the vital principle was established that no child should be held in prison, the next question inevitably became: where are children in trouble, whether awaiting trial or not, to be kept? By insisting that children must be transferred from jails to remand homes, activists may be prolonging the child's institutionalization in worse surroundings. The prisons are likely to be more accessible, and more open to inspection, than other institutions. Why, I asked Sinha, were the remand homes of Bihar so poor? Although he was clearly full of anger and frustration, he calmly described an appalling picture of disorganization, incompetence and neglect. "In the remand homes everyone is dissatisfied," he said. "In 1979 the administration of remand homes was transferred from the jail department to the welfare department. The idea was to improve them but the staff were not at all happy. The district welfare officers had too much to do already; the new responsibility of the remand homes had very low priority."

As few superintendents have ever been appointed, the homes are all run by housemasters. But a housemaster has very little power: if a child is sick he cannot send him or her to the hospital without the authority of a superintendent, who does not exist. The budget for running the homes is very low and allocations never come through at the right time. The blanket allowance for the children for the winter, for instance, would arrive there in summer. Some remand homes are a long way from the nearest court, and it is impossible to get the money needed for a child's transport or food on the journey, so many cases are delayed or ignored. The remand homes are nearly all rented by the state, rather than purchased or purpose-built, and they are in very bad condition, with leaking roofs and no sanitation. "They are regarded as unfit for humans, so they become remand homes," said Sanhat Sinha scathingly. The staff, even when well intentioned, receive little support or recognition. They feel their colleagues in the prison service are doing better, with promotions and salaries and benefits, while they are often not even reimbursed for sums spent from their own pockets on medicines or clothes for their charges. "They become angry, and the anger is transferred to the children," said Sinha. "The ultimate sufferer is always the child."

Not far from the center of Patna, down a side street, stands an unremarkable two-story house of pinkish stucco, set back from the street behind a wall. The house has open arcades on the ground and second floors with small rooms opening off behind. The whole place, like the street itself, is crumbling and dilapidated; but, unlike the street, where the usual lively racket is in progress, the house seems enveloped in a sullen quiet. The ground floor houses offices of the welfare department; the upper floor is a senior remand home for boys.

My guide and I found the superintendent, a severe-looking elderly woman with iron-gray hair drawn back in a bun, seated behind her desk, on which lay a large *lathi,* the Indian police truncheon. Outside her office two or three men in dirty white *dhotis* were standing around. There was no sign of a uniform or indeed of any official presence, apart from a glass case on the landing with small curling photographs of young boys pinned up inside it. I later learned that these were missing children. The superintendent was reluctant to talk about her job; it turned out that she was not far from retirement, having worked for thirty years at various jobs in similar institutions in Bihar, but she divulged a few facts. The house is rented by the state, and it can house up to a hundred boys, from infants to the age of eighteen. It now housed about thirty. The length of stay varied from a few days to a year or more. The welfare department ran the home. She herself had originally trained as a probation officer, but there were no probation officers attached to the remand home. In fact, she said, there were no probation officer posts anywhere in Bihar, though she believed that some were planned.

Three categories of boys were sent to her: "undertrials," boys convicted of an offense, and boys in need of care and protection—usually orphans, lost or destitute boys. All shared the same quarters and conditions. She was supposed to have a housemaster and six supervisors working under her, but as usual was understaffed. Two teachers were supposed to come daily to hold classes.

The place was bare and grimy. I was taken through a locked door into a larger inner gallery built around a central well. There was a strong smell of sewage. The superintendent said something to my companion about an unsolved drain problem. Around the open gallery various boys were hanging about staring at us. They were dressed in dirty white and appeared to be between twelve and eighteen. One boy, obviously disturbed, rushed up to us and started talking wildly, clutching at my Bihari companion and grinning. We went into one of the rooms. About ten wooden beds were crammed side by side; a few rags and towels hung on strings along the walls. We tried to talk to the six or seven boys in the room but a small, angry-looking elderly man soon intervened. One boy of about fifteen was telling us that he had not done anything wrong and was afraid he would never get out of the place. His face was contorted with anxiety and fear. "Of course they all say they are innocent," the elderly man broke in mockingly. "But the police are not blind," he shouted, leading us away. All the boys gazed after us.

Back in the gallery we paused to look over the parapet into the stinking yard beneath. Two older boys were planing wood; this was described as a carpentry workshop. Otherwise there was no sign of any recreational or educational space or facilities, and certainly no room for exercise. The boys never went out. Sensing their despair, it was hard to leave them there, but they were, in fact, the luckier ones, for at least they were not buried in the remote countryside where no one would ever know what went on.

Confronted with the enormous task of overhauling the remand schools of Bihar, Sanhat Sinha has recently been looking for a way around it. "Our first aim had been to get the children out of the jails; the next became to get them out of remand homes, because they are just as bad or worse." Was there no public demand for an improved system? I asked. Sinha looked at me tolerantly and shook his head. "Nobody makes any noise about it. The citizens are not much concerned. So we started to follow up cases ourselves, through the families where we could find them, and call individual cases before the courts. We had a very good response from the families, who in most cases were not even aware where their children were. This was very encouraging."

But if a child in trouble had lost touch with his or her family, were the parents simply not told what became of them? Were the authorities not required to inform parents? "Mostly the children are dumped in a jail or a home and forgotten. If they can write, perhaps they write a letter, which is often torn up. Sometimes the authorities say they tried to contact the families without success. But when we write to them they come forward. So what does that show? The parents usually reach us with empty pockets; where it is very necessary, we help them financially."

Was legal aid available in such cases? "None of the lawyers we use charge any fees, just their expenses. There are many good people in this society. We have found that, where relatives can be traced, you are on the way to solving the problem for at least thirty percent of the children kept in institutions. This percentage could go home right away. Thirty-five percent have more serious problems but, with help and support, they could go back to their families too. We feel that with a year's preparation they could be ready; they have the capacity, but they are uneducated and have never experienced love and affection. Many times, if they have done something wrong, it was not with a criminal intention but for survival. For the rest, about a third, it is more difficult. Perhaps they are orphans or perhaps their families don't want them back. These do need some institutional support. So now we are trying to identify groups and homes which might take such children and look after them properly and work on their problems with them. Of course it is very hard to find such homes. Usually they are religious, or voluntary, charitable organizations. We have to be very careful; we don't want to repeat the same old mistakes."

What, I wondered, were relations like between Sanhat Sinha and his team and the Bihar authorities: politicians, welfare services, police, the legal profession? "At first our approach was collaborative," he said, choosing his words with care. "Then we found that nothing was achieved. So now we are turning to the outside. Relations with the judiciary are good." And with the government ministers responsible for social welfare and prisons? For the first time Sanhat Sinha looked grim. "I cannot act on their liking. I act first on the needs of the child." He is now planning a workshop for policymakers, to try to get them to confront the reasons why so many excuses are made for not implementing national and state laws.

Since he came to Bihar, Sinha reckons that about two hundred cases, of children having been imprisoned or held in inappropriate conditions, have been directly dealt with by the Project. Many more have been helped indirectly. Of the children still in need of help, he calculates that fewer than before have been held for more than a year; previously, many had been in jail or unsuitable institutions for four to five years. It is plain that he now feels he knows the dimensions of the problem in Bihar and how to solve it, but that he is frustrated by the lack of interest or cooperation he encounters from the authorities. "There's no will from anybody from top to bottom to do anything about this kind of thing. I know that eighty percent of cases concerning children could be disposed of, provided everyone collaborates," he said with passion.

What were his next steps going to be? "We want at least some of the promised juvenile courts to be established; eight are supposed to be set up in Bihar. Meanwhile, we want a magistrate to go once a week to the remand homes, as an interim arrangement, to dispose of cases more quickly. Also we are going to produce a handbook on the Juvenile Justice Act, including recent Supreme Court judgments. Often the police, the welfare officers, the judiciary themselves don't know what the law is, or what they are required to do." Full of admiration for his tenacity, I asked if he ever felt the task was hopeless. The thought appeared not to have occurred to him. "There is no limit to patience," he said.

Sanhat Sinha was somewhat reluctant to give me examples of cases in which the Project had intervened, as they strive to respect the privacy of the people they are trying to help. However, he did outline for me a case that he hopes will establish a crucial principle: that, for an offense allegedly committed while the suspect was legally a child, the law applicable to children shall be invoked even if the accused has passed into legal adulthood while awaiting trial. This case is still pending.

Four years ago a man and his two sons, then aged about fourteen and twelve, were accused of murder. At first all three were kept in jail; after a while the boys were sent to a remand home. All three were then sent for trial jointly in the ordinary court. After protests, an age determination test was ordered. A board of doctors concluded that the older was then above sixteen and below seventeen, and the younger about fourteen and below fifteen. The examination, however, did not take place till eighteen months after the date of the crime. The judge then sent the younger boy to a remand home, and the case was referred to a higher court. There the judge suddenly declared the older boy to be over twenty and sentenced him and his father to life imprisonment. In Sanhat Sinha's opinion the father alone had committed the crime and had implicated his sons to shield himself and confuse the issue. Within three months the father died in prison; eighteen months later the younger boy was released from the remand home because no one knew what to do with him. The older boy, however, remained in prison, sentenced to life; he is now nineteen, by the doctor's reckoning, and has spent four years in prison for a crime he probably did not commit. The Project filed a writ and took his case to the Supreme Court, which ordered the Bihar High Court to dispose of it within three months. At the time of writing, the appeal had still not been heard.

"These boys' rights were violated by the courts, which did not give them the benefit of the Children's Act," said Sanhat Sinha. "We know of four or five cases of a similar type, where boys of fourteen have been sentenced to life imprisonment." How, in his opinion, could such cases occur when the law of India was so emphatic that no child should ever be sentenced to life, and recent Supreme Court judgments had confirmed that the Juvenile Justice Act should work retroactively? "Ignorance and carelessness. Everywhere children's rights are violated, and no one sees it as a great problem. But in this way we are making future criminals."

About six months before my visit the Project for the Protection of Children's Rights had conducted a study of a group of girls in a Patna residential after-care home. It made distressing reading. The researchers had interviewed about eighty of a hundred or so inmates; the others were deaf and dumb or mentally ill. Two thirds of the interviewees were under twenty-one, and thus legally termed children. Nearly half were between sixteen and twenty. Eight were under ten. Again, most of the girls came from very poor families: some of them had been working as servants from the age of nine, for between ten and twenty rupees (less than a dollar and a half) a month, and more than half were illiterate.

The Project reported on conditions in the home, which were found to be extremely primitive and squalid. The building was in a state of near dereliction and "stinking with filth." The roof leaked. There were no proper doors or windows, just holes in the wall, and the floorboards were broken. Some inmates had no bedding at all. Many had no clothes either, and walked around seminaked in dirty rags. Food supplies were erratic and of poor quality; often just four *roti* (pieces of unleavened bread) and one glass of water a day. The water supply was unhygienic and insufficient: one broken standpipe for the whole compound. There were no medical facilities whatsoever. Many of the inmates were physically and mentally ill. The leg ulcers of one girl had been so neglected that amputation was considered likely.

Most of the girls who found themselves trapped in this nightmare had not done anything wrong. Eighty percent had no cases pending against them. A typical chain of events would be as follows: a girl of about fifteen would run away from home after a quarrel. Because she had no money and nowhere to go she would soon be picked up by a man, or sometimes by an older woman, who would involve her in prostitution. She would then seek protection from the police or become the victim of a sexual assault, or get involved in a vice case as a witness. After a spell in jail she would end up in the home, either waiting for a case in which she was a victim or a witness to be heard, or sent there as the result of a case and because she had nowhere else to go. Poor families often do not want wayward girls back, and in any case a third of the girls were orphans.

After two or three years of enduring the conditions in the home, some girls were prepared to try the only way out available to them: a marriage arranged by the staff. These marriages were not preceded by an investigation of the prospective husband and no attempt was made at a follow-up. Some girls returned to the home in a worse state than ever. Several told the team that they would rather die in the home than endure such marriages. However, as the educational and training programs supplied by the home were totally inadequate, marriage was their only chance of ever getting out and living a normal life.

Late one evening in Patna, I called on a woman who had worked for many years in this same after-care home. She lived in a small house behind a high wall a little way out of the town, with two huge barking Alsatian dogs. While she confirmed the conditions described in the report and explained to me the pathetic amounts of money allocated for the care of each girl (less than three dollars and a quarter a week for food, about twelve dollars a year for clothes), she defended the arranged marriage system and said the report was unfair. "Most of the girls want to escape from the home by any means possible," she said. She described how the system worked. Men would apply for a wife; sometimes they were soldiers serving in the area; they were always men with a job, "not beggars. It is the best way for the girls. They are the daughters of the government," she said, implying that the government was responsible for arranging their marriages since no one else would. But she agreed that the girls' conditions were intolerable and that a crash program was needed. "The government should take proper action on humanitarian grounds; but the government is not very interested." She recounted one case that she remembered with horror. A girl had actually been reclaimed by her family from the after-care home, where she had been sent after a bitter quarrel over a love affair with a boy of a different caste. The girl was confused, and the staff at the home were reluctant to let her go back to her family, fearing that they might harm her. In the end she went. After a few months it was reported in the newspapers that she was dead. She was about nineteen.

Before I left Patna, I met two respected local reporters. They struck me as tired and cynical, and they told me that stories of unfair detention and terrible conditions in jails and remand homes were common. Most people in Bihar just took such things for granted. There had been a case recently of a juvenile "undertrial" committing suicide after being sexually harassed in jail. Was this reported? I asked. They nodded. Was there an outcry? They looked at me almost pityingly. "This issue," said one of them patiently, "is not seriously pursued here. Prisons are only well run when there is some benefit in doing so for the politicians."

Despite universal condemnation of the practice, children—and even babies—are in detention today in many parts of the world. They are there for theft; because of political repression; and because in some places the authorities judge prisons to be the safest way of caring for children who would otherwise be alone and on the streets.

While the overall world trend is to raise the minimum age of penal responsibility, in practice some countries are lowering it in an attempt to isolate juvenile delinquents from society. The most preoccupying aspect of the treatment of imprisoned children appears to occur during police custody and pretrial detention. Research indicates that more often than not children have no legal assistance during proceedings against them.

Recent reports from Turkey suggest that children are locked up in adult prisons for as much as a year before being sentenced, and that only rarely do they have access to a lawyer. Torture has been used in order to extract confessions and children have been known to have been held for so minor a crime as begging from tourists. Other evidence of children in prison that has reached Amnesty International in the last few years includes reports of three hundred Kurdish children detained in northern Iraq, and of a number of children detained without charge by the military in the district of Kitgum in Uganda. In the United States there were thirty prisoners on death row in 1987 for crimes committed when they were younger than eighteen, and in some cases younger than sixteen. They were waiting to be old enough to be executed.

The best-documented account of the imprisonment of a very great number of children in recent years comes from South Africa. In the six months following the imposition of emergency powers in June 1986, over twenty-two thousand people were detained; some eight and a half thousand were children who, through school boycotts and public demonstrations, had voiced their opposition to the South African authorities.

These children were picked up either at school or on leaving home, and taken to police stations for interrogation, often in an entirely random way. Most were aged between thirteen and eighteen, but some at least were under ten. At the police stations they were bullied and threatened and on occasion tortured into making a confession, or into giving the names of other "troublemakers." Arrested under the pretext of the emergency laws, they were then confronted with charges of criminal offenses based on their confessions. Parents were seldom notified of their children's arrest and discovered their whereabouts only by going from police station to police station, or by learning that they were appearing in court.

Those not released after preliminary interrogations were kept in police cells or transferred to prison, where some were kept incommunicado for several weeks. The more fortunate were put with children of their own age. Others found themselves with adult criminals, and were sexually assaulted. A number of these children are still both physically and psychologically maimed by their experiences.

Despite the fact that at least two international legal instruments state that children should be separated from adults both before their trials and after they have been convicted, children are imprisoned together with adults in many countries. At a seminar organized by Defense of Children International in December 1984, experts meeting to discuss the jailing of children with adults passed resolutions deploring the custom, suggesting that child offenders should be given community service and held in semiliberty, and proposing that children throughout the world be removed from the system of adult criminal justice, based on repression, and placed within a system of juvenile justice, based on social assistance.

C.M.

5

Child Abuse

in Great Britain

Sarah Hobson
with Peter

Northamptonshire, where I have lived for most of my life, is not well known outside its own boundaries, despite its royal connections with Mary Queen of Scots and Princess Diana. Once a rural treasure trove for the landed gentry, it has swollen its towns by importing labor in the last three decades: Glaswegians to Corby; Londoners to Northampton; and Asians to Kettering and Wellingborough.

In 1980 Northamptonshire had the highest rate of sexual offenses against children in Britain. At the same time, the county offers some of the most progressive services in relation to child abuse and has some of the best people working there. Yet the voices of those who were abused were hardly heard. Their experience was often shrouded by experts in a blanket of concern, discretion and protection. I therefore had the idea of working directly with a small group of people in and around Northampton who wanted to tell their own stories.

I was introduced to Peter, Sandy, Mary, Robert, Francis and others. Each contributed according to his or her wish, and within the limited space available in one short chapter. Peter wrote or dictated his own section, and helped to edit his own and others' material; Sandy wrote and edited her own section; Mary, Robert and Francis recorded their experiences on tape, and then commented on the material once it had been edited by me. Others wrote their own pieces. I prompted, asked, listened and selected. Before working in this group Peter had never met another male who had been sexually abused, nor had he met an abuser other than his own; Mary had talked only to her counselor about her childhood; and Francis had revealed to no one the details of his upbringing. All of them felt that it was time to speak out. Doing so is part of a healing process, provided the words and the feelings behind the words are honored by those who listen. This chapter is intended to be part of that process—both for the readers and for the writers. We are all sentenced to the memories of our childhood; who we are now is part of who we were then, how we were treated and how we responded.

Where appropriate, names have been changed.

AGE: three. SEX: male. Adopted.

Daddy got dangerous fingers. Daddy has. He's got some nails, big nails. Put them up my back. Make it bleed.

My mummy got the fag and burns me and Colin's back.
Right up there, up my head. And down my leg, and burnt my
shoes. My best shoes.

My mummy, her put a fag up my bottom.

My daddy in my bedroom. Him clown. Him getting me.

My daddy pull my willy. My bleed on my bottom.

Daddy hurt me. Him not love me. I horrible, him say.

Daddy, Kevin, Gary, Maxine, Glenys, Sam, David, Debbie,
Grandad. Them witches.

Them get spiders and worms in black boxes. Put them in
our hair.

Them witches burning me. Me and Craig and Darren.

Them witches make you go in the bonfire. It burns us.
When them splash you with water, you stronger and
stronger. Can't get burnt. Them witches splash you with water.

Mum know them witches.

I a boy one witch.

AGE: eighteen. SEX: male. OCCUPATION: nurse.

I used to hate my mum. She always made me do the housework. While she sat, she'd say, "This is my rest day." Every
bloody day was her rest day. She made us clean the front
room, and every week we had to move all the furniture out of
the rooms, then hoover, and put all the stuff back. The units
were ever so heavy.

My mum often gave me ten pence to spend without my
brothers or sisters knowing. It was as if she needed a friend,
and so tried to buy my friendship. She never helped me with
my homework: as long as I could peel potatoes and hoover,
she was quite happy. She used to say, "I'd rather have
twenty-two girls than one boy, especially like you.'

I have very few memories of my father. He was just a person that seemed to be there whenever my mum wished him
to be. She asked him to hit us if she felt we needed it. That

was all the contact I had with him. He hardly ever seemed to be home, he either worked long hours or went someplace else after work. When the family were together in one room, we had to sit dead still. We couldn't scratch an itch or cross our legs without disapproval. We had to accept everything he said without question. The only pictures I have in my memory are of my father sitting in front of the TV with his right hand down his trousers, even when my friends were there.

My memories about my uncle are very clear. It is my feelings and emotions that cause me conflict. He used to call us into his bedroom. He undressed and told us to do the same. His touch was cold and frightening; he made me feel ashamed of my body. He said, "You have a small willy." I looked at his face, but not ever into his eyes. He was happy, fulfilled. How could I make someone feel like that just by touch? One time when I was alone, I touched my own legs in the same place, but I didn't feel happy or fulfilled. Just sad that I couldn't go out to play.

I never told my mum with the intention of putting him in jail. It was just that I told on him because he was doing something painful. I was very ashamed and thought I was in the wrong. My mum was shocked and called in my dad. At first my sisters didn't say anything. I was crying hard and explaining what he had done. Then they started crying and finally backed me up. My parents sent us upstairs and confronted my uncle; he got angry, and overpowered them. On his way out he called up to me. There was anger in his voice. "I'll fucking get you for this," he said. He ran away. My parents phoned the police, who arrested him.

It was quite a nice day when the policeman took me and my sisters for a ride in his car. It was fun. He was really kind. When we arrived at the police station, we had to give our statements—to describe the first event and the last. Some policemen were laughing. I felt so dirty and small. They were making jokes. I could hear them, and I felt they were laughing at me. I was about nine at the time.

My father refused us having any professional help. He said that we were to forget. In two days it was an untalked-about subject in our house. It wasn't until we did sex education at school that I realized fully what had happened. Sitting there in the TV room at school, watching them show us how to use condoms, I could only cry. I was ashamed of myself, of my body. I felt so guilty. How could I tell someone this was happening and had been doing so for a few years? Also that at points I could not help but enjoy it? It was so difficult to admit that I'd let it happen for all those years. I had a sense that everybody was looking at me, that everybody knew. As if I'd been stamped on the back with a sign saying, "I was to blame, I've been sexually experienced. GAY." But I was only young.

My dad was sleeping around with other women. He was very unloving with my mum and sex didn't exist between them. I remember them arguing in the bedroom late at night, something to do with their love for each other. My mum was sleeping with another man. When she was beaten up by her boyfriend my dad didn't want to know, so she went into the battered wives' home with my sister. He asked me to make a choice between him and her. My mum was drinking heavily. She often used to hit me. She didn't ask me to go with her, so I stayed with him.

We lived in a normal house in a village near Northampton. It was a peaceful place: the usual village green, a river at the back of the houses and a woodland. I used to stay awake at night, looking at the lamppost, and the stars and moon.

I couldn't hear him enter my room. I felt cold as my blankets were removed. He didn't say anything to me. I hated him. I felt useless. I felt he owned me. I felt guilty as I tried not to feel pleasure. But the more I tried to hold my feelings, the greater the pleasure. I thought I heard him laugh.

The night I was mugged, he said I should have overpowered the muggers. Then he abused me again as if I didn't have any feelings. I hated myself. I searched the house for tablets. I don't know what I used. I lay back and waited. I'd never felt so peaceful. In about four hours I woke up. At first I didn't realize what I'd done. Then I phoned a policeman who took me to the hospital. He was really comforting to me.

The stomach pump was fun: I enjoyed the attention; I remember the nurses guessing what I'd had for lunch.

Things got worse at home. At school I was a bastard to get on with. I always got into trouble for being me, for being unhappy. People told me to cheer up even when I was happy. That made me feel worse.

I was possessive. I needed the abuse. My father was going to Spain with my elder sister. They only told me a few days before they were due to go. They never asked me for my opinion. What was I meant to do while they pissed off to Spain and left me all alone?

I worked part time at a supermarket, stacking the shelves. It brought in extra money to pay the electric bills. While I was working I was also cooking and cleaning, doing the housework, doing all the gardening, and expected to study for A levels. On the way home one night a lamppost toppled over and I crashed into it. I just couldn't believe it. It could only have happened to me. I was meant to be going round to a friend's house, but because my fucking bike was knackered I couldn't go. So instead I went home to kill myself. It was the best alternative.

It was six hours before I got into hospital—that's how long it takes for tablets to get into your bloodstream. They gave me some brown fluid that made me violently sick every twenty minutes, but there was nothing to bring up. I was discharged from the hospital into my auntie's care. She was really nice—I love her very much and I miss her very much. After the weekend, I went back to the house and stayed on my own.

A social worker from the hospital came to see me and referred me to Child Guidance, where I met this fantastic lady. She said I must bring my dad to a session. He was very reluctant. He stayed in the room for about ten minutes. He ended up shouting and swearing, and he fucked off home. He forbade me to see her again and told me I was to have no involvement with anyone in social services. But I kept on working with her. I talked about plastic surgery: I hated myself; I wanted my face to be changed because I wanted somebody to love me, not abuse me—but to me, abuse equaled love.

Several weeks, or months, passed. I can't remember which. But one weekend I left home. I moved all my stuff over to my mum's. It was like a divorce. I took the dining-room table, the video recorder, some other pictures off the wall, my bedroom furniture, some of the stuff out of the freezer, even some of the garden tools. As I was his lover, it did seem like a divorce.

I didn't want to take him to court because I felt he was my father. I owed him love and respect. And trust, that it was our secret. But I found out that he probably wasn't my father as my mum had had another boyfriend. So I didn't owe him anything except a jail sentence. And I wanted the world to know, to prove to his precious friends what a bastard he was. I made a statement at the police station. It was a green room, with really comfortable chairs. There were cups of coffee, flowers, pictures on the walls. We went in the morning and came out in the late afternoon. Walking out, I felt so relieved, as if I'd left that miserable, abused part of me in the station. But I couldn't have been more wrong.

I was told he'd be taken in for questioning straight away. It took about a week. After he'd talked with them, he was released. He bloody well wasn't kept in. They were concerned about his age and said there was insufficient evidence. Now I think about it, I felt as though I'd been the abuser after I'd made my statement. I remember I was asked to wait outside. I was pacing up and down. They think they've come so far forward, but they haven't, not when they do things like that.

I was lost. I no longer fitted in at school. I was the only kid in the sixth form that lived on their own. I wasn't being abused. And I wouldn't stimulate my own body as it felt wrong. I lived in a really grotty bed-sit. The school were good to me. They gave me extra grants: I was raking in a few hundred pounds every term, plus working on the side. I just had so much money, but it all seemed to go. Looking back, I know where it went. I was becoming quite depressed in my room. Just four walls to live in. It was enough to turn anyone to drink. So I drank.

There have always been incestuous tendencies in our family. The uncle that abused us had slept with his brother. My dad asked his sister for sex. History seems to repeat itself. My older brother was put into care by my parents. My mum was in care with all her living brothers and sisters—she was one of a very large family; my dad was also in care. I was sexually abused. I guess my uncle was sexually abused. I took an overdose and so did my mum. I was an alcoholic, so was my grandmother, and my mum to a lesser degree.

In the past my relatives lived in the country as agricultural laborers. They moved to the town and became artisans. My family are very handy with their hands. People think, Poor kid, what do you expect from the lower classes? Well, just as many kids in your upper- and middle-class families are being fucked by Mummy and Daddy. You may have all the money but your families fuck your kids as well.

I can't love or be loved, as to be loved you must respect and accept the person you want to love, and to do that you must be able to respect and accept yourself. I'm an object, not a man or woman—an object men use for their own satisfaction, to fulfill their sexual desire. I'm not human to them, I have no feeling. I feel dirty and very much alone. I feel people talk about me behind my back and say, "Oh, there's that kid that was sexually abused." So I was abused. It's not my fault. Nobody loves me, nobody helps me, I make a mess of things. I've never done anything except upset people. Self-pity, that's what this is: even doing this upsets people. It would be nice to be loved. It would be nice to sleep next to someone all night and not have sex. But I'm alone, wondering where I'm going in life, why I'm here. For eighteen years I've been alone. How much longer? I'm weak. The guilt is strong. Why did I not kick, punch, shout, scream, cry? I could have told someone. But why not? I've been abused. Why?

AGE: nineteen. SEX: female. OCCUPATION: shop manageress.

People ask: what kind of families? Well, my family was typically middle class with a detached house in the country, two cars, and holidays every year. There were two brothers and a sister, all a lot older than me. I was the baby, the only one that spent time with my parents.

My father was a large man who was physically very powerful. When he hit me I was flung the length of the room. He was a respected man, a manager who owned his own business. My mother was a quiet, cold woman who worked part time because she wanted to—not because she had to.

When I was small she undressed me and locked me in the coal bunker. When she took me out she told me off for being dirty and put me in a red-hot bath of water.

I was seven when my father first raped me. I was nine when he had anal intercourse with me. His visits to my room were part of my life. At fourteen I had a miscarriage. After that I tried to commit suicide several times. I was put in a psychiatric hospital for several months when I was seventeen.

When I left home at eighteen my brothers and sisters turned against me. I was the one who was in the wrong, I was the guilty party, and nothing I said or did made them change their minds, because they didn't want to lose their security and their parents. I lost everything. It was as though everyone in my life had suddenly died. It was worse—I couldn't mourn them because they weren't dead, I couldn't go to a grave. I didn't know what they were doing but I wanted to know what was going on in their lives.

When I saw John two weeks ago after almost two years, it

was as though we'd never met before. He was politely opening the door for me. No one would ever believe that he was my eldest brother. I used to watch him walking down the stairs on his hands as he was training for his gymnastics. I love John. He was my big brother, the one that protected me, the one that stuck up for me when my friends were picking on me. I fell off my bike once, and he came charging down the road, shouting at my friends because he thought they'd pushed me off. But now, as I walked back from the doctor's, the pain was so great, it was hard not to cry. Seeing his face and not being able to say, "Hello John, how are you?" I was thinking: I wonder if he remembers me, I wonder if he's feeling how I feel. I couldn't say anything because we're strangers now.

When I left home my body wouldn't stop feeling sexy. I needed sex as though it were an addiction. The only way I could make the physical feelings go away was to satisfy the sensations. I'd always associated sex and love with pain, so instead of using sex to make the sensations stop, I used pain. I got a knife and cut my arms and hands.

I also felt dirty when I felt sexy, so pain was a way of punishing myself. I hated my body. I couldn't bear to touch it or look at myself naked. I thought nobody could love me and that sex was the only thing I was fit for. For fourteen years I had been forced to do it.

I seem to attract people who hurt me. I got into a relationship with a man who beat me with a cane. I was so frightened, I didn't respond. He then got angry and hit me harder. It would have been easy to have stayed in the circle I'd been in since I was three. To me love equals sex equals pain equals love.

English society adds to our guilt. When I spoke with a Samaritan and told him my father came to my bed and fucked me, he said, "But didn't you wear any knickers or do anything to stop him?" That man's attitude to me was one of blame. He made me feel so dirty, I tried to put a knife inside me and cut out the evil in me.

Everyone I know who has experienced incest gets the same response, that when we talk to people the attitude is, "Why didn't you stop it and tell someone?" At the age of three? How? To whom?

I don't want people to think that because I've been abused I'm a failure. I got six O levels and two A levels, which isn't bad when I was under all that pressure. I've helped counsel in a rape crisis center, I'm now the manageress of a shop, I've got a sense of humor, and I enjoy life. I've got a new mum and sister who mean more to me because they love me for what I am and not what they want me to be.

AGE: thirty-four. SEX: female. OCCUPATION: campaigner for children's rights.

I'm the one who people see as successful. I'm on committees, I've built my own house, I'm a coper. I found my strength through my children. You have to be strong and do what you want for yourself in order to find your way through. I was always frightened I'd be an abuser, but I'm the one in the hundred that doesn't abuse, even though I was abused.

My mum loved to sing; she sang in all the pubs and clubs. She loved Cliff Richard and all the way through my childhood I loved him. Even in the 1970s, when he was going downhill, I didn't care—I liked his music and I liked him. He is what she held dear, so I have held him dear—he binds her to me.

My mum was seventeen when she had me. She came down from Glasgow with my dad—they were all from Scotland, from the steelworks. I was born by cesarean section—my mother was little.

She wasn't very good at caring for me, in fact she used me like an adult. It was my job to look after my brother and sisters. I did it without being asked. I climbed up the pram to lift my sister out. If they were jumping on the bed, I got the hiding for allowing them to do it. She chased me if I nicked the bread—I expect it was his sandwiches and she got a beating if she didn't have them.

God knows if she knew what was going on, but she didn't like to see me hurt. When I had an abscess she wrapped it up in bandages. At night she put hot things on it and only if I didn't cry did she give me a glass of milk. Sherry size. It was all the milk she had.

My mum worked in a factory from six till two in the morning. Once she'd gone my dad got me out of bed and sat me on a chair. He battered me before he went to the pub and said I'd pay for it if I moved. I was terrified. I didn't dare go to the toilet or turn the telly off, even when it finished and the coal fire burned out. Then my mum came home and said, "Has he gone and left you again?" And it was always "Here, have a packet of crisps." Then she'd put me to bed.

He used to use my sister to make me more unhappy. He cuddled her up on his knee and watched me stand in the corner, or wherever he told me I had to be. But there was something about me not wanting to be close to him either. He had a big belt, a strap. He made me smoke cigarettes. He was often drunk. What anyone did, it was my fault, and I always took the violence. The fact that I kept bouncing back and kept looking after my brother and sisters probably made him more violent.

When he lost his job through drink he went for work in another town. We packed the cases and spent the first night in a bus shelter; the second night, it was a room. In the middle of the night he came over to the couch and started on me, and of course I cried. She put on the light. It wasn't the first occasion but it was the first time he was caught. She might have known before, but now she was face to face with it she couldn't ignore it anymore. I was six at the time.

He left immediately. He just walked out and I've never seen him since. The next morning we went off in this little blue mini. My brother was left at one place and then we came to this great big house, like Dracula's, with big walls and trees. We went in and they said, "Would you like some dinner?" So off we went. We sat down and ate apple pie and custard. When we came out, I said to the lady, "Where's my mum?" She said, "I want you to go and play in the garden." "But where's my mum?" "She has gone away and she is never coming back, so get out there and play in the garden." We went out in the garden and I remember running up the drive, which was gravel, with nothing on my feet—they had taken our shoes and socks off so we couldn't run away. I shouted, "I love you. I love you. Come back. It doesn't matter. Please come back." The matron came out and gave me a bloody good hiding, and sent me back on the swings. Then she brought out two big dolls. They were china and she gave me the one that was a bride. It got broken in the end, but it was the best thing I ever had.

I wet the bed, of course, and had to wash my sheets. To stop us going to the toilet at night they said there was a ghost called George. I was terrified. I hadn't got my bloody dad, I'd got George lurking on the stairs.

I just lived and did as I was told. I just existed really. You had nothing much when you were in care. Nobody loved you. I was glad to move to my foster parents'. They only wanted one child but they were willing to have me too. It was very restricted, very enclosed; they let no outsiders in and had no contact with anyone outside the family. But it was almost God-sent. There was no violence, no alcohol; they were good with money; I was cared for, given warmth and spoiled in the family. I got a lot from them, their standards made me determined to do well for myself.

I had lost contact with my brother for a number of years. When I was sixteen I asked if they could find him. He'd been put in a temporary foster home and then moved to a big family, but they had so many children, he was just like a bit of cash. He didn't even get to go to school. He was about twelve when they found him: he couldn't read or write, so they sent him to school with one-to-one tuition to help him catch up. He was so severely disturbed, he kept wetting the bed. At fourteen he was fostered again. The foster father ran off with another woman and the foster mother had a nervous breakdown. My brother was left to look after their son and to run the off-license. On leaving school he got a job but the firm went bankrupt. He moved in with an auntie, but her marriage broke down and she got in with someone he couldn't stand. He moved away and got into lots of trouble and fighting. His body is scarred all over. He went to prison for petty theft and for drug abuse.

He deserved more and we deserved to have known him. When he comes, I know nothing about him so we can't talk. He is a stranger.

At sixteen I was back in a children's home. Oh, dearie, I was that innocent. A girl waltzed out into the garden, she had a bikini on and every part of her body was covered in love bites. She'd been found in a sailors' brothel. I didn't know what she was up to. The girls were all so free. They were coming in from the Northampton racecourse—grass in their tights, covered in love bites. And I looked at them and said, no, this is not for me. And they were saying, "Oh, he really loves me," and I thought, God, how nutty can you be. And I made my decision then that I wasn't going to go their way. I know a few of them now, and they've ended up fairly happy, but it's taken them a long time to reach their maturity.

I did spend one night with this lad. He didn't force himself upon me because I told him in no uncertain terms, "If you think you're getting your leg over, on yer bike." The room was smelly and damp, it was like the room I'd spent the night in when my mum had found out about my dad. When I went back to the children's home I was like a child again. I was ill for a good weekend—shaking at having been back in a smelly, damp room, alone with a man.

I had to make my first Communion in my school dress.

Everyone else was in white. It was a very unhappy day and I cried. As I got older, I felt guilty that I'd cried for not having a white frock. I knew that receiving my Host was more important, and the dress shouldn't have mattered. So when I got married, in order to put it right, I made a wedding dress in blue—my school dress had been blue—to show Him that I loved Him enough not to have a white dress. I made it all in secret, and when I turned up, they all went "urgh?" The priest was even more gob-smacked, because he thought, Oh, God, what is she doing in a blue dress?

In my heart I knew that I didn't deserve to wear white— the feeling of not being quite pure, and then holding it with me all those years. It haunted me that someone had done something to me and it shouldn't have happened. All the other bits were bad enough without doing that to me, without spoiling me as it were. Because he did, he spoiled me forever, and as much as I will come to terms with it, and manage to live a normal life, I shall never feel right about it.

With my husband, in order to be as normal as I could for the sexual occasions, I had to put myself somewhere else. That's what I learned when I was small, to remove myself from my body. I lay on the edge of the bed. If he'd been to the pub and smelled of cigarettes and beer, which was my dad's smell, I couldn't bear him to get in bed with me. He said, "Come off the edge of the bed, love, I'm not going to touch you.'

Once he said, "I can't stand it any longer. Whatever is the matter?" I said nothing, but that night I was on the cider. I got drunk. I crawled home from the pub and had a fit of the giggles—hysterical giggles—so he left me to it. After about an hour he decided it was no good, and he said, "Come on, I'd better put you to bed," and he started to take my clothes off. I went absolutely crazy. I told him something awful had happened to me as a child, and that more than anything I hated hands. We never talked about it again.

I feel safe with my husband though I'm not sure I'll ever

feel a hundred percent safe. There's such stability. He's had the same sandwiches for nineteen years, and if he never changes his sandwiches I don't think he'd change anything like a wife! He'd do anything for me, and I'm quite horrible, testing him all the way, a bit like a child, to make sure he loves me enough. When I talked about being sterilized, he went off and got it done instead. It was a bit hurtful for the old pride but I think he thought, Which is the worse, two weeks of discomfort or a year of her going off her trolley?

Children are my life. I've only ever wanted to care for children. I had nanny jobs after I was sixteen in order to have a sense of family. I feel things about children so strongly, and I sense immediately pain and distress, without them saying anything.

The first six weeks of my own baby were hard. I struggled to love. I wondered why the love wasn't brimming over. I was very mixed up about her, what would happen to her, and what I would do. I had nightmares that I would take her and put her in the bath, forget I had put her there, and come back to find her drowned.

I get scared when I feel angry and violent. I can't deal with it at all. I feel I mirror my dad with my feelings inside. I want to be reasonable, and he never was. His violence was unjust. I needed help from a counselor to sort it all out and let go of the fears of what I might do as a mother. Outwardly I was an ordinary, normal person; inwardly I was suffering, and I didn't recognize it was normal to have such emotions. I had never told anyone before. All those years I'd kept silent, I'd kept it hidden inside me. Even to myself, I hadn't been able to admit that it had happened.

I don't spoil my children, I have my head screwed on. They're nice kids and I'm going to have to learn about them leaving me. It was pretty hard when they went to school: I felt lost, abandoned, and I thought I'd better have another baby. But I couldn't go on having babies as each one went away to school. One day, they would all have to go away.

I have been for my children what I lost for myself. I wanted everything they have: to feel loved and secure; to be with one person who will be there for the rest of their lives—that's what I wanted for me, and that's what I've achieved for them.

I want nothing to do with my dad. The child in me would be too frightened to meet him. The adult in me might want to murder him; and the parent in me certainly wouldn't let him near my children. But I have no anger toward him. I don't wish him dead. He can go on living up there with his funny liver getting dried out. He'll eventually do himself in anyway.

From my experiences and from all the people who have looked after me—whether it was for bad or good—it was always the good parts that I liked, that I took to choose to make me who I am.

AGE: forty. SEX: male. OCCUPATION: factory inspector.

I've just rolled a cigarette from some tobacco bought cheap, a good deal, will save me pounds on cigarettes over next two weeks. Mother expressed disgust that I was wasting money on smoking at all.

Feel as though I am somehow cheating the system.

I am in a quiet place—I like being on my own with my own thoughts, it's peaceful—no arguments or opposite opinions to contend with. Mother going to be away for four months soon. Although this means I will have to do more for myself I am sure I am going to enjoy it. Freedom to please myself, however, a bit afraid I might go and get drunk a couple of times.

Miss my dad, have not come to terms yet with his death, feelings very sad, lump in my throat, watery eyes.

Just thought how different my mum and Sheila are. Poles apart. Mum domineering and forthright. Sheila quiet and submissive. Just wondering if I married Sheila for peace and quiet, but actually find it difficult to adjust to not being domineered.

I have always loved the idea of being my own boss for the reward it could bring, money- and satisfaction-wise, but have never had the guts to pursue it. Always giving myself reasons why I was unable to do it. Never have reached my potential and blame others and circumstances for that. Think of others as either incompetent morons or people who are out to stab me in the back. Wonder if that is why I have never kept any friends.

I remember as a teenager seriously contemplating suicide. I cannot remember the reasons for feeling that way but remember being very angry and frustrated with my lot in the world.

I was thirteen when my parents tried a reconciliation. My dad had bought a grocery business in Yorkshire. We all joined him for six months, but he still ran around with other women and then he went bankrupt. We lost all our possessions, including my push-bike, and we finished up living back at my grandparents' again.

I remember some talk of my grandfather exposing himself on a bus when I was about fourteen.

I started drinking heavily when I was sixteen, which got me into trouble with the law a couple of times. It wasn't long after that I started exposing myself although I was well into courting Sheila by then. I do remember that it was very important to me at the time that I might well be incapable of making love to her properly, a feeling I had held since my early teens. Even today I have misgivings about my sexual prowess.

Early on my sex life was okay, but as children came along it petered out. It had a lot to do with bad communication, not really understanding whether each of us got enjoyment out of normal sex. Because I couldn't get full excitement from normal sex, I thought of every sort of thing to pep my sex life up. Every time I committed a particular act, it got less exciting, and therefore less satisfying, and therefore I had to escalate it.

It takes years to cover that sort of ground. I could pick up one particular thing and concentrate on it for months. You attempt to do it, say on a weekend, but it doesn't quite come off. So then it's postponed until the next weekend to try and achieve what you've got in your head. And when you can't go any further, perhaps because it would get you into trouble, you switch to something else. It doesn't happen in months. It happens over years.

When you're enacting your fantasy, you don't realize that your wife or daughter don't realize the rules. It's a game, they take part, so it seems fairly equal—no imposition on anybody, until they say no, and immediately you have to reconsider the rules, and the game even.

I had no particular desire for my daughter; she just happened to be there at the time. I suppose eventually it would have been on the cards with my other daughter, because of the escalation of my sexual activity.

It's not easy to put myself in other people's positions and feel the way they feel about things, but I did get an inkling that underneath she had a slight hesitancy, which I overrode because I was much older. I'm the one looked up to—the father—my word is taken as gospel.

I never understood at the time that I was harming anyone because I was so wrapped up in my own fantasy world.

My own problem is in itself difficult, but the effect on my daughter is a bit deeper to grapple with. She must have a feeling of insecurity, she must be afraid of it happening again, whether with me or somebody else. She probably feels guilty, despite the fact that it's not her fault. I think she did think of it as a game, but as time goes on she will probably think it was an invasion of her privacy, of her as a woman, or as a future woman.

The way my wife and I react from now onward, how we reassure my daughter so that any damage that is done is not compounded—all that is critical. I spent a short time in as relaxed a way as possible telling her why it happened, that it was my fault and not hers. That was done within a couple of weeks of my arrest. Now it's difficult for me to follow on from that because I need to get information from her as to how she views it in order for me to respond in the right way. So I need to rely on my wife. It's a long process that we need to treat gently and steadily, as and when required.

I'm willing to change, but I don't understand what I have to do differently to allow something different to happen—I don't understand what I have to do.

I'm naturally a good person, I love my family, but you can't put that over to the general public because once you've committed a particular act you're condemned out of hand. If I'd gone to prison, I wouldn't have had to see a probation officer, I wouldn't have had to go through family meetings, and I would have served my prison term and come out with absolutely no different view whatsoever. I would have just picked up where I left off.

There ought to be something that is built into the system that ensures that perpetrators of whatever sort get medical and psychiatric help. After I was arrested, I was given no assistance by anyone in the system. On my own initiative, I started visiting a marriage guidance counselor. I went to see my doctor to ask for psychiatric help, and after six months I was given an hour. I went to the head of the social services department to ask them why my wife and daughter had social workers but I had no one. He said that perpetrators should have social workers but the finances of the department did not allow it, and there was nothing he could do. It took four and a half months for a probation officer to be allocated to me.

At the police station, when I was brought to book, I broke down. I spent three days in prison: I found it intolerable, I couldn't contemplate staying there again, it was so degrading.

I was released on bail with the condition that I go and live with my mother. A week after I got home, Mother put her arms around me and said she'd stand by me. That's the only time in my life she's held me. She isn't a cuddly sort of person.

In court, I was found guilty of indecent assault of a nine-year-old and was put on three years' probation.

I was always shot down by Granddad—not just me, but the rest of the family. If we differed from his opinion, that was it: no arguments, no reasons, only because he said so. He was a cripple, a short, stocky man who was very, very strict. At mealtimes, for instance, no talking was allowed, absolutely none, and if not engaged in using our knife or fork, we had to sit on our hands. I hated his guts at the time.

My father was very intelligent—five A levels. A fine big man, distinguished-looking. He seemed to be very business-like. I got very close to him in his old age, but when I was a teenager I felt cheated. Why wasn't he around to give us the things we wanted? We were hard up living on our own. We couldn't have a television like everyone else in the street. Instead, it was me who played the man of the house, filling up the tax forms, aged twelve.

So I was determined that my children would always have a loving, caring father who was there to provide for all their needs. I was always there. I've never had any sort of bad feelings toward them in any respect; I never hurt them; but, inadvertently, I have done. I know it's hard to put the two together. How could a caring and concerned father do that at the same time? But you can. You can. Tears again.

There's a danger I could drift back into the old ways because it was pleasant. My wife and I tackle it now by understanding how fantasy first builds up, how it drifts along, and how it can be diverted by conversation or normal sex. But it would be totally hypocritical of me to say that such fantasies, even in a mild form, have not started to rear their ugly head over the last eight months, because that wouldn't be true. They have.

AGE: middle-aged. SEX: male. OCCUPATION: company director.

Your Honor,

You will no doubt recall that you presided over our case. If you do not recall, I can assure you that the remaining pupils who were assaulted [by a master at public school] most certainly remember you and remember it most vividly. The other three witnesses are dead, two by suicide and one through cancer.

In presiding over this case you forgot that the witnesses against———were only eleven years of age. You hectored and bullied each of us in turn without mercy and implied that we were vindictive and lying. Several boys in concert? No, sir, that is not true and I am sure that if you are honest with yourself you would admit this. We were not lying: we started out frightened by the pomp and crass arrogance of your court; we ended up petrified by your callous and bullying manner. You allowed and encouraged (despite objections by the prosecutor) the defense QC to act systematically in the same way to each witness who you allowed to be ruthlessly confused, hurt, humiliated and brought publicly to tears. No doubt you felt that you were doing your job; today your cowardly and arrogant behavior would result in your being impeached—a disgraced and broken man. Instead you left us frightened, confused and scarred for life, not by the reason for the trial but by your despicable handling of the case and the anger shown in the adult world to what was to those children an insignificant event. I hope that you can feel proud of what you have done!

Do I bear malice? No, not for the unfortunate———driven by unnatural compunction, for I don't feel that he was a bad man. For you I feel hate: I despise you for what you did and for what you stand for; yours was a cold, calculating and callous way of inflicting pain, with intent, on those who were both in your power and unable to defend themselves from your cynical, self-righteous ego.

I find it easy to feel sorry for, forgive and pray for the defendant, even to like him. For you I find it hard to find the charity to pray—I do however pray to God for the Christian humility to feel forgiveness, not hate; to feel understanding, not disgust; to feel love, not pity, and that you too will ask for the forgiveness that you most certainly need.

Signed, The Writer (alcoholic, unsuccessful suicide)

AGE: forty-five. SEX: female. OCCUPATION: writer and psychologist.

My father had been born an "aristocrat" in a stately home which was duly lost in a sea of alcohol by his parents. He believed in honesty, integrity and passionately embraced the Roman Catholic Church in a particularly blind and bigoted way. He wanted us to be perfect, sinless. As he had lost his birthright he wanted us to regain it and marry into the "right class." He believed that we should be kept untainted by commoners.

We were forbidden to make friends with the "village children" or the children at school who were NOCD (not our class, darling). I held myself apart. I never played with my sisters who had close friends of their own age and didn't want me tagging along. I rarely spent time with my mother or father: Mummy, because she was always busy running the family and Girl Guides; Daddy, because he never spoke to me and I was afraid to speak to him.

The punishments were almost daily. We were sent to our rooms for not using the butter knife, not eating our food, being more than two minutes late for a meal, not tidying our rooms, not getting good marks for homework, being insolent and leaving our bikes out. Sometimes we were hit with a belt. Usually we were sent to our rooms between meals and, as we grew older, for longer. Most of the time I read books. By eleven I had read the whole of Dickens. I often thought about suicide.

Two other people increased my upset. One was the greengrocer who put extra fruit in the basket and fingered me; the other was our next-door neighbor who trapped me in the lane, kissed me and fingered me. I wasn't clear whether it was wrong or not, as I knew nothing about sex. I enjoyed the attention, as I had none in the family. I wanted to have physical contact, but no one at home had hugged or cuddled me since my nanny had died.

I longed to be found by someone who would take me away and love me and let me be human. I dreamed of being sent to a boarding school where everyone would be "our class" so I could have friends. I watched films and television avidly—I wanted to learn how people laughed and had fun, and wondered how I could do the same.

When I was about eleven my mother got rheumatic fever. The woman who came to look after her would not let me see her. I grew more difficult. One evening I was summoned by my father, who told me I was being sent away. I was put on a train and was met two hours later by my godparents, two people I hardly knew. They were already in their fifties and lived on a farm away from anyone else. I didn't get letters from home and very few telephone messages. I was too frightened to ask how long I would be staying. I was terrified of misbehaving and being sent away with nowhere to sleep and nothing to eat. I wandered around the fields and riverbanks, feeling horrendously lonely. But I wasn't hit, and I only stayed six months.

Coping strategies? Going to university so that I could create my independence. Becoming a psychologist in a desperate attempt to find out how people worked so I might learn how to relate to others.

The only way to heal myself was to heal "the child" and to repair my relationships with my parents. My father was already dead, but I embarked on a series of processes where I talked with him in my inner spiritual sanctuary. Gradually I began to understand some of his motivation and, as I did, my hate dissolved. With my mother, I sat down one long afternoon and asked all the questions I had always wanted answers to, and I discovered that her experiences of the events of my childhood were not the same as my own. I had drawn conclusions about her feelings for me which were absolutely untrue. Slowly I began to rebuild a relationship with her—to love her just the way she is and, more importantly, to build up my own internal strength and not depend on outside opinion about who I am.

AGE: fifty-five. SEX: male. OCCUPATION: Anglican clergyman.

I was abused by my male guardian, a bachelor cleric in a parish which provided him with an enormous rectory. He was withdrawn, even frightened of people. The only sociable thing I remember he did was run the Scout troop for the village.

I had been born illegitimate; my mother did not want me and sent me to a children's home. I was transferred to him when I was about four and a half. He had my mother's permission to take me away. The rumblings of the Second World War were taking place in Europe. Philanthropic bodies, including the Quakers, were organizing transportation for German Jews from Europe. My late guardian, learning of the needs of these destitute children, went to an Ipswich clearinghouse and filled his rectory with them.

He placed his mother, his sister and a houseboy in one wing of the house. The rest was his own domain. He ruled with a rod of iron. To look "wrong" was to be thrashed on the spot. Punishments were usually three times a day—morning, noon and night. If any work was found improperly done —such as darning or domestic jobs, or shoes not properly cleaned—you were pulled out of bed and told to do it again, and if you didn't get it right you were thrashed and sent back to do it again and again. Morning and evening we were led by "public" prayer in the study in the best Victorian way.

From April to October every year we had to go barefoot in and around the house and grounds. We did designated house and garden work; only when tasks were done were we allowed to go to bed. We cultivated about one and a half acres. I could scythe by the time I was ten, and was often scything at four-thirty in the morning. My hands were scabbed and scratched. Two or three times I lost all my nails to dermatitis. I often had running sores on my face and thighs.

I was frequently told I was evil and demonic. I was going to grow up to do nothing better than follow the plow. After a time that became the sweetest sentiment of my life, that I would be left alone, day in and day out, holding the handles of a plow, looking at the horse's arse, listening to bird songs with the sun on me. I could think of no better heaven.

I was the youngest of all the boys. When the others went to secondary school, I was left at home alone. I had had about eighteen months of primary education. I was put into the garden room. Among the flowerpots, broken toys and tennis rackets I spent the day learning sums and English without tuition. I was given an exercise book and a pile of lined paper and was told to learn things by a specific time. If I didn't, I was thrashed. I learned the use of language by reading Victorian novels. That's why I speak the way I do.

My childhood years were totally contained within the rectory. Occasionally I wrote letters to my mother and, if these were found, I was thrashed. They were torn up in front of me. I was told I had no appreciation of where my loyalty lay, that I was ungracious, that I had no sense of social decorum.

Thrashings were always with clothing removed. I could often feel blood trickling down my legs. I was frightened of pulling up my trousers in case I got blood on them, and then getting thrashed again for dirtying my trousers. I was told to go into the kitchen and rub salt on myself. Sometimes I was punished with a stiff hairbrush which swiped the buttocks, bristles downward. I bled extensively and the burning pain lasted for hours and hours.

When I was about ten the old man asked me and another boy into an unused, bare bedroom on the third floor. But first we were told to go into the garden and make birches—they were straight and very flexible. He undressed and lay on the bed; then we had to hit him. He got angry because we were frightened, but the older boy got into the act with some enthusiasm and really did swipe him. I did it in halfhearted fashion. I was very confused. He then stood up and said, "Yes, well, that's enough of that. Leave those there and go and play." He was always easier on us after it had happened.

When I was about eleven I was mysteriously invited into his bedroom and told to take off my pajamas. I was told to bend over the side of the bed. It felt painful and odd. I didn't like it one little bit. He ended up with a large, wet, silk handkerchief—a white one, the old-fashioned sort, napkin size. After that, I was for a long while let off any undue horrors. It was the only time I felt so free that I could move about or sing or hum, and not be worried about punishment.

After the war we moved to a much smaller house. I was virtually on my own and desperate to get away. The two boys next to me in age used the house as a base—all the rest had gone into the world. I wanted to go into the Boys Service of the navy, but that was forbidden. I was allowed to bicycle into the nearby town every Saturday morning, where I made friends with an antiquarian book dealer. I loved old books and I developed a penchant for old armor.

I had another go at asking to leave home. He said, "You can't." I said, "I'm going to take myself away and find a job." I stormed into my little attic bedroom, which was an arsenal of swords and a suit of armor. He came up to my room and demanded I let him in. I had a Scottish sword, an ancient piece I'd picked up for next to nothing. I thrust it straight through the door. He was on the other side and I didn't give a shit; I hoped to run him through. Then I kicked open the door because I was going to have his bloody head off. I went out there, a four-and-a-half-foot knight in shining armor; I went out to slay the dragon and he was bent double looking to see if he'd been injured. His clothing was cut and he knew it was only sheer luck that I hadn't run him straight through. From that moment, I had no problems. He never punished me, never castigated me. He became a quiet, subdued, withdrawn old man.

As time went by I became quite close to him in endeavoring to understand him. I remember many of our talks. Long silences used to find him in tears. When I was at theological college I started to question him, about his faith, concepts, his place in society, his background. I found him exceedingly touchy, terribly guarded and most uncomfortable when challenged on points of faith. He called me grossly impertinent, to presume a position of inquiry that was not my right and, indeed, was not the right of any person at all. He was answerable to Almighty God, and God alone.

It was with a sense of sorrow for the man that I felt a tenderness toward him. He wasn't the great, powerful, all-knowing overlord that he presented himself to me for all my childish years—his great six-foot figure, lean and black, constantly towering over me and invading every moment of my life. I came to see him as a man curled up, bent double, badly dressed, unkempt, disregarding himself, broken in spirit and probably broken in heart.

I think probably what happened with my guardian was that he was a man conditioned by his class, his code of ethics, his job, his religion, his position of responsibility, by the fact that he had appointed himself custodian and guardian of a group of boys. And all those contradictions must have put enormous pressure on him and simply triggered the detonator. He was his own land mine. I don't think he can be blamed. Who the hell had repressed *him?*

I think people who are repressors are those who have the

power and the authority to persuade society to maintain a form of social order that protects their power positions. A leader well placed in any institution, whether legal, political, religious, commercial or familial, who has been entrusted with a position of responsibility is interested in preserving himself and his position of privilege. The weakest man very often is the one the world calls powerful. You only get to the top by obedience and subservience.

Speaking as a man, I would say you can't put your sexual energy into anything else but sex. I'm not a Tantric yogi. It's no part of my culture or my forebears' culture. I was never educated about sex. I would say that a combination of sexuality and sensuality is perhaps the strongest force in my life. And when its expression is not possible, I imagine or fantasize about it. I suppress my desires, but for that suppression I pay a price: resentment, anger, grief, illness or a subconscious vendetta.

I'd say of my life that I've dismissed what I can't contain and those things I haven't been able to get my emotions round. There's something in my nature that says I'm not to be broken. If those who have influenced my life have left a bad wake, and I have it in my power to give them some sort of absolution, then I have a duty to do so. I don't feel it right to perpetrate the evils of one generation onto another. I do have the right—indeed, the obligation—to purge myself.

With special thanks to Sandy, Mary, Robert and Francis; and also thanks to many others—particularly Gill Freeman, Helen Kenward, Tony Baker, Liz Brayne and James Fitzgerald.

In 1961 an American pediatrician from Denver called Henry Kempe coined the purposely emotive phrase "battered baby syndrome" to jolt the public into taking notice of the fact that a great number of children's injuries were being wrongly diagnosed as accidental. Doctors in Britain and the United States began to watch out for Dr. Kempe's battered babies and, toward the end of the 1960s, reports of child battering were increasing on both sides of the Atlantic. A series of tragedies, in which small children were found dead, killed by parents or stepparents, focused attention further.

According to figures gathered by the National Society for the Prevention of Cruelty to Children in Britain, where much of the research into child abuse has taken place, cases of parental violence toward children in Britain grew steadily in the late 1970s and early 1980s. In 1983, 7,038 children were reported physically abused in England and Wales. One child a week was found to be dying at the hands of its parents or guardian, making it the fourth most common cause of death among infants. It was usually a boy, less than a year old, who died of head injuries. These figures have more or less held constant in the middle and late 1980s, with slightly more children being battered, but slightly less seriously.

Figures for parental violence in other countries are harder to come by. Outside Britain and the United States research is limited. In the United States (as in Britain) the number of reported cases jumped dramatically: from sixty thousand in 1968 to a million in 1978, according to one report. More recently one hundred and fifty children have been dying each year from family violence in New York City alone. In France recent surveys have put the number of abused children at fifty thousand a year, and the number of deaths from ill-treatment at five hundred. In the Federal Republic of Germany severe cases are estimated at between fifteen thousand and eighteen thousand a year.

Child abuse has generally been viewed as a Western phenomenon, but it would seem that some degree of parental violence is universal, even when you take into account the vast differences in the way children are brought up from one country to another. This alone makes comparisons difficult. It is also clear that the greater the public awareness of abuse, the greater the number of cases reported. In 1970 the state of Florida registered seventeen cases of child abuse. In 1971, after a hot line had been set up and widely publicized, there were 19,120.

Until five years ago there was widespread reluctance to accept the fact that children were also being sexually abused, and that what had always seemed an unbreakable sexual taboo was, in fact, being broken on a very large scale. It was only when people began to discuss their experiences more freely in the more open climate of the 1970s and early 1980s that sexual abuse became a real issue. As they began to discuss it, so the scale of the problem became apparent.

In Britain—a country in which, as with child battering, much research has been carried out—reported cases have risen steeply in the last few years, from a handful in the late 1970s to 7,119 new cases registered in 1987. The sharpest rise came in 1986, with a 127 percent increase. How widespread sexual abuse will eventually be found to be worldwide, no one knows.

C.M.

6

Trafficking in

Children for

Adoption

Tim Tate

Asunción International Airport is an angular, concrete building set in several acres of lawn. From the outside, Paraguay's only airport creates an impression of a modern, prosperous and efficient nation. Inside is very different. The dusty, flyblown arrival and departure lounge, supervised by dozens of unsmiling state security officers, is extremely basic. Every few minutes a shabby peasant Indian slouches across the

143

room hawking a tawdry collection of tribal souvenirs. In the middle of the hall a haphazard huddle of stalls sell branded whiskey at impossibly low prices, up-to-date video equipment and counterfeit Cartier watches.

Paraguay is not a regular tourist destination. The country is the world's longest-surviving right-wing military dictatorship: on every corner, the legend runs, there is an informer, while every cab driver is a free-lance state snooper. Those who come to Paraguay come on business or specifically to shop. Prices in Asunción are a fraction of those in neighboring Argentina or Brazil. This was due in part to General Alfredo Stroessner's laissez-faire attitude to international trade, and in part to an officially relaxed view of contraband.

Corruption is endemic in South America, but in Paraguay it has become organized and routine. Police officers near the border with Brazil have a semiofficial crime concession. Senior military men have it built into their contracts that work finishes at 4 P.M.: this allows them time to concentrate on their tobacco or alcohol cartels supplying consumer contraband to neighboring nations.

On any day of the week those waiting at the airport, in the endless queues for passport and visa control, will consist of businessmen, the occasional journalist and a few local people traveling to visit relatives in Brazil or Argentina. Almost invariably, each will be clutching a souvenir from the airport's ramshackle *souk*—a bottle, a camera, a watch.

But some travelers stand out from the rest. Most are European or Israeli, traveling in pairs and—even by Paraguayan standards—extraordinarily nervous. They are met by escorts who guide them past the stares of the security police. When they leave, a few days later, they are guided through passport control to wait for their flight in a screened-off VIP lounge. These couples have also come shopping in Paraguay, but their souvenir comes gift-wrapped in diapers and blankets. They have come to buy a baby.

The official definition of child trafficking is deceptively simple: the exchange of a child for financial reward. Where that child ends up—in prostitution, the drugs business or to be sold for transplant surgery—can be horrendous. But even its better end, that of the buying and selling of children for adoption, is born out of the extreme poverty and destitution of parents and is rapidly becoming a practice attacked by police and human rights experts all over the world.

And yet it is a growing Western trend. There are no official figures for the number of children who have been sold to the First World by the Third—trafficking is a uniquely one-way trade—because there have been no international surveys. Individual Third World states have periodically released figures showing the transfer of thousands of children to new lives in the prosperous corners of the globe. But these have been ad hoc and unreliable. They have taken no account of how the transfer was achieved, whether money changed hands or even where the children were sent.

At the heart of the trade is a simple economic equation: the First World is rich but has a low birthrate. In Third World countries the position is exactly the opposite. What has transformed trafficking from an occasional bit of business to an international trade, which—according to some of its participants—rivals cocaine smuggling in scale and value, is air travel.

The comparison with cocaine is an apt one. Child trafficking is at heart no different from any other form of illicit trade. If you substitute drugs or pornography for children, the essentials, to the trafficker at least, remain unchanged. Frequently the same people are involved in all three trades and use the same shipment routes. Interpol has identified a series of trails from South America to Europe used for trafficking drugs and children; the same brutal methods figure in both. Drugs, in one shape or another, are a common feature in most forms of trafficking, and the trade in children is no exception.

Defense of Children International maintains records of all reported cases of child trafficking in the world. Their files are the best—probably the only—indication of the extent of the trade.

Guatemala: 1987
Government officials have alleged privately that high-ranking military officers are implicated in the export of children for illegal adoption. The trade is highly lucrative, as U.S. families are prepared to pay over five thousand dollars for a child obtained for a few dollars in Guatemala.

Yugoslavia: 1986
Many street children in Italy have been virtually sold into slavery by their parents in impoverished regions of Yugoslavia. Once smuggled into Italy, they are forcibly tutored by their gypsy captors in the ways of a life of petty crime. The slave traffic from Yugoslavia has existed for years. Five years ago Italian authorities sent four hundred children back to Yugoslavia, all of them thought to have been held illegally. Over recent months one and a half thousand have been sent home. Some officials in Rome estimate that more than ten thousand Yugoslav slave children have been imported to Italy and held in gypsy encampments outside major cities. The average price of a child is a hundred and fifty dollars. They can earn up to two hundred dollars a day begging.

Philippines: 1984
The Japanese mafia, Yakuza, imports young girls from the Philippines for purposes of prostitution. This business grosses about $1.5 million per day, and imports about eight to ten thousand girls per year.

Honduras: 1987
The Secretary General of the Junta Nacional de Bienestar Social [National Council on Social Welfare], Leonardo Vil-

leda Bermudez, charged today that Honduran children adopted by foreign families had been used for the purpose of the sale of body parts. "Many families came forward to adopt children with physical defects. At first we thought they were decent people who loved children, but in time it was discovered that they wanted to sell them for body parts —for example to remove their eyes for the sake of other children who needed eyes; in short it was a case of trafficking in bodily organs of children adopted here." Villeda Bermudez referred to previous reports suggesting that children had been used by foreigners for sexual abuse and as couriers in drug trafficking.

Various branches of the Honduran government subsequently disowned Bermudez's allegations. Nonetheless, the trafficking of children for spare-part surgery is known to occur in other Central and South American countries. Equally, Justice Department officials in California have confirmed several cases of Mexican children being sold to American pedophiles for prostitution and child pornography.

As to the trafficking of children for use as drug couriers: in June 1987 members of Thailand's Center for the Protection of Children's Rights (CPCR) took gruesome testimony from an established child seller.

Southern Thailand had, for several years previously, been the hunting ground for organized gangs of child stealers. CPCR estimated that around six thousand children had been stolen from the area since 1980. They had subsequently been smuggled into Malaysia and sold for illegal adoptions.

On June 26 CPCR officers interviewed a fifty-four-year-old Thai woman living in a red-light district of Mahachai in Samut-Sakhon Province. She had trafficked at least eighty children between 1969 and 1977. Most had been unwanted babies of local prostitutes unable or unwilling to look after them, and had been sold, through middlemen, to "respectable" couples looking for babies to adopt. What made this trafficker abruptly give up a trade she admitted was lucrative was the discovery in 1977 that rival traffickers had used babies to transport drugs across the border.

"Around that time there was news that some people had killed babies, strangled them to death, cut their stomach open and then stuffed it with heroin . . . when I heard about it I decided to stop looking for babies right away. I don't do these sort of things anymore, you know. But some prostitutes still come and ask me to take their unwanted children. Just a few days ago, one woman asked me to take her baby, but I refused."

Killing babies to use as inanimate heroin couriers may be an extreme case, but the Thai trafficker's story illustrates a basic truth: there are a number of mothers who either wish, or are forced, to part with their children, and there is a corresponding demand from rich infertile couples for babies to adopt. Putting the two together is, to the trafficker, simply good business. To circumvent awkward questions as to the ethics, or occasionally the legality, of selling children, traffickers have developed a creed which insists that the removal of any child from the poverty-stricken Third World to the affluent First World is automatically in that child's best interests. It is a creed the West has been quick to adopt. Television coverage of drought, famine, war, plague or sheer poverty almost invariably prompts a significant rise in the number of Western couples seeking international adoptions.

Some countries have grown tired of what they see as a new brand of colonial exploitation—the stripping of a nation's greatest potential asset, its children. Indonesia, for example, has passed laws requiring foreign couples to be resident there for seven years before becoming eligible to adopt. But other countries, particularly in Central and South America, condone or even assist in intercountry adoptions. From there it is but a short step to illegal, but highly profitable, child trafficking.

Piet Stoffelen is a Dutch Labor MP. In 1987 he produced a

report on child trafficking and exploitation for the Council of Europe:

> The adoptable child is—bluntly speaking—a commercial object commanding five-figure prices. In such circumstances the interests of the child are not even of secondary consideration. The profit motive leads many parents to sell their children for adoption. Pregnant mothers are persuaded to sign away their future babies in exchange for a few weeks' food and shelter in the immediate prenatal period.

By 1985 the kidnapping and trafficking of children from El Salvador had become a major scandal. Two judges were discovered to have been involved in a highly organized network turning over millions of dollars a year. Lawyers were found to have retained hospital workers to kidnap babies from maternity units and to have paid their "scouts" $50 for every child brought in.

Gradually El Salvador brought the problem under control. Although the government today officially approves, and assists intercountry adoptions, by January 1988 the trafficking rackets had been largely shut down. But by then the trade had simply moved elsewhere.

Brazil produces coffee, rice, sugar cane, soybeans and cotton. It also produces babies at a tremendous pace. The latest available government statistics put Brazil's ever growing child population at around sixty-three million. At any given time more than half of those children will be officially classified as *carentes*—the needy or underprivileged. Seven million of those—nine percent of the total child population—are registered as abandoned. It is the sheer scale of poverty that has led to Brazil's new role as probably the world's largest exporter of children. In Rio de Janeiro the federal police admitted earlier this year that in the last three years at least a thousand children were taken abroad.

Irene Rizzini, once an adoption worker, now heads a research group at the Universidade Santa Ursula in Rio. She has watched as the traffickers have become ever more organized and ever richer. "They make a lot of money out of these children. They find a pregnant girl—no husband, no money, no food. They talk about how cute the baby will be, about education. They say maybe he could grow up to be a doctor or a lawyer: they paint a picture of a wonderful future away from Brazil. And then they give the woman food and a place to stay. When the baby is born they may also give her a few dollars and make her sign the paperwork—and that's it: another baby is sold."

There is no provision in Brazilian law to prevent foreign nationals taking children out of the country. A civilian working with the police, Geovanni Azevedo, describes the problem: "Brazil has a long frontier—sixteen thousand kilometers in all. We know babies are being smuggled out across our borders; we know the gangs are making millions of dollars. But we don't know exactly how many children are involved." As a statistical base, the only document Azevedo has to work from is a computer printout of two thousand children who had left the country before 1986. The list gives no clue as to whether the children went abroad for tourism or were trafficked. Brazilian-based social workers involved with legitimate intercountry adoptions suspect that at least some of those on the list were quite properly adopted through officially sanctioned programs.

Adoption in Brazil is a complicated business, made more so by an obsessive, and frequently corrupt, bureaucracy. Officially the government has no objection to intercountry adoptions, provided all potential domestic options have been tried first. In theory, Brazilian law should make intercountry adoptions very simple: Article 3 of the Juvenile Code specifically requires that all adoptions should be "free and secret." Some juvenile court judges have used this to encourage adoptions from abroad. They see them as an arm of social policy, relieving pressure on the state organization that deals with street children, and offering a chance of a better life to underprivileged children.

Many individual courts operate their own official, or semi-official, schemes to send local children out of Brazil to a "better life" in Europe or Israel. The Swiss charity Terre des Hommes has an office in Rio handling intercountry adoptions. Claudia Cabral runs the program. "The problem with official intercountry adoptions—and our program is officially recognized—is that they generally take a long time: four years is the average waiting period. In some ways that is a good thing: the courts, the judges and the social workers get to know the adoptive couple during that period. There is time for proper social inquiry and psychological reports. But many couples in the West don't want to wait that long. They are desperate to have a baby and are prepared to do almost anything to get one."

This is where the traffickers step in. The going rate for an "easy-to-place baby"—a euphemism for a white, blond-haired, blue-eyed male child less than three months old—is twenty-five thousand dollars. Older children, female or dark-skinned babies cost proportionately less. This sliding scale of "desirability" worries Claudia Cabral. "I think it shows these people are not really interested in the welfare of the child: they are primarily trying to satisfy their own needs and desires, not help an underprivileged baby."

Terre des Hommes is not allowed to arrange intercountry adoptions for children under three years old. Cabral works frequently to place handicapped or disabled children. Neither of these categories falls into the highly desirable bracket favored by child traffickers. Their market is supplying the most sought-after babies for the highest price.

"Although they work secretly we are able to get an idea of how big their operations are by the drop in numbers of this type of baby coming into the state child-care program," says Cabral. "In the last couple of years there has been a very noticeable decrease in the numbers of blond, blue-eyed babies. We can only assume they are being snapped up by the traffickers."

The state of Paraná in the south of Brazil has traditionally produced fair-skinned children: historically there has been a strong Germanic presence. Dr. Carlos Cesario Pereira is a lawyer in the small resort town of Itajai. Lawyers in Brazil have a certain elevated social status and an income above the national average, but Pereira could never have afforded his ranch or his horses on the salary of a small-town solicitor.

Pereira was the first alleged big baby trafficker to attract police attention. From 1984 to 1987 he arranged a hundred and fifty intercountry adoptions, charging between five and ten thousand dollars per child. Late in 1987 federal police raided his ranch house and found twenty newborn babies installed in a custom-built nursery unit, together with a corresponding number of Israeli couples who had paid to adopt them. Pereira was promptly arrested.

According to Judge Bruno Carlini, who heard the case initially, Pereira's operation involved more than sixty people, including doctors, nurses, baby-sitters, notaries and court officials. He also ran a team of "scouts"—women who masqueraded as social workers and convinced pregnant girls to sign over the unborn babies for a handful of cruzados. Some girls received the equivalent of five dollars; others food in lieu of payment. The "scouts" were paid seventy-two dollars for every baby signed up.

"We discovered Pereira's operation was based around the public baths. Babies would be taken there and subsequently taken away by Pereira's gang for adoption," Carlini has explained. "At first Pereira had operated within the law, and within the judicial system. But then he started charging money and working illegally. We estimate Pereira made at least five hundred thousand dollars. His organization began performing irregular acts: there was no bona fide proof of the particulars of the adopting couple, there were no affidavits.

Furthermore we know that the natural mothers were taken to a certain registry office in a particular district to sign the adoption deed. These women came from many different districts and areas within the state, but they were all taken to this one office for the adoption deed to be approved."

Was Carlini saying the official who notarized the deeds was corrupt? He is no longer in office. What worried Carlini and the federal police more than the likelihood of corruption was evidence that some of Pereira's babies had been kidnapped.

By February 1988 Pereira was out of jail, pending a full hearing of his case. He said that he was out of the baby business. The lawyer has denied any misdemeanors and claimed the police are making him a scapegoat. "I don't have any doubt that the police picked on me for political reasons," he says. "Our government knows the country is in a very bad economic situation, and it is very embarrassed that Brazil has become an exporter of its children. Hundreds of thousands of children die each year from hunger before they are one year old. The government does not take care of them."

Pereira went on to claim that he was performing a public service, a humanitarian act, by exporting the children to a better life abroad. It is a claim echoed by every trafficker. Pereira was also at pains to stress that he never actually "sold" a baby—he simply charged reasonable fees for his legal expertise in arranging the adoption formalities. It was a claim belied by the purpose-built nursery unit and by the lavish ranch house.

Whether such fees are lawful remains to be decided. A 1984 federal law makes it illegal to arrange adoptions for profit. Pereira argues that his legal fees do not fall into that category. The irony is that such "fees" are unnecessary anyway. From his courtroom in Itajai, Bruno Carlini arranges his own intercountry adoptions. "Our program is a model for all Brazil," he claims. "It is completely free, and we take great care to make sure that the foreign adoptive parents are suitable. Only through the proper legal procedures can we be sure of placing the child in a genuine, bona fide home. In illegal placements the child can be taken into a harmful environment because the parents have not been thoroughly checked out. Surely that is a terrible destiny for our children?"

Carlini also demolished the traffickers' myth that Brazilian families will not adopt Brazilian babies. "When the television pictures of the babies in Pereira's nursery were shown I was in charge of placing them in good homes. All of them were placed within ten days: the interest from ordinary Brazilians in these babies was intense."

To Carlini and to his colleague, Dr. Jobel Araujo, trafficking in babies is dangerous and morally despicable. Araujo, the equivalent of a resident prosecutor in Carlini's court, knows he could have grown rich on bribes—bribes which persuade other court officials in other districts to falsify birth and adoption certificates.

"I believe in God. I don't think you can put a price on life. The people who exploit a human desire for children are terrible criminals. I have had some foreign couples come to me who have paid up to twelve thousand dollars for a baby, and then found there is no baby for them. In one group of twenty-one couples I saw, only five had actually received what they paid for.

"Typically the trade works something like this: a 'scout' will obtain a baby—sometimes by kidnapping—and take it to a notary public or some other corrupt court official. There she registers the baby as her own. That way she can sign 'her' baby across to the foreign couple under a process known as 'simple adoption.' I will give you an example of how easy and how widespread this can be. In a town nearby, in one year, the judge there sent three hundred babies abroad for adoption. In that same period Bruno Carlini and I allowed just ten foreign adoptions from Itajai. Now we have managed to get a law passed in this state that notaries cannot make these adoptions without the involvement of a judge.

"Also the federal police here will not issue a passport for

the baby unless he has a copy of the judge's agreement to an intercountry adoption. That is good, because the federal police operate all over Brazil. But it does not stop the trade. There are many ways to get false passports and the traffickers are now sending foreign couples to Paraguay to collect their Brazilian babies. The traffickers smuggle the baby across the border."

Two hundred miles northwest of Itajai, in the federal prison near Curitiba, Arlette Honorina Victor Hilu makes children's clothing. A suitable punishment, perhaps, for an unrepentant trafficker who, according to the police, became a millionaire inside two years. "Arlette Hilu," says Dr. Renato, head of Curitiba state police, "was the first person to turn baby trafficking into really big business. She traveled around the world seeking couples who wanted to adopt, she held several false passports and she ended up a very rich woman."

Hilu's operation was remarkable for its scale, its value and for the speed with which it developed. In 1983 Hilu was an accountant in the office of a female lawyer. An Israeli couple walked in off the street wanting to adopt a child. When the lawyer declined to help them, Hilu offered her services. As Carlini and Araujo point out ("You must remember, in Brazil adoptions are free and secret"), juvenile courts do not require the involvement of a lawyer to agree to an adoption. Hilu, by her own account, successfully arranged a child for the Israeli couple.

"This couple told me of another five Israeli couples who wanted babies. So I went to Israel and the word spread that I could arrange adoptions. It was like a snowball: it just grew and grew." From then until 1986 Hilu became Brazil's leading baby trafficker. She admits to arranging a hundred adoptions. Curitiba police put the total much higher—fifteen hundred by the time of her arrest in 1986. As the investigation closed in, Hilu increased her prices: at the end she was charging fifteen thousand dollars per baby.

Hilu still protests that she is basically innocent. "They

wanted to frame me, so they said that I committed a crime, that I charged dollars for the adoptions but that was not so. I had to charge something due to the costs in the adoption process itself—for example, traveling—and I charged my own fees. As a professional I am entitled to charge a certain rate but it is not true that I became a millionaire."

Hilu's traveling expenses involved her in crisscrossing Brazil to find judges who would sign her increasing number of adoption certificates. The accountant from Curitiba flew across country to Paraná, to Santa Caparina, to Florianopolis, to Itajai, to Rio—anywhere, in short, where she could find a judge who was prepared to sign.

"There was never an Arlette Hilu gang as has been reported. I did it all myself. I taught several people how to do these adoptions, and other people saw how it was done and that it was profitable. Toward the end I saw myself in the newspaper called a trader, a gang leader. I saw these banner headlines and found it unpleasant. I began to think it wasn't worth it. Many people worked in the shadows, using my name. I would hear of babies disappearing from hospitals and people saying, 'It was Arlette Hilu—she has taken the baby.' Of course, I hadn't."

The case of Janice de Souza Macedo illustrates the point. In June 1986 she gave birth to her third child—a girl—in Petropolis, a hillside town thirty miles west of Rio. A day later, as she lay in the maternity unit, a woman dressed as a nurse walked up to her bed. "She said she had to take my baby Rafaella to put some drops in her nose. I agreed, of course. She walked out of the unit with my baby. That was the last time I ever saw her."

Petropolis police at first linked the kidnapping to Arlette Hilu. Now they are not sure. The *favela* where Janice Macedo lives, in a dusty yard attached to a two-room shack, is the main center for cocaine dealing in Petropolis. These police, armed and nervous, are considerably more interested in the possibility of attack by local drug barons. Alicione

Santana, the federal police officer with most experience in baby trafficking, is more forthcoming. "Five or six gangs operate throughout Brazil. They are rich and ruthless."

In February 1986 Hilu fled to Israel where, because of the number of babies she had provided, she was something of a national heroine. In Curitiba the federal police obtained a warrant for her arrest, effectively barring her return to Brazil. But by October she was in business, based in the safe haven of Asunción, Paraguay.

When she was finally arrested by the federal police it was in Foz do Iguaçu. She was found to be carrying several false passports, diapers and baby bottles. She was sentenced to four and a half years in prison for handing over a juvenile to an unfit person. The charge arose from a raid three years earlier when police had found five babies in a run-down house near Curitiba. All were in poor health and suffering from diaper rash. One was rescued from a wardrobe where it had been hidden when the police moved in.

Documents in the house linked the babies to Hilu. All were to have been delivered to her customers in Israel. More babies were subsequently found in another house and seven people were arrested. One, Hilu's former pupil Maribel Da Rosa Pereira (no relation to Itajai's retired trafficker), turned informer and assisted the police in Hilu's arrest.

Hilu insists that she was never a baby trafficker, simply an expert doing a social service: "I do not consider it as selling babies or human beings. I consider it as the placement of abandoned minors with an excellent family, whereas if the child were to be left in Brazil it might die. To deliver a child for adoption would mean one child less dying in Brazil. I do not think the situation should be considered as the sale of children."

Hilu's protestations might carry more weight were it not for the inescapable truths of all child trafficking: adoptive parents, even those "excellent families" Hilu dealt with, want healthy, white babies. Those babies are among the least likely to die in Brazil's slums. The view of Hilu as an international child welfare officer also conveniently overlooks the condition of the five Israel-bound babies found by Curitiba police, and the complicated paraphernalia of fraudulent passports and birth certificates found on Hilu when she was arrested.

Delegado Azur Pinto has no doubts about the nature of Hilu's operation: "Arlette Hilu was the first person to turn baby trafficking into a big business. We have information that she sold around two thousand babies before she was arrested, at a price of ten thousand dollars each. We don't know for sure how many people were in her gang but a good source tells us there could have been two hundred people involved. But the arrest of Hilu didn't put a stop to the trade. We hear of other gangs operating in other states, and we have information that Maribel has taken over Hilu's business." If Arlette Hilu was bad, her pupil was (and still is) worse. Maribel Pereira has taken the trade to its ultimate conclusion: theft, drugs, corruption and death in a business worth millions.

Rudolfo Jaime Garcia was a member of Maribel's gang. His brother is married to Maribel's sister, and he was recruited to the family business late in 1985. Among other tasks he was responsible for showing her clients, who were generally from Israel, around Brazil, and he came to know precisely how the business operates. "The children are obtained from the three states in southern Brazil. Maribel only works with white children with blue or green eyes. But not all of those sent to her in Paraguay are white; any dark-skinned children she sends back to Brazil through her suppliers.

"Normally the child travels for three days to get to Paraguay, arriving very tired, and she sends back the black ones the same day. That often causes the death of the child."

Nor, it seems, is Maribel too particular how her stock is obtained. "She doesn't always know whether the children have been kidnapped: she works from Paraguay, and her suppliers work here so she can't have total control. But generally it is published in the newspapers when a child is kidnapped here, and even in those cases she does not return them."

One delivery to Maribel's Asunción base included a thin, undernourished black baby covered in sores. "Maribel said, 'I don't want this baby: it is rubbish. Throw it back in the ditch where it came from.' It had been drugged and it was in a coma. I took pity on it and nursed it, dripping milk into its mouth. On the third day it cried and eventually I persuaded an Israeli couple—who really wanted a white child—to take it. That child would have died if it had been sent back to Brazil."

Eventually Rudolfo left the gang after a highly publicized kidnap. He fled to Tel Aviv where former customers hid him for six weeks. He was persuaded by Curitiba police to return to Brazil and help track down members of Maribel's gang. It was a dangerous move. "Maribel found out where I was and one night she grabbed me from a restaurant. I was thrown into a car and a gun was put to my head. As the car took a bend on the road I took a chance and threw myself out onto the pavement. I only just escaped with my life. I am sure Maribel is the largest trafficker in Brazil today. She must have between two hundred and two hundred and fifty people working for her, here and in Europe. She receives European people in Paraguay—between five to ten couples per week.

"The price for a child is relative to its color and to the people buying it. She is a very shrewd businesswoman and those who are prepared to pay most are Israelis. She charges them thirty thousand dollars. I don't know the exact breakdown of the bill, but around five thousand is for false documents, two thousand goes to the people who take the child across the border into Paraguay, and another two thousand is for the police at Asunción Airport to let the children out. I reckon Maribel earns an average of seventy thousand dollars a week."

All of these allegations are confirmed by the federal police and the team in Curitiba charged with investigating

Maribel's gang. Some members of the operation have been arrested and have independently backed up Rudolfo's evidence. The key to the business is Paraguay. Once babies leave Brazil from Foz do Iguaçu the rule of law is effectively suspended. "It's cowboy town over there," one senior Brazilian policeman said. "We only go across the border if it has been fixed in advance and we have a guarantee of safe conduct."

British Embassy officials in Asunción confirmed the Brazilian view. Maribel operates in partnership with a man who is known to most European diplomats in Asunción as a well-connected organized-crime figure who has a semiofficial concession on false passports. "He takes the false Brazilian passports, the documents from registry offices and so on and legalizes them in Paraguay," says Rudolfo. "The children leave as Brazilian citizens with Jewish names. They travel on false passports, but it is seen to that this does not cause any problems."

Who, then, are the adopters, the people whose demands ensure a constant and lucrative supply? The simple answer is that they are ordinary couples denied the opportunity to have their own children and driven by a desire that overcomes any scruples about paying for a baby.

They come from America, from Britain and Europe and, particularly in the case of Brazil, from Israel. They are pushed toward adopting from the Third World as the pool of adoptable babies diminishes in the First. The trend began in the early 1970s when the contraceptive pill drastically reduced the numbers of healthy children available for adoption. Simultaneously most European countries began setting up official intercountry adoption agencies to assist, monitor and regulate adoptions from the Third World.

Britain chose not to, and remains officially uninvolved in the process. Adoptive parents turn for advice and guidance to agencies like Parent to Parent Information on Adoption Services (PPIAS). Philly Morrell is the organization's coordinator for intercountry adoptions. "Intercountry adoptions can never be outlawed: there are many, many people who want to adopt from abroad, but there is no guidance from the government. This can mean that people fall into the hands of child traffickers and end up paying thousands of pounds for their baby. PPIAS tries to provide information on the legal agencies and steer people away from anything that sounds seedy or is charging any amount of money."

PPIAS provides would-be adopters with a list of legitimate organizations working abroad to place children. But, according to Philly Morrell, many are pushed unnecessarily into a foreign adoption. "It can take several years to adopt a baby from abroad," says Maggie Jones, author of the handbook *Everything You Need to Know About Adoption*. "Usually you have to go to the country in question, taking all your documentation, find the baby, wait while the adoption is legalized there, and then begin the process of applying to bring the baby home. All this can take a very long time, and applying for entry clearance here can take months on top of that while the Home Office and the DHSS [Department of Health and Social Security] are considering it." It is not surprising, then, that many couples prefer to spend a few thousand dollars to bring home a baby—any baby—within a matter of weeks.

Israel has a policy of allowing and encouraging intercountry adoptions: the state has even allocated a unique identity number prefix—20—for children born abroad but adopted by Israelis. By the summer of 1987 forty thousand such ID prefixes had been registered.

The kibbutz movement is registered with legitimate official adoption agencies in Brazil. That allows couples like Shelley and Irwin Stenzler to take part in the scheme run from Curitiba by Bruno Carlini and Jobel Araujo. On February 3, 1988, the Stenzlers formally adopted a baby girl, after a two-year wait and many social and psychological reports.

But other Israeli couples are less prepared to wait. Perry and Raquel Rosemberg paid four thousand dollars to traffickers involved with Arlette Hilu and Maribel Pereira. The couple were arrested in August 1986, attempting to take the baby home on forged passport and papers. "We came here because we were desperate for a baby," they told federal police. "It was going to be so happy for us—the baby is so beautiful. Now we will try to adopt him legally."

The Rosembergs should perhaps have known that the papers for their adopted son were forged and that the traffickers they were dealing with operated outside the law. They could not, however, have known that the leaders of the gang had lengthy police records for drug smuggling. It was a point not lost on federal police chief Santana: "Once again child trafficking is linked with drug trafficking. But what can we do? The babies are simply driven across the border into Paraguay and we cannot control it. And there are always people willing to buy."

Rough figures released by Israel confirm this: in the summer of 1988 state officials admitted that at least two thousand Brazilian babies were now living in Israel. Of these, the majority came from the southern states like Paraná—the source of highly marketable blond, blue-eyed children. According to adoption workers like Claudia Cabral, those children simply do not come up on the legitimate adoption market. The conclusion is inescapable: the Israeli figures represent the best estimate yet of the scale of trafficking for adoption.

In January 1988 an American citizen was arrested in Rio de Janeiro by the Brazilian federal police. His business card revealed him to be the president of a children's charity. He had been caught in possession of a false Brazilian passport for a young Brazilian boy.

When Geovanni Azevedo's men broke into his apartment in Copacabana they discovered two boxes of homosexual child pornography. A phone call to the United States authorities produced the information that the man had already served a long jail sentence in America for child molestation.

Inquiries at the orphanage where he obtained the boy revealed further evidence of sexual misconduct. "Now tell me," said Azevedo, "that taking this boy out of Brazil would have been good for him."

Two miles away in the same city, Irene Rizzini, the researcher at the Universidade Santa Ursula, added: "What can I say? This is the danger of selling children: the traffickers don't check up on their customers. If you sell a baby, using false papers and corrupt officials, how do you know what sort of person is buying it?"

Until not so very long ago, and certainly well into the 1960s, adoption was widely seen as a good solution for children left homeless as a result of war, natural disasters or personal family tragedy. World population growth, the spreading social and economic ills of Third World countries, and the liberalization of abortion laws in the West have caused an unprecedented number of babies to change hands and with this has come a dramatic shift in views. In the 1970s the numbers of children taken from Third World countries by childless and affluent Western couples quadrupled. They have been rising steadily ever since. In 1986 alone, sixteen hundred Sri Lankan babies were said to have been adopted abroad. With this escalation have come growing doubts about the practice as a whole, about the issue of separating babies from their culture and their background and about the methods by which many are currently being removed from their natural parents.

In May 1987 a California law firm sent out a letter to two French agencies specializing in intercountry adoptions. "We travel frequently in Third World countries," they began, "and have developed sources of children and contacts within government and private sectors of these countries. . . . [Prospective adoptive parents] usually have a child meeting their specifications in their home in less than a year. The cost is approximately US$10,000, depending upon the country where the adoption takes place. . . ." While their contacts may indeed be legitimate, many, or perhaps most, are not: kidnap-

ping, bartering, sleight of hand or simply the payment of money by middlemen to parents reduced to desperation by poverty are feeding a vast international market in babies which has its roots in South Korea, Sri Lanka, India, Chile, Colombia, the Philippines, Thailand, Hong Kong, Bolivia, Taiwan and Indonesia. At the other end, Israel, the United States, the United Kingdom, Scandinavia and West Germany have become often extremely unscrupulous receivers in marketed babies.

One of the most blatant and unpleasant cases of trafficking in children this century was that carried out by the German "Lebensborn" Society which, during the Second World War and the progression of Nazi soldiers across conquered Europe, arranged for desirable-looking children to be seized from schools, institutions and even parks and streets, and sent off to a clearing station where supposed "experts" tested them for racial characteristics. Those selected for "Germanization," and considered suitable for reproducing the master race, were sent to childless German families for adoption. The real anguish, often, came later, as haunted parents combed liberated Europe looking for children they had last seen as babies or small children and who were now often perfectly integrated Germans.

The first United Nations study of the subject was published in 1953 and led to a cautious set of rules. Further guidelines about the international adoption of children came in 1978, when information was gathered from sixty-five member states about their policies. But it was not until December 1986 that the UN General Assembly unanimously adopted a "Declaration of Social and Legal Principles Relating to the Protection and Welfare of Children, with Special Reference to Foster Placement and Adoption, Nationally and Internationally." Like all similar declarations, however, this one was not binding on states. Furthermore, its very wording permits any number of escape clauses for governments reluctant to intervene in certain areas of child protection. Twelve out of its twenty-four articles are phrased only as wishes or qualified recommendations.

In many countries established adoption agencies have looked on appalled as the market in international babies, unchecked, unregulated and largely morally unquestioned, has boomed. Most people concerned with this field now seem to agree on at least two basic points: that international adoption is not a satisfactory long-term solution to the problems and needs of the most deprived children and that abuses of the practice have now become so widespread as to make it imperative that the strictest possible international monitoring system be set up to protect the interests of the children involved.

C.M.

7

Migrant Children

in France

Anne Chisholm and
Caroline Moorehead

"I was born here in Paris. At seven months, my parents took me home, to Portugal. At three, they brought me back. At eight, I went to my grandmother's, in Portugal, once again, fifteen kilometers from the sea. She has a farm where she grows oranges and has goats. I was always ill here, you see, with a bad throat, and the woman my mother left me with while she worked couldn't keep taking a sick child." Séverine is fifteen, a neat, self-contained girl with an anxious smile. She arrived back in Paris last year, though her parents had been living there all the time. For six years she saw them only during the summer.

"At home we speak Portuguese; or sometimes French and Portuguese. My father's French isn't very good, so sometimes I correct him. At school I'm in a class for foreign children. There are three of us Portuguese, three Moroccans, a Pole, a Yugoslav, two boys from the Cameroons and a Peruvian girl. It's not too bad now because when we make mistakes no one laughs. Next year, when I join an ordinary French class, everyone will laugh at me.

"My father is longing to leave France. He says that he has had enough. His hands hurt in the winter from his work. He wants to go home to the farm. In Portugal, with the money he has made, we have bought a house by the sea and an apartment. He loves the sea. He wants to run a café on the beach.

"I'm going to be a hairdresser. My parents are going to wait for me here in Paris until I get my diploma.

"In Paris we go on living just as if we were still in Portugal. Nearly all our friends are Portuguese. The apartment is so small, just two rooms, that we can't entertain much, but on Sundays we try to see friends. My father wouldn't like me to be out on the streets late, so I'm always inside by six-thirty. I feel funny each time I come back to Paris from Portugal. There, in our village, there are lots of people we know and who come up and talk to us. In this block of apartment houses, there are people who have been living here for twenty years and still they don't talk to each other.

"No one is nasty to me, but I can't wait to leave. We have our home in Portugal. It's ours. No one can throw us out. Here we might have to leave any time. It's hard to have roots if you live like this. At school, in my class, we tell each other what our real homes are like and how much we want to be there. It's interesting when you hear the others feel just like you do, but it's also sad.

"At school I try to pretend I'm really French. At home I'm Portuguese. Sometimes I get so muddled in my head I can't think. If I make a phone call to a friend, I go silent. I can't remember what language I'm supposed to be speaking. Inside the house, with my parents, I feel fine. But in the streets I look at all these French people and think: What am I doing here? My father says: 'We're strangers here, but then in Portugal we're now also strangers.' Yet we dream of the day we'll go home."

During the first round of the French general elections early in 1987, posters of the political candidates were pasted up in the schools of Paris. In one secondary school in the eighteenth arrondissement, the area that runs north and west from the Gare du Nord, teachers arriving in the morning would notice that bits were being torn off the bottom of the poster of the Le Pen National Front candidate. When they stopped to watch, they observed how the children would pause below the poster and rip off a scrap before darting on and into their classrooms. The smaller ones had to leap into the air to reach. Day by day, while Jean-Marie Le Pen could be seen on television telling the French voters that the migrant workers should be sent home, the posters shrank, little by little, from the bottom up. Well before election day, all that remained of Le Pen's man were the tacks that had held him in place.

The eighteenth arrondissement is Paris's most foreign quarter. It is here, in the Rue Livingstone, the Rue Richomme, and the Rue de la Goutte d'Or, in the last thirty years, since France's empire started to shrink and her former colonial citizens prepared to answer the call for cheap labor, that the migrant workers settled. The First World War had seen the arrival of some one hundred and twenty thousand people from the Maghreb, the strip of North Africa colonized in the nineteenth century by the French. But it was only in the 1960s that the migrants came from the souks and small villages of the Maghreb in great numbers to feed France's expansionist economic dreams. In those years Tunisians arrived and Moroccans and Algerians; after them came Malians and Senegalese, Guineans and Somalis; after them again, Portuguese and Turks and Spaniards. Between 1975 and 1982 the foreign population of France grew by seven percent. Today there are four and a half million immigrants, almost half of them from North Africa; three quarters of them live in the French cities. The most numerous are the Algerians, then come the Portuguese. Three million are Muslims, and one million of these are French, either because they were born in France or because they fought for France in Algeria and were "repatriated."

Many are young. Recent research has put the numbers of those under twenty-four at some two million. Neither French nor foreign, these are the children of migration: the young who grow up with no roots or with muddled ones, who are obsessed with the new laws which govern their future, and who are uncertain about both staying and going. They are at home nowhere; both to stay and to leave feel wrong.

The eighteenth arrondissement no longer feels like a French city. Only the bakers have retained their atmosphere of Frenchness, with their baguettes and croissants and cakes, though many of them are now run by the migrant workers. Grocers have come to look like shops in North African souks, with all the food displayed on the pavement and up the window. Bars have become cafés. In the street market behind the Métro station called Barbès, sheeps' heads and coriander have taken the place of country cheeses and pâtés. The smell, spicy and rich, is quite different.

Not far from the market, up a side street and past a modern school of concrete and orange steel girders, is a tenement building, one of a row of what must once have been elegant town houses. It was in this neighborhood that Nana, Zola's courtesan, lived. Number 5 Rue Richomme is shabby, derelict and damp. A pale light, which flickers for a few seconds and then goes out, shows a dirty, peeling hall; above the letter boxes a message has been nailed to say that because of non-payment the water is to be cut off.

Opposite the door leading to a Malian tailor are two rooms belonging to Moncef Ben Lakhal and his family. The bell was answered by a child's voice, squeaky with apprehension. No, his parents were not at home. Yes, their name was Ben Lakhal. No, he hadn't been told to let anyone in. I said that I would wait. For the next half hour I listened to the scratch-ings and gurglings of a second, much younger child. The Ben Lakhals had been shopping. When they unlocked the door they explained that they always closed it by key from the outside, preferring the risk of fire to that of a break-in. Their French neighbors sometimes shouted abuse at the children. In the hallway, they said, they also often found syringes. It was not a good thing for children to see.

Moncef came to Paris in 1972, from a village in northern Tunisia. He was sent by the National Office for Immigration, to finish his studies in France. He was a bright boy, with his eye on a law career. To live, he had to find work. Working, he had no time, no will to study. Mathematics was abandoned for a job in a factory. "My father was old and when he stopped working I became responsible for him and for the education of my younger brother and sister. I had hoped for something better. I could not have believed that this could happen to me."

He moved from the factory to an electrician's shop. He has never left it. In 1979 he went home to Tunisia, to a bride he had never met, and brought her back with him, to one room not far away from where he now lives. When the third baby was born they moved here, to two rooms, twelve feet by six, with no natural light; the kitchen and bathroom are boxes. "I had hopes. . . . I liked the idea of the law. . . . But it's too late now. It doesn't mean that I don't read a lot." His wife, an affable, big woman in her late twenties, reminded him that he had once talked of aviation. He nodded.

The eldest boy, Ahmed, is eight. His parents talk to him in Arabic and, after his day's schooling in French, give him classes at home in the Koran. He is now bilingual. The little girl, Fatima, is at nursery school; her French is faltering. The baby is too small to speak. The parents have a sad, protective air. "You have to have one foot here and one at home," says Moncef. "That way, if one gets trampled on, you still have the other."

Moncef has long planned to go home. He accepts that he will never, now, find work of the kind he once dreamed of. And yet he hesitates. "It's like being a smoker. You can't suddenly stop. That's my position. I am addicted to being here, in France. I can't break the habit. So I shall just wean myself very slowly. We are sending the boy back first, on his own, to my mother, then, bit by bit, over the years, we'll try to make the move.

"It's a completely new world there for me. It makes me frightened. I would have done better, far, far better, never to have come here in the first place. The things I believed I would find, for me, for my children, I never found. My friends? They are all Arab, all North African, like myself. We talk about how we have been deceived. So much was promised. I came thinking that France was superior. But they have treated us like things. We are not just poor, the French think we are inferior human beings. They just assume our children are backward. Nothing is expected of them except failure.

"Now I'm going to save my children. I'm going to get them home, back to Tunisia where we belong, before they too are bitter and disillusioned. We are a close family and we will survive. It's very hard for my son. He comes home and talks about all the people he has seen taking drugs. At home he has nothing to fear. Even just in the few months we spend in Tunisia every summer I watch the children alter, flourish. Because they can go outside, without danger, they look healthy. Here we spend all the time at the doctor's. I can't accept the fact that we have to keep them barricaded, day after day, in the half-dark. People are best off in their own countries. If you take a pygmy from the forests and put him in a city it's bad. We, too, are just pygmies. It's bad for us too here."

The Lakhals have never allowed their image of home to pale. They carry it in their minds, like a vision of perfection against which they measure the poverty, the bleakness and the continual slights that fill their lives. They exude an almost tangible air of apartness.

Three streets away, up a steep slope, in three narrow rooms above a grocer's shop, live the Omramas. Their experience of France has been good but, like the Lakhals', their life is separate. Success does not mean integration; it means, for them, the preservation intact of what they arrived with. They, too, know that one day they will leave.

Leila was born in Tunisia in 1972, as were one younger sister and a brother. Ben Omrama, their father, had been working in Paris since 1966 but, until his third child was born, he preferred to keep his family in Tunisia, in the house of his parents in the south. Two more children, a boy and another girl, were born in the two years that followed the family's arrival in Paris. Today, the five teenagers are remarkably alike in build and manner, and curiously untouched by their experience of migration. When not in class they stay near the shop, replacing their mother at the till. Madame Omrama has never learned French.

Leila is the most talkative; a demure but direct girl, with brown hair in braids, she has watched the migrant families who make up their friends very closely. She has strong views about what migration can do to people, held with a comfortable certainty which comes from knowing that one day she and her brothers and sisters will be back in the large house and garden near the sea that has been built for them in their absence with money from the shop. "It's been easier for us. We watch other children who never learn to fit in. You have to be very clear, you have to be able to select only what is good and useful in French culture, and avoid everything else. We all want to go home, all five of us and our parents. We know, we've seen, that however well we may appear to fit in here this is not our place. We will leave when my youngest brother has finished his schooling. We are preparing, every day, our departure. It's far better to go than to be pushed."

Their plans are ambitious. Leila wants to go into business, so as to be able to start something of her own in Tunisia; her two sisters both want to be doctors; the elder boy a chemist. "We have a good chance of succeeding. You see, when we go home, we'll be different. We'll go home with a lot of useful baggage. We are not like the Chinese and the Vietnamese who live in the *treizième* arrondissement. Did you know that when someone dies they don't report it but burn his body in the house and keep his papers for another immigrant?" This same story, with varying degrees of horror and contempt, was repeated to me by almost every immigrant I spoke to. In each case, only the nationality of the corpse was different.

Ben Omrama is a wiry figure with a small mustache and uneven teeth who smiles politely all the time. He is a man of certainties. His children will not marry outside Islam because it would be wrong: they do not follow the lax manners of French teenagers because that too is wrong. He has always been content in Paris, but now, with Le Pen, something is different. *L'effet Le Pen,* as they call it, has shifted some fragile balance that held him and his children safe. Maria, the second daughter, explains: "It's only in the last few months that we have come to understand, with certainty, that we are foreigners. Or rather a strange mixture, foreigners with a French life. At my *lycée* there is a boy whose parents vote Le Pen and who says that he cannot bear Arabs, but that of course I'm different, I'm not like the others, I'm intelligent and clean and when the others go I should be allowed to stay. We never go to his home. We know what his parents think. It disgusts us, just as it disgusts us when we see the National Front candidates on the television. In the shop, this last winter, we have had customers who come in and stand talking to us for hours, just as they have always done, only now what they talk about is how the Arabs and the migrant workers are taking jobs from the French, how they are responsible for the rise in drugs and crime and how they must be made to go. They seem to forget that we are Arabs. When they remember, it's like the boy at school. They say: 'You're nice, you're different, you can stay.' "

Leila says: "I think what is hardest for us is going back to Tunisia in the summer. We have to adjust. We have to behave like other Tunisian girls of our age. But we don't really get on with them. They have all left school, long before us, and we're not like them anymore. We try to be calm, moderate, wear sober clothes. But always we can see that they are thinking how rich we are, and lucky, and that Paris must be Paradise.

"I take a bus to school. When it goes along the Rue Barbès and I see the Africans, still wearing the clothes they wear in Africa, I want to lean out of the bus window and say: 'Why don't you dress like the French? Why don't you at least pretend to be like them? Then you'll fit in better.' They look absurd. In front of them I feel French. But as the bus moves on, to another street full of ordinary French people in ordinary clothes, then I lose my sense of identity."

Mohamed, a compact, enthusiastic young man in his late twenties with a great deal of energy, is studying anthropology in Paris. He arrived in France with his family in 1974, when he was fourteen. "I already knew French a little, from school, and in one way I was glad we moved to Paris because the family was reunited. My father had left Morocco in 1966 to find work. He had always intended to return to Morocco when he could afford it, but that never happened. It's hard to say if I was happy when we got here or not. After all, I had no choice in the matter, and I didn't realize the significance of it. One can put up with it, as with an accident or an injury. One does the best one can.

"As a young foreigner, at once you confront a society in which you feel inferior vis-à-vis French children. Being foreign is a handicap. The child has to face and deal with different values from the ones he has grown up with; he feels a sense of loss and of frustration. He is also humiliated. Suppose he has done well in class in Morocco; he arrives here, and just because of the language difficulty he is bottom of the class. This shows him his language has no value in France, and that the educational system has no respect for it or him. English is also a foreign language, but it is one that is respected and taken seriously.

"I feel the same problem affecting children born here. They feel the same devaluation of their own language and culture the moment they cross the threshold of their home. As a result it is very hard for them to respect their parents' culture and customs. To me this is the result of a monumental error in the school system, and it should be put right by including Moroccan and other languages in the school curriculum.

"I remember very well my first day at school in France, how I stood in a corner with the other immigrant children. What I felt was: Here my experience doesn't count. Everything I know means nothing. As for racism, I didn't know what it was until I came here. It's the same with the kids I talk to today. When I ask them what they think racism is, they answer something like: 'Only the French people are racist.' The other assumption they make, of course, from their own observation, is that to be a full citizen and have all legal rights you need to be a pretty color.

"I have a younger sister who was only seven when she arrived in France, so she knew not a word of French. She was put in with the five-year-olds and hated it. I would see her coming home from school in tears; my baby sister. I felt terrible. I tried to help her and to protect her. All she needed was access to the same education as French girls her age. Eventually she got her *baccalauréat*, won a scholarship and went to medical school, but even so, financially things were impossible. My father has retired, and of course my mother has never worked. She shared her scholarship money with them and took a job, but it was too hard. She has dropped out, although she hopes to go back to it one day. She still studies, at night. My mother, who can't read or write, sits up with her to keep her company. For all the immigrants, family solidarity is very important, and parents have a deep need to see their children rise and succeed. If they fail, the parents tend to revert to the old, traditional ways and try, for example, to arrange a marriage for their daughters, who by this time of course do not want such a thing. All the time there is a conflict. I feel it still, between the values I have inside me and the values I see outside and aspire to. The contradictions are very difficult.

"In bringing the workers they needed here, France forgot they would have children. Who am I in French society? Just a laborer, like my father, or a French citizen, second class? Or do I have the same rights as my French contemporaries?"

Until about ten years ago the migrant workers of France seemed to be a temporary, transient phenomenon. They came to the country to work in jobs that paid well by their standards and that promised even more. And they lived in hostels which they knew to be appalling but which they continued to think of as lasting no more than a few weeks. They kept thinking how, soon, they would go home, back to the Maghreb, with the money they had made. It all seemed so brief that no one, particularly not the French, minded about the extreme discomfort and squalor in which many of these men lived. But then, extraordinarily quickly, people's perceptions of what was happening changed. With the oil crisis France's economy languished; the valuable foreign workers were suddenly not quite as vital as they had been. What was more, they had taken to bringing their families with them. In the 1960s the authorities talked about work. Now they speak about housing, schools and pensions. When Le Pen talks about giving France back to the French he arouses a warm feeling in people who have never really liked the look of all these foreigners but have never managed to focus very clearly on what went wrong.

Last year, in an attempt to capture votes from the far right, Jacques Chirac pushed through, at least to a first stage, a new law on immigration. The *loi Pasqua*, as it is known, modifies all existing French laws on the subject of migration—laws which, human rights experts agree, were very good laws, the fruit of twelve years of fighting. The emphasis now has shifted, not even very subtly: things were once easy for the immigrants; now they are very hard. Furthermore, a sword of Damocles has been wielded: any breach of state security or contravention of public order by an immigrant can result in deportation. The trouble is that no one quite knows what this means. All that they know is that, under its umbrella, troublesome young immigrants have already been expelled from France and sent home, though home is not what many of them consider the birthplace of their fathers to be. Under the *loi Pasqua* children born in France of migrant parents can be expelled if their father is expelled.

The law is now being fought by the many small and precarious organizations, spawned in the last few years, that deal with foreigners. In these crowded places, many of them in the apartment houses that surround the Gare du Nord, Tunisians, Moroccans, Algerians, Turks and Portuguese come and go, in search of advice and help, addresses or just companionship. It is here that the sense of terrible injustice is kept alive. France, say the men who come here late after work, was once the country of welcome; it was the first place, after the French Revolution, to take in persecuted Jews. Where has that hospitality gone? Why is it that one in five of all Algerians is now out of work? That French workers have more refrigerators, cars, hair dryers, irons and sewing machines than they do?

At the Office for Tunisian Workers, Mohamed Chaouih told his story. He was a thin, sallow man in his fifties, with a bony face and ears that stuck out, who wore a heavy suit and overcoat, despite the spring weather. But Mohamed Chaouih did not want to talk about the hardships of the migrant men; what he really minded about was the effect of this migration on his children.

"I have lived in France for thirty-one years. I was twenty-three when I came and I'm now fifty-four. The French authorities brought me here to work in a car factory in Lyons. Seventeen years ago I came to a factory outside Paris. At fifty they sent me packing. There wasn't anything more for me. Ever since then I've been searching for work.

"My family lives in Tunisia. I have four children. The youngest is six. I have never lived with them. I kept thinking this way of life was only temporary and that I would soon be home with them, so that there never seemed any point in bringing them here. In any case my wife never wanted to come. At one point, if I had gone back, I know I could have found work in Tunisia. But then I met people who had tried to go back and never found a job. I lost my nerve. Now it's too late. I can't ever go back. I have my pension here and I have to be here to get it. I draw it, and then send most of it back to my family. It's a terrible way to live.

"My oldest boy is sixteen and dreams of coming here. I shall never let him. I was hurt, badly hurt, by the promises of migration. It's not going to happen to him. I don't really know my children. Every time I see them they are different people. I think that they are all right. At least they speak French and are learning English. Life in Tunisia is very different from the way it was when I was young. But I wouldn't really know how they are. They don't seem to be my children anymore."

In the past few years the immigrant communities in Paris have started to organize themselves and establish a network of support for their people. One of the most active is the Association of Moroccans in France, which runs a Center for Activities and Interests in Puteaux, once a village on the outskirts of Paris which is now dwarfed by the huge skyscraper development of La Défense, about half an hour to the northwest of the city. On Wednesday afternoons there may be as many as twenty children, boys and girls aged between six and sixteen, in the basement room. Some are doing lessons or reading, some are playing computer games, and the television is on.

Two shy Moroccan boys were aged twelve and thirteen. They were born in Morocco but have lived in Paris since they were very small. Both speak Moroccan at home, though their fathers speak a little French. Both boys said that they preferred to eat Moroccan food, and that they would never think of marrying a non-Muslim girl when they grew up. It was, after all, forbidden by their religion. A larger, more confident boy from Haiti called Hari, aged fourteen, said that his family were political refugees, that he had a brother doing well in America and that he intended to be a construction engineer and to travel. When asked whether it was going to be hard for him to find a job in France, it became clear that he has some muddled ideas: "Jobs should be first for the French, then for foreigners," he said firmly. But then he agreed that if the foreigner was as intelligent, as well qualified as the French person, and spoke good French, he should have the same chance. As a volunteer later pointed out, these provisos would rule out most immigrant children. Their aims are often, he finds, unrealistically high; it is important to make them more realistic without destroying their dreams entirely.

Misha, aged fifteen, had recently arrived from Zaire. He said, with some bravado, that it was fine by him to be in France because the education was better. Asked if he found the language difficult, he spoke at length about how he wished that his family would speak French at home because it was so hard for him to improve otherwise. He badly wanted a good accent and to sound like a proper French person. The language of Zaire, he said scornfully, was a poor language, very rough. Misha is a boy in the process of learning to despise his own culture.

On the other side of Paris, in the eighteenth arrondissement, not far from Moncef Ben Lakhal and his family, is the center called Children of the Goutte d'Or, named after a street renowned for its cluster of immigrants. In this center a handful of determined young French teachers run after-school coaching classes for children of all nationalities who have learning problems. Two harassed-looking French teachers, a young woman in dungarees called Corinne and a man, were attempting to control a group of children aged about seven.

"We are in touch with about thirty children, and we work with the school welfare service," said Corinne. "We are open for all the kids of the quarter, but ninety-five percent are children of immigrants, or of mixed parents. They come after school, between five and seven; the times are flexible, which is not ideal, but the ones who are keen get into a regular pattern. Some just come to play, not work. Sometimes their parents bring them, sometimes they come with friends. The main problem is reading and writing. We try to improve their vocabulary, because often they may sound fluent but their range is very limited. It's good for them to have a place to come to, otherwise they are often left alone in the street and conditions round here are not very safe.

"At about thirteen or fourteen the psychological problems start, when they wake up to the situation they are in and start to look around. Often as small children they have great potential. But it's hardly ever realized."

A large, dark girl of around fifteen from Haiti came up to talk to Corinne about a tea party arranged for later that week. The school year was ending and the center was celebrating with a special tea. Her mother would make a cake, she said. She had arrived in France as a baby, and came to study twice a week. She liked the other children. Asked whether she would like to go back to live in Haiti, she nodded. "Oh, they all say that," said Corinne ruefully. "They all want to go back."

The people who work with the migrants, who run the little national offices around the Gare du Nord, are cynical about the dream of going home. Migrant workers, they say, never go home. It is all talk. Only the very successful, those who have done extraordinarily well in their new life, so that they manage both to save money and to conserve a memory of home that can be translated into reality, ever make it back. The others, those who have had troubles, those who have lost their jobs, or never found a proper apartment, whose children have done badly at school or been in trouble with the police—the very people in short who should go home—never actually get there. Their migration is forever. This is what makes the position of the children so poignant: they live in limbo, often in squalid surroundings, hearing stories of how wonderful everything is at home, and yet never get there to enjoy it. Even so, these are perhaps the lucky ones. French law demands that a migrant worker must show evidence of work and fifteen square meters of housing for every member of his family. Often a man can only find thirty or maybe forty square meters: he has no choice but to bring only part of his family to Paris and leave the others at home.

In a modern block of apartment houses beyond the Porte de Clignancourt, where the migrants who have not found rooms in the eighteenth arrondissement or who cannot face the high-rise apartment houses of the suburbs have come to settle, live the Bouamanas. Their block was built ten years ago, in the shape of a pyramid, and painted with zigzag lines of olive green and ocher. The entrance hall is roomy but dismal. The French tenants will not travel up in the elevators with the migrant families.

Said Bouamana came to France in 1969. He brought with him his wife of eight years and two children. At the end of the first three months his wife, who could not seem to learn French and spent her days alone with the babies in the apartment, had a nervous breakdown. Three more children have since been born. Said Bouamana is an invalid on an invalid's pension. For them migration has meant a divided family, neatly split down the middle.

Khali, who was two when the family moved to Paris, believes himself to be purely Tunisian. He hastened through his studies and went as an apprentice to a garage. Last year he made the great journey home: telling his parents he was going back to pave the way for the rest of the family, he sold his motorcycle, packed all his possessions and caught the ferry from Marseilles to North Africa. With him went his sister Fatou, who had trained as a secretary and who also felt herself to be wholly Arab. They left jubilantly. France, for both of them, for their entire childhood and adolescence, had been a holding station, somewhere to mark time before getting on with the proper business of life. Both spoke perfect Arabic. It was their French that was poor.

They stayed away for three months. The Tunisia they found was not the one they had been anticipating. They had imagined that they would find many friends, but no one knew them: they felt themselves to be strangers. Fatou complained that when she went to swim men followed her; she could never be alone. Khali could not find work. And so they came back, angry and disappointed, to the pyramid block of apartment houses.

Abelfatah, their younger brother, speaks no Arabic. He is fifteen. His French, as well as his French jeans and leather jacket, and his French friends, are all a matter of necessity to him. He is a lanky, purposeful boy with thick glasses who has found a niche in computers. "The Tunisian way is not my way," he says. "My mentality is different." He understands neither the despair of his older brother and sister nor the lethargy of his younger sister who, at fourteen, is in a class for ten-year-olds and whose dreamy gentleness conceals either confusion or stubbornness—no one knows which. Psychologists tell the mother that the child is bright. Year by year she slips behind, mild and vacant. She is interested neither in being French nor being Tunisian.

Few children face greater difficulties across the entire spectrum of basic needs and rights than the children of migrant workers. Arriving in the suburbs and cities of foreign countries in search of a promised better life, migrant families find themselves relegated to a second-class existence in unskilled, badly paid jobs, living in dismal housing with all the consequences that stem from poverty. For children, what migration means is a new language, a new culture and profound uncertainty. Uprooted children feel displaced, isolated, unable to communicate or to understand the enormous changes that are taking place around them. They feel unsettled by the new food and the different climate. As they grow older, many are excluded from higher education.

As northern Europe began to rebuild itself after the Second World War, mass migration from the Mediterranean countries brought millions of workers from Italy, Spain, Turkey, Portugal and Greece. By the late 1970s there were estimated to be some ten million migrants in Europe, three and a half million of whom were children. By then migrants were also flowing from Asia into oil-producing countries. Today large-scale migrations continue to take place between all continents. In many countries migrants have become vital to economic prosperity: in 1980 it was estimated that one car in every six produced in Germany had been made by migrant labor.

The economic crisis of the early 1970s did something to halt the flow, particularly where it was backed up by tough new policies intended to persuade migrants to return home to their own countries, as in France, Germany and Switzerland. Few, however, did go back, not least because for many of them, and especially the second-generation immigrants, there were no homes for them to return to. Instead the speed at which new immigrants had been arriving slowed down. Those who were already there made further efforts to bring their families to their country of adoption, so that by 1975 at least half the migrant workers of Europe had their wives and children living with them. And, as immigration rules became more restrictive, so the numbers of illegal immigrants—or "undocumented aliens," as the authorities prefer to call them—rose. When parents have no papers, children are seldom able to go to school. Infants have been found tied to bedposts to prevent them going out and alerting people to their existence.

The need for efforts to regulate immigration and, occasionally, to improve the lives of the migrant workers and their families, has been voiced in regional declarations, International Labor Organization conventions and by a United Nations working group. More importantly, perhaps, people have increasingly come to see how essential it is to develop special programs of education geared toward immigrant families and more humane policies to make their lives easier.

C.M.

8

Los Desaparecidos

of Argentina

Isabel Hilton

Clara Anahi, my little one, today is August 12, your birthday. You are five today, my life, and I can only imagine you. . . . Four years and nine months ago dark forces carried you away. You were just a baby in a little pink dress, with a wide mouth that laughed and laughed and sharp eyes that searched anxiously for the faces of your parents, to laugh, from pure love. . . .

185

I have searched for you, my Anahi, ceaselessly, to overcome the tearing grief of my deaths. Ignoring the guns, the
threats and the insults, I searched for you for a day, then
another and another, then a month and many months.
Clenching my teeth, burning my tears. In rage and despair.
With my heart bursting I thought of your first tooth, of
your first steps. . . . You were growing and I had to find
you, now, at once. I would imagine your first clothes and
your dolls and the kindergarten. And I couldn't find you.
. . . I bought you dolls, you know. I have them in boxes. I
had to change them for bigger ones. The dolls accumulated
. . . and I didn't find you.

(Letter to her disappeared granddaughter, 1981. María
Isabel de Mariani.)

The rooms they work in are cramped and dingy, four floors
up in an office building in Buenos Aires. The walls are covered with photographs, some of them fuzzy snapshots of
groups squinting into the sun, frozen moments of family hap-
piness; others are solemn ID pictures, already showing that
indefinably remote quality of a photograph growing old.
Mostly there are photographs of children, of babies held up
for the camera by huge adult hands, of babies lying in their
cots, their double chins lopsided, of toddlers captured on a
beach on a summer holiday that nobody now remembers.

The parents of these children are almost all dead. The children themselves, some two hundred of them, have vanished,
disappeared into the nightmare that was Argentina's Dirty
War against dissidents. The fate of the adult victims of the
Dirty War is now widely accepted. It can be presumed that,
of the nine to twenty thousand who disappeared and have not
reappeared, the vast majority did not, as Argentina's former
military rulers used to insist, go into hiding or abroad, but
were secretly eliminated by their military captors as the final
part of the gigantic, official lie which claimed that they had
never been detained.

The majority of the missing children, however, are presumed to be alive somewhere, cut off from their real families, from their real identities, living in ignorance of the fate of their real parents or the role their adoptive parents may have had in that fate. The middle-aged and elderly women who crowd into these cramped offices are their grandmothers, women who, over ten years ago, were precipitated into the unassuageable grief for the disappearance of a son or daughter. The grandmothers began by searching for whole families, a search that has now been reduced to the hope that one day their grandchildren will be restored to them.

This is the Casa de las Abuelas, the House of the Grandmothers of the Plaza de Mayo. There is one phone line, frequently out of order. There are filing cabinets stuffed with papers, affidavits, reports of cases, anonymous letters. The House is full of people, mostly women, who exchange kisses as they arrive and leave. And, among the women, one or two children, children who, miraculously, have been found and returned. These children are a source of renewed hope and renewed pain: a child found is a promise that others might follow, but for each woman whose grandchild is still missing a returned child renews an individual sense of loss.

A pretty, dark-haired girl of nine is the latest arrival in the Casa de las Abuelas. Dressed in a bright pink track suit, she is passed from hand to hand to be kissed and embraced. She climbs onto María Isabel de Mariani's knee and hugs her. "I have nobody of my own to hug yet," says Señora Mariani to the girl, "so I hug you." The child smiles, indulging the adults.

Señora Mariani, universally known as Chicha by the grandmothers, is the president of the grandmothers' organization and has been one of its driving forces since her own life was torn apart on November 24, 1976. It was a Wednesday, the day her daughter-in-law, Diana, always brought Clara Anahi to see her. "I was waiting for them after lunch. I had everything ready, as usual. . . . I used to give Clara a bath and Diana and I would chat."

But that day the peace of the early afternoon was shattered by a series of explosions, followed by sirens and the clatter of a helicopter passing overhead. The sounds filled Chicha with fear. For months she had been aware of the toll that repression was taking on the young, many of them students at the high school where she taught. But as she waited for Diana through the afternoon her main concern was that the battle she could hear was raging near to where the family lived. "I never for a moment imagined it could be them." Later that afternoon Chicha's mother rang her to tell her that her father was ill. She went to her parents' house and spent the night there, an act that almost certainly saved her own life. The following morning the newspapers carried the official version of the raid on her son's house, described as a terrorist headquarters, though there was never any evidence that he had anything to do with the guerrillas.

Chicha returned to her own house, where she found a crowd of neighbors outside the demolished front door. Inside she found her home destroyed, the floor covered with her smashed possessions, strewn with a disgusting mess of oil, sugar and the rest of the contents of the kitchen shelves. Chicha recalls that her visitors had paused to eat the contents of the refrigerator. Everything else—her records, books, furniture—was wrecked or stolen.

At first she believed that all her son's family had been killed. Her daughter-in-law had, in fact, died in the raid, and her son had survived only to be killed nine months later. Of Clara Anahi there was at first no trace, dead or alive. But as the weeks went by rumors reached her, whispers in corners from frightened officials, that her granddaughter was alive, that she had been removed from the house by General Ramón Camps, the notorious chief of police of Buenos Aires Province, and that she had been given to a couple in the security services.

So began the months of loneliness, of despair, of desperate confrontation with an officialdom that yielded only threats, denials, blankness. Day after day Chicha went to the barracks of the army unit that had raided her son's house, handing in letters that never received a reply. The friends who had thronged her home fell away, the neighbors were afraid to talk to her, people she had known for years crossed the street to avoid meeting her. Her musician husband, who had been in Italy when the nightmare began, could not bear to return to live in Argentina and Chicha could not bear to abandon the search for Clara Anahi. So she passed her days picking through the wreckage of her home, repairing and restoring what she could, and searching for her missing granddaughter.

In August of the following year she learned that her son Daniel had been killed. She never discovered the details or knew what had happened to his body. She remembers only that the news filled her with new despair. In the courts, in the police stations and even among her friends she was treated as though she was either mad or dangerous. Occasionally she would be encouraged when some official or a priest took her case in hand and seemed to offer hope. But each time the trail petered out and she was advised to drop it. There was no doubt that Clara was alive, that some official had her, but to pursue the matter, she was told, was too dangerous.

There was one consolation in the nightmare. As the repression continued, Chicha began to meet other women who were in search of their children and grandchildren. "On this long road we grandmothers got together and organized a group to look for the disappeared children, at first thinking that there were just a few of us, and then realizing to our horror that there were hundreds of us." Some, like herself, were looking for children who had disappeared with their parents. Others, mothers or mothers-in-law of women who disappeared when pregnant, could only guess at the existence of their grandchildren, presumed to have been born in captivity. Gradually these women began to act together, to meet in secret, to demonstrate in the Plaza de Mayo, to pool resources and to offer each other emotional and practical support. They became the Grandmothers of the Plaza de Mayo.

"When we began this work of looking for the children we didn't have the remotest idea of how to go about it. We began in the logical places—in orphanages, in barracks, police stations, courts of the districts where they had disappeared. We weren't detectives then, we were just using our common sense to try to find them," said Chicha. "It was after the first children were found (in 1979, in Chile, we found two) that we began to follow threads and began to develop our intuition as well as our reasoning powers. We have a fact, we examine it —birth dates, likely dates, names—we examine all of it and devise a plan."

In spite of the refinement of their technique the grandmothers admit that such success as they have had has been almost by chance. "Nearly all the children who have been found were discovered as a result of an anonymous tip-off, with the aid of the public," said Chicha. "Whenever we get publicity we get calls and anonymous letters from people. Without that we wouldn't have found any of them."

It was an anonymous tip-off that led to the discovery of María Victoria, the child that Chicha has been hugging. Her parents, Alfredo Moyano and María Asunción Artigas de Moyano, had been sweethearts since their schooldays. They married in December 1973 and lived for a time in the same building as Alfredo's mother, Enriqueta Santander. While they were living there, Enriqueta and the couple were detained for thirty-six hours in the police headquarters. Both Alfredo and his wife were tortured, but then all three were released. Their arrest, their captors said, had been a mistake.

By December 1977, however, the security services had a change of heart. By then the couple were living in a house in the Berazategui district of Buenos Aires. They studied in the evenings and during the day Alfredo worked as a painter and decorator.

On December 31, 1977, Enriqueta was waiting for her son and daughter-in-law, who were expected for the family's New Year celebrations. When they failed to appear, Enriqueta's niece went to look for them. She discovered from the neighbors that the house had been raided at dawn on New Year's Eve by about a dozen armed men. Alfredo and María Asunción, who was two months pregnant, had disappeared. "The house was destroyed, completely turned over, and all the neighbors in a state of terror," said Enriqueta. "That night my niece came to tell me what had happened. I had been worried all day. The neighbors said that they had been taken away with hoods on their heads. I was terrified . . . at the time I had no idea that people disappeared, that these things went on. It was only later that I found out that it was happening everywhere.

"I went to the local police station to ask about them. They were polite to me but said they didn't know anything. I went to the Ministry of the Interior the same day and to the local barracks, but nobody would tell me anything. Two to three days later I got a lawyer to present a writ of habeas corpus in the federal court and I kept going back there for news, but I was always told there was no record of their arrest. Finally, at the court, I met another mother who told me that other people were looking for relatives and that they had started an organization called Fedefam which might be able to help me."

Enriqueta made contact with Fedefam and finally found at least some emotional support. She was unable to continue her work as a seamstress because of the pressures she was under and thought of little else than her missing family. "My health deteriorated, I was in a state of permanent anguish. The only thing I could count on was the solidarity they offered me." She continued to believe that the couple would reappear. She would spend Sunday afternoons keeping the garden of their house tidy for them, until the day a neighbor told her that what remained of the couple's possessions had been taken away in a van and she became afraid to return to the house. Shortly afterward a "For Sale" notice appeared on the house. She never went back.

When the grandmothers' organization was founded Enriqueta made contact with it. She knew that her daughter-in-law had been pregnant and she wanted to find the child as well as the parents. In April 1978 a released prisoner contacted her to tell her he had seen María in prison and that she was still pregnant.

In 1979 a couple were released from Pozo de Banfield, one of Argentina's clandestine concentration camps, and they telephoned Enriqueta. They told her that they had been held with Alfredo and María and that María had given birth to a daughter on August 28, 1978. The child, the couple had been given to understand, would be left in a certain orphanage where her grandmother could collect her. She went to the orphanage but there was no trace of the child.

The conditions in such camps as Pozo de Banfield have since been described in detail by the commission of inquiry set up under President Raúl Alfonsín's government to investigate the disappearances that occurred during the Dirty War. In the commission's report, *Nunca Más* (which means "never again"), the authors explain: "Disappearance began with admission to these centers and the suppression of all links with the outside world, hence the name of *pozos* [pits], used to designate many of the centers. . . . It was not just a case of deprivation of freedom which was not officially acknowledged, but a sinister form of captivity which pushed daily existence to the limits of cruelty and madness."

In Pozo de Banfield another inmate described how "the regime was much harsher [than in the police station]. We were only let out to eat once in two days. There were three or more women in each cell and the lavatory consisted of a bottle of bleach with the top cut off."

Prisoners were kept chained up and blindfolded, forbidden to speak or to look at each other or their captors. The only break in the routine was when they were subjected to torture, or when a prisoner was "transferred," the preferred euphemism for the final disappearance. The prisoners, according to one survivor, had no doubt what transfer meant. "The transfers did not take place on set days, and tension reached untold heights for most of the prisoners. It produced a strange mixture of fear and relief, given that one both dreaded and longed for the transfer that on the one hand spelled certain death, and on the other meant the end of torture and agony" *(Nunca Más)*.

Pozo de Banfield was a three-story building in the suburbs of Buenos Aires. It is currently a police headquarters. In those years, according to *Nunca Más*, one of its functions "was that of housing prisoners in their last months of pregnancy." In unspeakable conditions, with minimal medical help, young women gave birth to their babies. Her daughter-in-law, Enriqueta was to learn from her informant, gave birth to her baby wearing manacles, blindfolded and tied to the bed.

The next stage, according to the report, was that of "separating the newly born from their mothers and disposing of them." Disposal of the mothers was by "transfer." Before her transfer the mother was encouraged to write a letter to her family asking them to take care of the baby. But most families never heard of either mother or child again once they had disappeared. The newborn infants were given to childless families in the security services.

These infants were treated in the same way as the rest of the property of the Dirty War's victims. Just as the cars, the houses or the valuables of the victims were regarded as legitimate trophies, to be distributed among the clandestine task forces which carried out the raids, so the infants were distributed among the agents of the security services, without concern for the rights of the children or their families. The children of those defined by the security services as "subversive" had no more rights than their parents.

Enriqueta's informant told how they had lived in Pozo de Banfield. "He said there were a lot of people in the camp, that they were tied up and hooded all day, surviving as best they could and trying to talk to each other. He said that on August 15, 1978, my son had been taken away and never came back, so he never knew about his daughter, but that they had been with my daughter-in-law when the child was born. Both my son and daughter-in-law had been tortured, although apparently they mistreated María less when they knew of the pregnancy.

"I was desperate when the man telephoned . . . it was the first news I had heard and I wanted to meet him, to ask him more questions, but he was afraid to come here. He telephoned twice and then we never heard from him again. The day after the child was born, this man said, two men came and took her away. One of them said, 'This is the child we told you about.' They asked my daughter-in-law about her medical history—what illnesses she and Alfredo had had." The mother was sent back to her cell and never heard of again.

One of the two men, the grandmothers now believe, was a senior police officer who gave the child to his brother for adoption. It was nearly ten years before Enriqueta was to see her grandchild. "I came every day to the Abuelas . . . people came all the time, to give bits of news. At the end of December last year Chicha told me that she thought we had found her, but they needed a blood sample for the courts. I couldn't believe it, after all those years when I had all but given up hope, but the judge ruled that it was her."

A team of doctors and psychologists began to work on the case in December. Enriqueta prepared a room for her granddaughter and bought her clothes. "I saw her for the first time on December 31, 1987. The judge brought her in . . . she was very shy, very silent. . . . It was extraordinary, that afternoon. At 5 P.M. I was in heaven, but still not entirely awake and crying all the time. I told her that I was her grandmother and that the other family was nothing to do with her. She had known from the age of four that she was adopted."

The child is now living with Enriqueta and Enriqueta's second husband. By their account she has settled well, but the joy of her reappearance can never erase the damage done to Enriqueta or her granddaughter. "Sometimes she remembers the 'mother' . . . she doesn't cry but she has moments of sadness. She seems to be recovering. I have other grandchildren, but they are far away so it is not easy for her just to live with two old people. Those people took away my best years. . . . The judge told her what had happened to her parents and when she asks about it I tell her the truth. . . . She has been lied to so much, I must tell her the truth.

"She has photographs of her parents and toys that once belonged to them and she seems to understand; she's very adult for her age. I believe these children know that they are not really the children of the people who had them. She is not allowed to see the other family . . . that is a stage of her life that has passed."

For each grandmother the search is a race against time, a race to find the child before it has grown to adulthood. For the Ross and Rossetti families that race has an added poignancy. They know exactly where their missing children are, but so far they have been unable to reclaim them.

Chacobuco represents all that is good and bad about small-town life in Argentina. A flat, regular little town of some twenty-five thousand inhabitants, it lies off the long, straight road that leads through the cathedral town of Lujan and, eventually, to Buenos Aires, two hundred kilometers away. Its regular grid pattern of streets is deserted by midevening, except for a few young men who gather in the pizzeria to pass the evening over a beer.

The road to the capital is heavy with cattle trucks, taking

the produce of the pampas to the metropolis. Back in Chacobuco everybody knows everybody; it is not a town for secrets or excitement and young people with ambition dream of escape to the capital or to other cities, like the sprawling university city of La Plata.

That was the route that Adalberto Rossetti took in 1972 when he went to university in La Plata to study law. He was nineteen and his childhood sweetheart, Liliana Ross, was seventeen. Two years later Liliana joined him in La Plata and began training to be a health visitor. "Adalberto was the only boyfriend Liliana ever had," said Lucía Ross, Liliana's mother. "He was the reason she went to study in La Plata."

Both had a strong social conscience. In Chacobuco they had been active in a church youth group run by a progressive priest. "We did the usual social work, visiting old people, health promotion, helping people with housing problems," said Adalberto. "There were about fifteen to twenty of us at the time. After we went to La Plata we would go back in the summer to Chacobuco to work with the group." The priest was later transferred out of pastoral work at the request of the military authorities. In the late 1970s a social conscience was regarded by the military authorities as one of the many symptoms of a subversive disposition.

The couple married in October 1976. Adalberto had graduated and was working in Buenos Aires, commuting from La Plata. Liliana was shortly to complete her studies and was pregnant. On December 12, 1976, when she was four months pregnant, Liliana was seized on the street, one block from her home, by a group of armed men and bundled into a car.

Adalberto's suspicions were aroused when Liliana failed to meet him off his train that evening. He went to a friend's house and heard, by chance, from a witness what had happened. He had been politically active and knew the dangers. "I was in a terrible situation. I knew that my own life was in danger and I knew what her disappearance meant." The next day a friend went to the Rossetti house and found it had been raided. Adalberto stayed with friends for three or four days and then went to Buenos Aires. After a year underground in Buenos Aires he left for Brazil and then went into exile in France.

Lucía Ross only heard of Liliana's disappearance fifteen days later. "Nobody had wanted to tell me. Adalberto was in hiding in Buenos Aires; four or five boys had been taken from Chacobuco. They took a relative of Adalberto's and held him for five days to try and find Adalberto and they raided his parents' house here in Chacobuco."

Señora Ross and Adalberto's mother, Elda Rossetti, began the long search for Liliana. Now Señora Ross is haunted by the conviction that her daughter died in place of her son-in-law, that her daughter had committed no crime and that her family's peace has been destroyed without cause. Back in 1977 she still hoped to find her.

"When I went to the Ministry of the Interior they said to me that I could have my daughter back if I could deliver Adalberto. It was a lie, but I think about it nevertheless."

Five months later, toward the end of April 1977, the two women had trodden the familiar path around the prisons, the barracks, the police stations and the courts. Then, suddenly, they picked up the trail. "We went to Military District 7 in La Plata and asked where a pregnant prisoner would be," said Elda Rossetti. "They told us she could be in the Los Olmos women's prison and we decided to go there."

They asked their way to the bus stop, looking for the bus that would take them the ten miles to the prison. At the bus stop they had a dramatic stroke of luck. "A young woman joined us at the bus stop, a thin, petite little thing," said Señora Ross. "We asked her if we were at the right bus stop for Los Olmos and we fell into conversation. She told us that she worked in Los Olmos and asked why we were going there. I told her that we were looking for my daughter and she began to ask me questions. Eventually she said she was the midwife in Los Olmos and that she thought there was someone there who answered Liliana's description."

The woman, Hilda Delgadillo, told Señora Ross that the person she thought was Liliana had just given birth to twin boys in the prison, blond babies with blue eyes. "I said, 'But how do I know this is true?' She told me that she had asked Liliana if there were other twins in the family as it struck her as unusual that a first pregnancy should be twins. Liliana said that her aunts were twins, which is true, I have two twin sisters." The midwife and the two women took the same bus to Los Olmos. "When we got to Los Olmos she pointed out the window and said Liliana was in that room."

Señora Ross and Señora Rossetti asked for permission to visit Liliana and the twins, but they were refused and told that they needed authorization. Thrilled by the discovery of Liliana, they decided to ask for help from the Church. They went to the cathedral to ask the bishop to help them gain access to the prison. "How naïve we were," Señora Rossetti remembers. "We didn't know what he was like." At the cathedral they were received by the bishop, who told them that he would look into the case. When they returned to see him he was frosty but told them to go and see the prison chaplain, Father José Hapo. "Father Hapo knew about the twins and said that they were in an incubator because they had been premature," said Señora Rossetti. "He said he would try to arrange a visit, but later said it had not been possible and that the twins were out of the incubator."

As the women ran from pillar to post trying to gain admission to the jail, Liliana's captors moved. As the two women later discovered from the midwife, Liliana was "transferred" at 3 A.M. on the morning of May 17. The twins were taken away in a separate car.

The little family had vanished and, in spite of their efforts, the two women failed to pick up their trail. They did, however, glean further details of Liliana's imprisonment: they managed to track down the doctor who had attended her and he told them about the birth. They learned that the twins had required a blood transfusion and that blood was supplied by a soldier. They were told that the babies had been well dressed, that clothes had been brought for them by a couple who seemed to have an interest in them. Señora Delgadillo supplied them with further details: she told them Liliana had called the twins Gustavo and Martín; she also told them that she thought, from a conversation with one of the drivers that night of May 16, that Liliana had been shot. She had put up a terrible fight when she was separated from her babies, the women were told. "It seems they had to drag her by the hair," said Señora Ross. "With all the pain she was in from the birth, poor thing, they dragged her by the hair."

Señora Delgadillo had told them too much for her own good. On August 3 she herself disappeared. "They took her husband later," Señora Ross remembers.

Another two years were to pass before there was any further trace of the twins. Of Liliana, the news never reached beyond the night of her transfer, though Señora Ross later met released prisoners who were able to tell her of the first two weeks of Liliana's detention, in the headquarters of the cavalry unit in La Plata. But in the twins' case there was an exciting breakthrough—an anonymous tip-off to the grandmothers that a certain Samuel Miara, a policeman living in Buenos Aires, had twin boys who were not his.

The two mothers went to the house on the pretext of looking for an English teacher. Just as they arrived, the twins appeared with Señora Miara. For Señora Ross it was a heart-stopping moment. "We stood there looking at them, quite close up . . . you can imagine what I felt," she said. "There they were, so like my daughter. We watched them for quite a while." The visit impressed Señora Ross, not only because of the emotion of seeing her grandchildren. She also saw that they were well cared for and that Señora Miara seemed extremely fond of them. "I have a difference of opinion with the Abuelas over this. They don't accept that I say this, but I saw that that woman really loved them. The husband is a shameless piece of work, a torturer, but she loves those children."

Once again the quarry was in sight, but once again the political situation created insurmountable obstacles. Señora Ross had opened a case in the Minors' Court in La Plata, but while the military still ruled Argentina the two women knew that a case against the Miaras—who were part of the security services—would lead nowhere.

By now there was a further complication which was to divide the two families and increase the bitterness of this tragic situation. Adalberto Rossetti, Señora Ross discovered, had formed a new relationship with a young woman, also from Chacobuco, whom he was to marry. The news came as a terrible shock to the Ross family and only served to strengthen their conviction that Liliana's disappearance was due to Adalberto's political involvement.

The Ross house in Chacobuco is festooned with sporting trophies: Señor Ross is a *pelota* champion and always encouraged his children to direct their energies into sports rather than politics. "In this house we never talked politics," Señora Ross insists, "never. That's why we are so indignant. . . . Why has this happened to us? They never bothered me, never. No searches, nothing. . . . The other house, yes, they searched it and they stole things, but here, no. When Señora Rossetti went to the ministry they told her that her son was the guilty one. . . . I am telling you this because I want the truth to be known, that my daughter was innocent."

When Adalberto formed his new relationship Señora Ross all but severed links with the Rossetti family. The enforced intimacy of small-town life meant there was no escape from an awareness of her son-in-law's second family. "Chacobuco is very small and they put the birth announcements of their children in the paper. These are things that hurt, that hurt me as a mother . . . there are so many things that hurt. I decided that I would have little more to do with them, that I would look for my daughter in my way and they in theirs.

"In Chacobuco people were kind to me, offered me sympathy, some solidarity. People had to be careful, but nobody turned their back on me. After my son-in-law began his new relationship I traveled by myself . . . I traveled everywhere by myself. I was a little crazy, asking questions everywhere. At one point some policeman took aim at me, thinking I had something in my bag. But I didn't ever really have any trouble. . . . Everywhere I went they told me that my daughter was innocent, innocent."

By this time Adalberto was living in Paris. When the elected government of President Alfonsín finally replaced the dictatorship in December 1983, he returned to live in Argentina and to attempt to recover his sons. The two families had covered a lot of ground while Adalberto had been away. "As a result of my mother's and mother-in-law's efforts and with the help of the tip-off we knew that the children were in the house of a certain policeman," said Adalberto. "We knew that an investigation would show that the birth certificates were false." The birth certificates for the "Miara" twins, known as Gonzalo and Matías, are dated May 16, 1977—the day, according to the late Señora Delgadillo, that Liliana and her babies were removed from Los Olmos prison.

With Argentina's return to democracy and the installation of a president whose personal record on human rights was impressive, hopes were high in the human rights organizations that there would be a rendering of accounts for the Dirty War—that parents would discover the fate of their disappeared children, that those guilty of wholesale torture and murder would be brought to justice and, for the grandmothers, that their grandchildren would be found and returned to their families. But, although the government had changed, and although the armed forces were chastened as a result of the Falklands debacle and their subsequent ignominious scramble from power, the return to democracy was to disappoint the Mothers and Grandmothers of the Plaza de Mayo. The civil authorities remained nervous of the residual power of the armed forces and were reluctant to risk confrontation.

President Alfonsín made two important gestures in the direction of human rights: he set up a commission to investigate the disappearances—a commission whose report, *Nunca Más,* was to shock a nation that had looked the other way during the events of the late 1970s; and he ordered the trial of the nine members of the three military juntas that had ruled Argentina under the dictatorship. But, although a mass of evidence had by then been collected on the conduct of the Dirty War, the government declined to involve itself directly in the prosecution of individual cases, preferring to leave it to the courts. Nor, as the Grandmothers of the Plaza de Mayo were to discover, was the government willing to undertake the search for the missing children.

Under the military dictatorship, as the grandmothers had discovered, few judges would investigate a case of disappearance. The judges were military appointees and, even if an individual magistrate wanted to conduct a serious investigation, it was common knowledge that the trail would lead, in the end, to the barracks. There was little doubt in anybody's mind as to what the outcome of a confrontation between the courts and the military would be, and it was a rare judge who would put it to the test.

When Adalberto Rossetti returned to Argentina the climate was considerably relaxed, but in the nation's courts business was much as usual. "In March 1984," he said, "we started the court case in La Plata. All the appearance of a court investigation was put in train, but the judge did not pursue it . . . in fact he did virtually nothing." The families themselves had traced the children and had no doubt that scientific tests would confirm the twins' real identity. "When the court's investigations were clearly going nowhere," said Adalberto Rossetti, "we decided to ask for blood tests. The judge turned us down, but we went to the appeal court and finally he had to accept it. In spite of that, there was a further delay of a year."

Alerted by now to their danger, the Miaras took their own evasive action. The blood tests were ordered in mid-1985, but in September 1985 the Miaras disappeared from Buenos Aires. The setback was all the more frustrating because the pursuers had known that it was likely. "We knew they were planning to leave and we even sent a telegram to President Alfonsín, to try to persuade him to intervene, but he didn't do anything," said Adalberto. "For some time, for almost a year, we didn't know where they were . . . then we got another anonymous tip-off from Paraguay, telling us that they had moved to Asunción." Finally the courts did try to take action. The case was moved from the La Plata court to the federal court in Buenos Aires and the new judge, Dr. Miguel Pons, asked for the Miaras' extradition. In April 1987 he flew to Asunción to serve the extradition notice personally.

The trip began well: a Paraguayan judge agreed to the extradition and ordered the children to be placed in Dr. Pons's custody. Dr. Pons went to the Miaras' house with a Paraguayan official and, finding the family absent, began to pack the children's belongings. But Señora Miara returned and, after a dramatic confrontation with the two officials, summoned both her husband and a senior Paraguayan police officer who overruled the judge's order. The plane that had been dispatched from Buenos Aires to collect the children was turned back and the case was transferred to another court. Dr. Pons returned to Argentina empty-handed and the case became stifled by the thorny relations between President Alfonsín's Argentina and the Paraguay of the long-serving dictator, Alfredo Stroessner.

In spite of their efforts, the relatives have had to watch time going by, aware that with each passing month the twins are growing up, which complicates still further the effects of their eventual restitution. The relatives talk of their bitterness against a government that has moved grudgingly to help, acting only when spurred on by the adverse publicity the case aroused and, even then, doing too little too late.

For Adalberto such emotions reflect his own difficulties in coming to terms with a society which may have rejected the methods of the Dirty War but which has not come to terms fully with what happened. Few Argentinians are willing to embrace those political activists whom many blame for provoking the savage repression. "We represent all that political current that was repressed after 1976—all the intellectuals and professionals, those who wanted reform. All the political program of this time was seen as a group failure and we are part of that failure. We are symbolic of something that people prefer to forget, of something that failed," he said.

"About the twins? Of course I am bitter. I am against the government's policy on human rights but it's the reality that we must live with. After all our efforts we have achieved nothing and all the time the children are growing up. It's very difficult to know what will happen now. . . . The Argentine government talks of national reconciliation as the way forward after the Dirty War, but in Argentina reconciliation is not the answer because there has been no act of contrition."

For Adalberto's mother-in-law, Señora Ross, the issues are more personal—a grief for her daughter that will not diminish and a longing for her grandchildren, a longing complicated now by the realization that, even if they do return to Argentina, they will belong not to her but to their father.

"After they took Liliana away that night I was never able to discover what happened. I want to talk to that couple, to the Miaras, to find out what happened to my daughter. If they can only tell me where she is. The grandmothers believe that that man is responsible for what happened to her. Can you imagine what it means for a mother to lose a child and lose her the way I lost mine? I used to say to the soldiers, 'If my daughter has committed a crime, put her on trial, sen-

tence her to whatever is appropriate, tell us what she did,
what her crime was.'

"I still live with a little hope that I will find her, but if she
is dead, I want her body. I want to know how she died. How
could I not want that? How could I stop looking for her after
eleven years of this anguish? There's no peace in this house,
not for me or for my other children. Poor things, they have
grown up in the atmosphere of a funeral here. My poor children who have helped me, who loved their sister so much,
they have no forgiveness."

Señora Ross is willing to forgive Señora Miara for what she
did because she believes that Señora Miara has brought the
twins up with real affection. But for Señora Rossetti, and for
most of the grandmothers, the love of people like the Miaras
for the stolen children is just another cruel perversion, another punishment inflicted on the innocent. "One day the
boys will come back," said Señora Rossetti, "and they will
punish those people themselves. When they know what really
happened in Argentina they will never love those people. But
what fills me with despair is that they are nearly twelve years
old. If we get them back soon, perhaps they will understand."

The grandmothers have no doubts that returning the children to their original identities is the right policy, in spite of
fears that the psychological effects on the children could in-
flict further damage. That is an argument they reject absolutely and they are convinced that experience has proved
them right. For them the difficulties are in locating the children, not in deciding what to do then.

"Everything about the children has been changed," said
Chicha. "It makes them so hard to find and we do it without
the help of the government. We can't use the police because
they are part of the problem . . . in many cases the children
are in the hands of policemen." The grandmothers, according
to Chicha, have located forty-four children to date. Four of
them have vanished again, six are dead, twenty-two have

been restored to their families and twelve continue to live with adoptive families, with the consent of the original families. These are cases, Chicha explained, in which the adoptive families were judged to have acted in good faith.

The courts are moving faster now on these cases, the grandmothers say, and there are fewer doubts now about the justice of the search. The grandmothers have never lost a case in court, according to Chicha, but they have made mistakes in identification. "One of them was mine," Chicha says. "Four years ago we thought we had found her, but the tests said she wasn't mine." Since that disappointment she has continued to work for the restoration of all the children. In some ways their work is easier now: they are no longer actively persecuted and have won the sympathy and respect of both the press and the public.

But, even if all the children were recovered tomorrow, the scars would remain: the lost years and the murdered parents gone forever. Like all the grandmothers, Chicha suffers the attrition of the passing years and the apparently endless search. "I do get tired . . . at one point I was so ill and tired that I stopped doing this for a couple of months. But I can't really stop. I think we will all die in this work. When a child reappears, it is like a piece of our own grandchild.

"I seem calm, but I cry a lot . . . we all cry, we cry at night, under the bedclothes."

Men, women and children have "disappeared" throughout Latin America since the early 1970s, and the term itself was first used by human rights organizations and the Latin American press in 1974. It was soon adopted in other parts of the world, as the tactic of abducting people and holding them in secret detention while denying all knowledge of their existence was taken up by other governments. In 1986 the United Nations Group on Enforced or Involuntary Disappearances noted that, as a tool of political repression, it had been in use in thirty-six countries. It has reached its highest level in Argen-

tina, El Salvador and Guatemala, but it is also to be found in Brazil, Chile, Peru, Mexico, Sri Lanka, Honduras and the Philippines.

"Disappearances" have the double function of acting as a deterrent through inspiring terror, and as a form of repression that leaves no martyrs. They are a particularly ingenious way of allowing a government to maintain a facade of legality and to feign innocence. "Disappearances" prove useful to weak regimes, who can arrest opponents without evidence and execute them without the process of the law. They are to be found in countries where long-lasting dictatorships have distorted the entire legal structure and where human rights organizations are very weak (Paraguay); in military dictatorships where the armed forces find it preferable to have their enemies vanish (Guatemala); in countries still struggling to reorganize along democratic lines but where the restoration of justice turns out to be very hard (Argentina); and in countries with elected governments, but where the military controls the security forces (Peru). In all these countries, children and babies—some of them born in detention to women destined themselves to "disappear"—have "disappeared" over the last decade.

"Disappearance" is a peculiarly dreadful occurrence, and possibly the most comprehensive denial of human rights of our time, bringing anguish to those abducted, ruin and tragedy to their families and havoc to the societies in which it takes place. Unlike torture and genocide, no specific provision for "disappearances" has been made in the international legal instruments that relate to human rights. Yet "disappearances" infringe on the right to life, the right to liberty and security, and the right to humane conditions of detention, all of which are enshrined not only in the Universal Declaration of Human Rights but in a number of subsequent conventions. In the case of children, the tactic also infringes on the right to a personal identity— as with a baby born in a secret detention camp and farmed out to adoptive parents—and the right of every child to the care and protection of its parents, both of them clauses covered by the 1959 Declaration of the Rights of the Child.

A "disappearance" can affect a child directly, when it is abducted with its parents or born in prison, and indirectly, when it witnesses the abduction of its parents but is not taken with them. Doctors who have worked with children of this kind have reported that they can be put into a prolonged state of shock, mental anguish and fear and that some suffer from lasting psychological and behavioral problems. In China a study of 203 children under twelve, at least one of whose parents had disappeared, showed 78 percent to be withdrawn, 70 percent to be depressed, and 78 percent to be intensely frightened. The younger the children, the more serious their condition.

Where individual action has proved ineffective, and where courts have totally failed to provide legal protection, a common response has been for relations of the disappeared to form themselves into associations, both in order to exert pressure on the government and to attract the attention of the public. The Chilean Association of Relatives of Disappeared Persons has organized hunger strikes, and the Mutual Support Group for the Return of Missing Relatives Alive in Guatemala has staged marches and demonstrations. In Chile, PIDEE (Protection of Children Affected by the State of Emergency), which was set up by foreign aid, uses doctors and psychologists to try to bring help to the children of parents who have "disappeared."

It cannot be said, in the late 1980s, that any major breakthrough has been made in eradicating the occurrence of "disappearances." The numbers of those who vanish drop in one country (where they are perhaps replaced by assassination) only to rise in another. Like torture, it has become too valuable a weapon to be discarded.

C.M.

9

Refugee Children

in Somalia

John Shaw

In the last ten years or so, many maps have acquired new colors and symbols, showing refugee camps and refugee zones in Africa, Asia and Central America. The shadings and statistics vary with the flow of people fleeing from violence and hunger, or both. But the patches on the maps persist and spread, seemingly as permanent now as the more familiar markings of terrain. The 1988 maps showed that seventeen nations in eastern and southern Africa were sheltering refugees. They came from eleven countries—some countries both generating and receiving refugees. Most of them, more than two million, are children.

While food production, economic growth and exports decline in these countries, national debts and regional droughts get worse. And the refugee totals multiply as armed conflicts continue, political enmities persist and crops fail. Guerrilla wars, political and racial pogroms, drought and famine drive people from their homes, usually across frontiers, emptying some areas, crowding others, changing the maps and changing the lives of millions, many of them children.

Halimo is twelve years old; she is a tall, thin girl with sad, dark eyes. For eight years she has lived in a camp for Ethiopian refugees at Sabaad in northwestern Somalia. With her parents and three brothers she lives in the hut that has been their home since the family, ethnic Somalis, fled from fighting in the Ogaden region of southern Ethiopia. She has no shoes, one cotton dress and she says she is sometimes hungry. Halimo can hardly remember home. She says, "I was young then." She still is, but does not live as a child.

Every day she does the manual work of an adult. Her parents are ill and she is the oldest child, so the family work falls on her. She rises at dawn, makes a cooking fire with twigs and sticks, then walks two hundred yards or so to a standpipe and carries back a heavy plastic jerrican of water. She prepares breakfast for the family, cornmeal porridge with milk mixed from powder. Then she fetches more water, grinds some of the camp ration of corn for a later meal, and then sets off, barefoot, across the arid hills beyond the camp to forage for firewood with other girls and women. Sometimes they are stoned and chased away by farmers and have to walk hours for fuel. Halimo trudges back late in the afternoon with her load, fetches more water and lights a fire to cook gruel for the family supper.

This day in the life of Halimo is not untypical of that of all refugee children in Somalia. Patterns of survival vary, but they are all part of a community of hardship. Sometimes Halimo's day is a little different: if there is enough firewood saved from the day before, she has time for a few hours of lessons at one of the primary schools in the camp.

There are about twenty thousand refugee children at Sabaad and about three thousand go to school for some of the time. Halimo is one of the few girls who go at all; more than eighty percent of the pupils are boys. Few families encourage daughters to attend, for at Sabaad the status of women is set by Islamic practice as well as by African rural traditions. This conservative combination intensifies the special poverty of refugee life which, as always in Africa, puts the heaviest of its burden on women and girls.

Halimo's dutiful drudgery is common among girls in the Somali camps. Their brothers, as is customary, do little of the family fetching and carrying. However, all of Africa's millions of child refugees share the plight imposed on them by the continent's political and military conflicts, as well as its droughts and famines. And their future, if it is to be other than life sentences as numbers on ration lists, is at best uncertain. Indeed, for most of the refugees in Somalia the word "future" has no real meaning. More than three hundred thousand children are growing up in the forty-three refugee camps there—a generation of children for whom any other home is no more than a vague memory of a parent's sad story, for whom a temporary resting place has become a place of exile, a place of endless waiting to return where some have never been.

Halimo's own wish, she says, is "to leave the camp and return home with my family." Home was on the rangeland of southern Ethiopia: "We were nomads and my father had many cattle and sheep." Meanwhile she would like "something which I might not get—better food rations, to go to school, a cart to bring the firewood, a water pipe in front of our house so I can get water every time I need it, and some new clothes." Sometimes, she says, she thinks of a future: "About escaping from this life. But if I leave who will take care of my parents? I cannot leave them." Both her parents have failing sight and, apparently, also suffer the paralyzing depression that grips many adult refugees after some years in the camps.

Halimo worries, "What will become of us?" Recently she confided to a visitor from UNICEF: "I dream of finding a nice place for my parents, going to school, getting a job. I know that might not happen. But miracles can happen. So I pray secretly. I've never told anyone of my dreams before—I was afraid they might laugh at me."

Several hundred miles away, at a camp in central Somalia, a boy named Abiib, who has lived there since the Ethiopian drought of 1984 made him a refugee, also longs to leave. But his father is away, his mother is often sick and his four sisters are still too young to carry water and collect firewood. Abiib explains: "My father left us two years ago to find work and we haven't heard from him since. I don't understand why he left us but I think he did not like this life. He will be back one day with money and clothes for us. When my father comes back, maybe I will be able to go to a town and get a job. And sometimes I think that it would help my mother if I left because it will be one less mouth to feed." Abiib is thirteen.

Meanwhile, "school is the only thing I like about the camp." Abiib reads well and gets good marks in math. He has one school problem: he fills his exercise books quickly and cannot always afford new ones. Abiib is the first member of his family to become literate: refugee children in Somalia have more chance of primary education, which starts at the age of seven, than most of the country's village children. The camp classes may be in tents, they may be in mud-brick sheds, they may have fifty to sixty pupils to a teacher, and they may be in two shifts to cope. But all camps have basic schools—funded by foreign donors and staffed by local teachers—whereas many Somali villages do not.

For Fozia, who is ten, school is the best thing in her life at the camp where she has lived since she was two years old. She says: "I don't remember anything from home but I know all about it because my parents talk about it and tell us how nice home was. My mother cries sometimes when she remembers home. It is not good here at all. When it rains it is muddy and messy and hard to walk around. There are mosquitoes and other insects which bite you and you can't play outside."

She has four younger brothers and sisters: "I am the oldest girl in the family so I have to work." But she manages to get to school most days. "I only go part of the time. I don't usually go back after the first break because I am needed at home. I wish I could go full time. But my mother goes to the fields when I get back from school and she leaves me to look after my brothers and sisters and cook for them. But I get the lessons I miss from friends and do my homework at night. I like school very much. I would like to go all the time but I have to help my mother."

Fozia lives at Qorioley, one hundred and twenty miles south of Mogadishu, the Somali capital. Qorioley is one of the oldest and largest refugee camps in Africa. After ten years it has some of the appearances of a permanent settlement which, at first glance, is not unlike any other in tropical Africa. The aid agencies have put up low concrete buildings—schools, clinics, workshops—and around them refugees have improvised several thousand wooden and patchwork family huts which straggle for miles along the Shebeli River. About thirty thousand people live in them, but Qorioley does not feel like a community. It has "camp commanders," not village headmen or a mayor. It is divided into Camp I, Camp IIA, Camp IIB, and Camp III rather than neighborhoods with names. This is useful for the Somali officials who administer the foreign aid which supports Qorioley. It also serves, despite the relaxed, even languid, manner in which they run things, as their daily reminder to the refugees—if one were needed—that Qorioley is an official place, a dependency.

There is a ramshackle main gate but the fence peters out in the fields of corn and the plots of vegetables and bananas along the river, some of which are worked by refugees as sharecroppers or tenants of the local Somalis. The settled look of their old villages—weathered mud-brick walls daubed with white clay, fruit and vegetable sellers sitting in the deep shade of tall trees—is one contrast between the traditional and the transplant. There are other differences.

One of the fruit sellers asked me for aspirin for her children and insisted on giving two mangoes in return. "Over there," she said, pointing across the fields to the huts of Camp I a mile away, "the dried-milk children all have medicines. Here we don't." The "dried-milk" children are the young refugees who are given that disparaging name by many Somalis because camp rations include imported skimmed milk powder which Somalis, lovers of rich fresh camel's milk, despise.

In a few material ways the refugees—particularly the children—are better off than some Somali villagers. In the Qorioley camp, for example, there are twenty clinics, two doctors, and scores of health workers. This system of primary and preventive medicine, funded by international agencies and donors, is not without delays and shortages but it is far better than that which the Somali government can afford to provide for its citizens in the surrounding Shebeli Province, or elsewhere in the country.

Qorioley also offers more primary schooling. In the nearby villages government education is collapsing; its funds are low, classrooms abandoned and literacy rates falling fast. In the Qorioley camps there are about five thousand children of primary school age and about half attend, taught by a hundred teachers in sixty classrooms. The demand for staff and space is likely to grow for some years yet. Another thirteen thousand of the camp children were under school age in 1988

and are growing up with siblings who transmit the new social habit of going to school. How long the habit will last is
another of the uncertainties endemic among refugees. Since
there is little prospect of education above primary levels and
little outside work even for those who complete secondary
school, education is seen to have a low economic value, if it
has any value at all. It fills some years but does not promise a
future. So, for the refugee children, their access to schools is a
benefit more apparent than real. Nevertheless, for many of
them it is the only light in camp life.

Baaq is fifteen and has just finished school at a camp called
Horseed near the junction of the borders of Somalia, Ethiopia
and Kenya, a semidesert region scoured by sandstorms for
much of the year. Although Baaq has been there most of his
life he still feels a stranger. He is not only a refugee but also
an Oromo—a Muslim, but not one of the ethnic Somalis who
comprise the refugee majority. Like many Oromos, he claims
discrimination at the hands—and fists—of the majority in his
camp. Perhaps the stress of refugee life sharpens tribalism.
Baaq says that some Oromos feel "they fled from one enemy
in Ethiopia only to find another enemy here."

After almost ten years as a child refugee, Baaq is seeking an
adult life and livelihood amid formidable obstacles: exile, dependence and tribalism reduce his prospects for more education or for any job. He solemnly recalls that "at the age of six
I was a camel man." At that time, in Ethiopia, "all I knew
was the nomadic life. Here I have had the chance to go to
school and learn something." Learning more is his next challenge. But there are very few secondary school places for
anyone in Somalia.

"Home" for most of the refugees in the Somali camps was—
and in their hearts and minds seems to remain—in the three
southern Ethiopian regions bordering Somalia. These areas,
Ogaden, Sidamo and Bale, are largely Somali in race and language and, like Somalia, Islamic in religion and culture. That

215

ethnic and religious kinship, straddling an arbitrary border drawn in colonial times with no traditional basis, is, ironically, part of the origin of their ordeal.

Modern Somalia was patched together in 1960 from territories formerly ruled by the British and Italians—but leaving out the adjacent ethnic Somali areas in southern Ethiopia. The retiring colonial powers (and the United Nations, which did not insist on more sensible arrangements) left behind a political time bomb. Independent Somalia inherited a border 994 miles long but excluding the million or more ethnic Somalis in Ethiopia, related also by language and the Islamic religion.

Somalia's leaders, sometimes for political distraction but always with nationalistic fervor, called for a "Greater Somalia" whose borders would include their ethnic cousins and coreligionists in Ethiopia. In the 1970s the Western Somalia Liberation Front, with bases in Somalia, waged a guerrilla war for possession of the Ogaden region.

In 1977 the Somali government, in an outburst of nationalism which quickly produced tragedy, launched a full-scale military invasion of the Ogaden. After initial advances the Somali forces were routed. In the wake of the retreating troops came the refugees, escaping from the fighting or from fear of retribution by the Ethiopians. Thus promised "liberation" became, instead, a flight for life, turning hundreds of thousands of peaceful nomads and farmers into refugees. As an act of political and military folly the Somali invasion of the Ogaden has few equals in the turbulent history of postindependence Africa. It turned Somalia into a huge refugee camp. In relation to its population, which may be about five million, Somalia has more refugees than any other country in the world, a ratio of one in eight, according to the 1988 estimates of UNICEF.

A government that had dreamed of a great ethnic gathering-in by expanding its borders did indeed acquire people, but not territory. In the face of triple defeat—military loss,

political humiliation and economic burden—the Somali government was at least consistent in nationalistic philosophies.
It opened its border to the refugees, said they could stay, did
what it could for the first arrivals and called for international
help for them. It has been a lasting lesson for the Somali
government; for the refugees it created an ordeal which has
no end in sight.

In Somalia the human tragedies and political complexities
inseparable from the African refugee phenomenon are present and likely to persist. In Somalia you can see what refugees become when they are left to languish, when waiting
becomes a way of life. In Somalia the camps are the sad pattern for many others springing up elsewhere in Africa, from
Mozambique to the Sudan. Somalia has more than half a million refugees from Ethiopia—or is the total nearer one million? Some have left the camps for home—but how many?
Many thousands are "invisible" refugees, filtering from the
camps into Somali villages and towns. Others straggle in
daily from Ethiopia—new or returning refugees, or simply
nomads sheltering until the rains return? Can anybody really
know? Does anybody really care?

There are few firm figures; and attitudes and emotions are
also hard to measure. The refugees in Somalia, the victims of
conflict and drought, long ago faded from the headlines.
They have sunk into a limbo land where politicians and bu-
reaucrats squabble over head counts and aid budgets, and fatigue erodes compassion. Occasionally the refugees in
Somalia attract a flicker of outside attention: a cholera epidemic strikes, or a few are formally repatriated to Ethiopia
(whence many thousands more, new crops of refugees, leave
in other directions). But the first waves of TV crews, relief
teams and aid volunteers have long gone, moved to Mozambique or the Sudan or wherever there is some new African
emergency or exodus, some bush war or environmental collapse. In Somalia the aid organizations, having coped with
crisis, have now settled in for the long haul of handouts, the

"care and maintenance" programs. They talk and plan, with no great conviction, about repatriation, resettlement and integration. They write rather wistfully about the future.

At the center of this ordeal are the majority of its victims—at least three hundred thousand children, perhaps as many as four hundred thousand. They are in danger of becoming a lost generation cast up on the margins of the wider human crisis afflicting much of sub-Saharan Africa. They could be lost if they are forgotten. Such a fate is only too possible.

Any summary of the events which dumped these children in the Somali camps reads, on one level, like a conspiracy of fates and, on another, indicates the difficulty of rescuing them or giving them hope. The drought of 1973—which caused the first of Africa's televised famines, and also ensured the fall of the crumbling Ethiopian monarchy—drove the first wave of Ethiopian refugees into Somalia. Drought followed them south, becoming so severe in 1974 that it also forced several hundred thousand nomads from their rangelands in Somalia itself. Many joined the arrivals from Ethiopia in relief camps until the rains returned.

Although Ethiopia's modern droughts are more famous (or more infamous) because of their international impact, Somalia has suffered the same cycle, and worse. Drought, defined here as the failure or lateness of two or more consecutive rains, seized Somalia fives times between 1973 and 1987. In those fifteen years the land would barely recover from one blow before another fell upon it.

Across the scorched, exhausted landscapes moved political as well as environmental refugees. In 1976, although the rains had returned to Ethiopia, there was an exodus of Oromos (non-Somali Muslim herders and farmers) from Bale Province in southern Ethiopia. They trekked into Somalia following clashes between Oromo separatists and the new Communist government of Ethiopia. A year later the worsening of the long guerrilla struggle in the Ogaden drove the first war refugees into Somalia. In 1978, following the repulse of the Somali invasion of the Ogaden, the stream of refugees became a flood which did not subside until 1981.

A recent report by Refugee Policy Group (RPG), an independent, Washington-based organization for research and analysis of refugee issues, said of those crisis years:

> The Somali government initially attempted to assist these refugees with little or no outside help. As the numbers mounted into the hundreds of thousands its capacities were overwhelmed. In 1979 Somalia had, arguably, the worst refugee situation in the world, with reports of refugees dying of malnutrition-related diseases, and even starvation, in the refugee camps. Somalia, therefore, turned to Western countries, UNHCR [the United Nations High Commission for Refugees], and other international organizations for help. Ironically, the major US assistance began to arrive in 1981, shortly after the major influx ended. The combination of the arrival of massive assistance, the ability of CARE [Cooperative for American Relief Everywhere] to establish an effective transportation and logistics network, and the arrival of the rains in Ethiopia meant that the major assistance crises had ended by late 1981.

The emergencies subsided. Most of the foreign doctors and nurses were able to depart, leaving UN agencies and donors to establish camp systems for rations, primary health care, water supply and basic schooling. The number of food donors dwindled from twenty-two nations and groups in the starvation-haunted days of 1979–80 to a dozen or so. It became necessary then to count heads—and ration cards.

In 1981 the aid agencies attempted a census, despite obstruction by the government, which at that time claimed a refugee total of 1.2 million, in the hope of profiting from extra aid. The census failed—truckloads of villagers who officials claimed were refugees were moved from camp to camp, to increase the count—but a "planning" figure of seven hundred thousand, owing more to diplomacy than facts, was negotiated between UN agencies and the government. The major donor countries did not accept it and instead based their food deliveries on their own estimates of about five hundred thousand.

That argument had not been settled—it never has—when a new influx, driven by drought in Ethiopia, began to cross the northwest frontier. About thirty-five thousand came in the first wave in mid-1984, creating near chaos and bringing with them cholera. An outbreak of the disease within a relief center became an epidemic, spread by local Somali villagers who had infiltrated refugee queues. In seeking free food many of them found death as well. About two thousand people, refugees and villagers, died before cholera was controlled there in April 1985.

A year later yet another rush of refugees crossed the border. In six months some thirty thousand were counted into a new camp. Most were Oromos, Muslim farmers who usually said they had left the highlands of the Ogaden because the Ethiopian government was imposing rural reforms. These reforms included "villagization" and resettlement in order to gather small farms into cooperatives, which were claimed to be more productive.

This destructive decade of drought, war and political upheaval—a catalogue of national conflicts and natural calamities—was played out in a region where life is difficult even at the best of times. Somalia itself is a desperately poor place, always among the worst global statistics for income, maternal and child mortality, life expectancy, literacy and public services. Economists describe its subsistence economy as "unconventional" and "informal." Half the population are pastoral nomads, roving with their herds—not the sort of people who keep accounts. The hardships of their poverty are clear enough, though: by UN estimates, one third of rural Somalis exist in a state of chronic hunger and weakness, unable to grow or buy the 2,200 calories considered to be minimum daily sustenance. More than half the country has no health service at all. Malaria, cholera, typhoid, bilharzia, eye diseases, diarrhea and anemia are common.

With Somalia able to offer refugees little but space, the UN agencies and foreign donors had to assume responsibility for everything else. This has meant food and care for the refugees—indeed more food and care than the Somali government can give the neediest of its own citizens. But, ironically, this shouldering of the burden helps the Somali and Ethiopian governments to postpone the full political settlements which alone can bring sustainable solutions. The agencies and donors realize this but they are faced with a dilemma: for humanitarian reasons they cannot leave, but the longer they stay the more the refugee question hardens around them.

The refugees face a dilemma too: the camps offer food but not a future. In contrast, for the Somali and Ethiopian governments the existence of the refugees in Somalia has economic and political advantages which both governments are reluctant to lose. Both, quietly but effectively, play the refugee card for all it is worth—which is quite a lot. Indeed, the two governments have interests in keeping things much as they are.

In theory, any of the refugees—at least those fit to travel—could leave the camps for home. The camp gates and the frontiers are open. Ethiopia says its citizens can return, and the Somalis cannot overtly detain them, although they do not encourage them to leave. But apparently the refugees prefer the austere stability of camp life to uncertainties beyond the border. Most stay in the camps, not because they are content but because there is nothing to make them confident enough to return to homelands which they know have changed. There is also the habit, insidious but inevitable, of dependency.

In the camps many of the refugees are undergoing social and psychological evolutions—a sea change in the desert mentality of the former nomads, in particular—which work against their capacity and will to return. Food security—the buzzword of the late 1980s among development and environment agencies in Africa—has an older significance for marginal farmers and herders. Camp rations (a daily half-kilo "basket," usually of grain, flour, powdered milk and vegetable oil) are sparse but assured. Dependency is eroding or replacing traditions of self-reliance. There are other factors: family structures have been damaged and expectations and aspirations have changed.

The Somali government, the aid agencies and donor governments do not agree on how many refugees there are—in and out of camps—in Somalia. In mid-1988 their claims ranged, respectively, from 860,000 down to 490,000. But they do agree that in the camps sixty percent are children (from infants up to the age of fifteen), thirty percent are women, and ten percent men. Thus the forty-three refugee camps are largely societies of children living without fathers, and women without men. (Outside the camps the "invisible" refugees are impossible to count in any way.)

Except for the elderly and the sick, men are rarely present in the camps other than on visits to sire more children or to take, deposit or divorce another wife. The practice of polygamy, traditional among ethnic Somalis, has become cheap and less onerous for refugee men with camp connections. Wives and children can be parked, or abandoned, with assured rations and shelter. Thus a family ration card is for many men a passport to a new nomadism: itinerant work in Somalia, occasional jobs across the Red Sea in the Gulf states, and seasonal treks with camels and other stock to and from clan rangelands in Ethiopia. Most refugee men choose itinerant ways of living and earning, which are apparently preferable to the routines and restraints of camp life and the odor of foreign charity. Men who were once nomadic herders or were farming family or clan lands are unlikely and unwilling camp dwellers. And many others died in the Ogaden campaigns or, later, of their wounds. One result is that sixty percent of camp families are single-parent families headed by women.

Recently UNICEF recorded a unique series of conversations with 387 of these women, conducted in thirteen camps by six Somali-speaking researchers. They extended fifty-eight of these extraordinary interviews into detailed case histories which revealed some of the psychological and social stresses, as well as material problems, of camp life.

Among those interviewed was Habiiba. She is thirty-eight and has six children, three of them born in the camp where she has lived for almost ten years. She said: "We left everything behind when we fled from home. In the panic, my husband and one of my sons ran in one direction while I and two of my children went in another. It was two months before the family were reunited in this camp. My husband left us when he couldn't take it anymore. He was a man used to hard work and taking good care of his family. In the camp he felt useless, not able to do anything. He was always depressed. He changed both physically and mentally. We are like vegetables used to plenty of water, but we don't get enough water anymore. Now I am always depressed. I don't have relatives or friends in the camp. I feel very lonely and I cry all the time. I am afraid I will lose my mind. Sometimes I don't go out of my hut for days and days, but my children cook and collect the water and firewood. . . . I miss my husband even though he wasn't doing anything for us. Now I have no one to talk to. I get so fed up with hardships and depression that I sometimes feel that I will cut my stomach with a knife."

Mumina is thirty-five. She has seven children. She described the impact of camp life on her marriage: "We lived in the interior of Ethiopia and we had cows, camels, sheep and donkeys. One night I heard shouting and shooting and I saw troops killing people and burning huts. They killed one of my sons who tried to run away. When they had burned all the huts and there was nothing left except ashes, they took the men and left the women and children. I stayed one night to see if my husband had escaped or to hear about his death, and then I left with my six children. My husband eventually joined us on our walk to Somalia.

"In the camp my husband does nothing to earn any money. I think he is irresponsible and escaping from reality and I tell him that he has to do something to improve our situation. But then he shouts at me and beats me, saying that I am a crazy woman who can't understand. He has no relatives here and he has no skills to work here because he is a man from the interior.

"This life makes me depressed and I cry like a mad person. Crying is a medicine for me because it gives me relief for a time. Things are worse since my husband took a younger wife. I am always pressing him to give something to my children because I feel that he gives whatever he gets to his other wife. Also, since he married again he has lost interest in me, and my last child is ten years old. My children sometimes come home and tell me that my husband's other family are having better food than we are and that also makes me upset."

Some of the refugee women are war widows who have not remarried. One of them is Fadumo, who is forty-three and has three children under fifteen. She left Ethiopia in 1978 during the Ogaden war, in which she lost her home and her husband: "One day airplanes killed many of our camels and only twenty-five were left. The airplanes started firing at seven in the morning and continued until the afternoon. At night I and my children escaped. We were walking for seven days till we reached the border. In Somalia we got food, medical service and peace. At first the camp was good, we got food and medicine; but now everything is getting worse. We don't get enough food. If my children get sick, I don't get any medications from the camp. The best things in the camp are the water system, schools and being at peace. If these were not here nobody would stay."

Another widow who told her story is Naado, aged forty. She has nine children, aged between ten and eighteen. They have lived for more than nine years in the Qorioley camp. She said: "Life back home was good but there was no peace, so we gave up everything we had in order to live here in peace. My husband was killed by the Ethiopians, and I escaped with my children. My children got sick when we first came. I was scared but there were some good doctors. I kept the children close to me. All of us used to sleep on the same mat. My children used to cry all the time, asking me to take them back. Camp life was hard but we could sleep peacefully without hearing the guns and screams and killings.

"The most difficult thing for me was to cope without a husband. All of a sudden he was gone and we had to flee, come to a new place not knowing a soul, and I was responsible for nine children. The oldest was ten then. I can't tell you the hell I went through at that time. It was hard to get used to being a single parent. I had to do everything by myself. While husbands were building shelters for their families I had to do it all alone. I carried on my back all the wood to build the hut. I got some help from neighbors, but I had to do most of the work. Finally I built the hut for them and attended to all their needs myself. It was a tough time, but God was with me and we got through somehow. In fact it made me a stronger person.

"The food rations are very small, so I do any work available to get more food for my children. I sell firewood and some farmers hire us daily and my children go with me to work. I never thought I would see the day I would work for someone as a laborer. Back home we used to hire people to work at the farm. We used to look down on them because there was only one particular tribe supposed to do these jobs. Well, today I work for someone. I am not complaining, but life is strange.

"The school system was good at first. When things were bad it was the only positive thing in my life. At least I thought that my children were getting educated and it pushed me to struggle more and dream about their future. Now I have two boys and a girl who have finished school but are not allowed to go to secondary school. Seeing them hanging around the camp with no school and no job is bad. I struggled so much to put them through school. For what? I hate to see them wasted like this. Young people who have nothing to do but hang around the camp will cause some problems. I sensed my two older boys becoming restless and I got a few complaints about them. They were nice boys when they were in school. Now they have changed and I am worried about them. . . .

"I belong to a group of women, twelve of us, who have a credit union. Everyone pays one hundred shillings a month, and then each month one of us takes all the money. It goes around. If one of us has a problem and needs the money when it is not her turn we talk about it and give it to her. The amount is not much but it helps.

"There are some women who are mentally ill. They start with depression and as problems increase they can't cope. I know many women who were strong and healthy but are crazy now. Some of them don't come out of their huts, don't clean or care much about their children. They seem to give up. . . . The most difficult job for women is collecting firewood. We walk a long way to get it and we have only our backs to carry it. How much can a woman carry on her back? Most of the women in this camp have backache. There are many miscarriages caused by carrying the firewood. Some women have to take their babies with them when collecting firewood. It is a dangerous job.

"I think women can do a better job than men if given a chance to run the camp. We know more about the reality of camp life. We are aware of the weak, sick and needy people and we could give more justice. Men don't know much about the difficulties. They are only aware of their families—some even don't know this—and the political part of the camp. But women know the people."

The UNICEF study revealed many such little-known or hitherto invisible aspects of the camp lives of refugee women —and thus of their children. But this information is not likely to be used. It was optimistically intended to help devise ways to meet what the study called the "psychological needs" of refugees. But even while the study report was being written it was made to seem, at best, irrelevant. Events elsewhere pushed Somalia's refugees further into the shadows. New or renewed conflicts and famines erupted in Ethiopia, Sudan and Mozambique in 1988, throwing several million more refugees or innocent fugitives into the whirlwind. The aid agencies and donors scrambled to meet their desperate needs for the ingredients of survival—food, water, medicines, shelter. Amid the priorities of these emergencies they had little time or inclination to look ahead very far, least of all to consider the mental health of refugees.

A conference of UN and other agencies in Africa was arranged for late 1988 in order to plan for 1990, a year in which the experts in relief and refugee matters expect that Africa's need for food and other refugee aid will be double what it was in 1988. The increase may be more than that, or it may be less, depending on wars and weather. And by then the number of child refugees in Africa—displaced within their own countries or across borders, forced from their homes in either case—could well reach four million. A nation's worth of children on the refugee roads: an unimaginable total perhaps, but not imaginary, for that is what African events are leading to at the end of the 1980s.

The African nations whose actions, ideologies and circumstances are at the core of this deepening nightmare are Ethiopia and Sudan, both of which have civil wars, and South Africa, which controls and finances the guerrilla war against Mozambique. Their governments are not without powers to stop or limit the wars, all of which are also producing or worsening famines; nor are their principal allies, creditors and trading partners: the United States, the USSR, Japan and the EEC; nor are the pan-African political organizations. But all seem without policies or ideas for solutions. A feeling that parts of Africa, and therefore many Africans, are expendable seems to be growing. A terrible paralysis of political will seems to set in. Few outsiders have moved much beyond Band-Aid assistance—some not even to that level. Some encourage and arm the conflicts; arms purchases are delivered much more quickly than food donations. Others maintain, or tolerate, apparently endless racial and separatist disputes about pieces of land which are useless to anyone except those peasants who, left alone, can scrape a living from them.

All, in different ways, are observing and assisting a children's Calvary in Africa. Parents and elders suffer, too—but children suffer more.

In 1988 there were said to be more than twelve million refugees in the world, most of whom were women and children. Southern Africa's refugee population alone was put at 1.3 million, and it was growing steadily. One eighth of the population of Mozambique were refugees living in camps outside the country. When the UNHCR was set up on a temporary three-year mandate in 1951, refugees numbered two to three million. Today they make up a kind of nation, and not even a particularly small nation at that; an invisible and floating country of displaced people.

Refugees are made by wars and by natural disasters, made worse by man's handling of them. In the past eighty years some one hundred million men, women and children have been forced to leave home because of war, political upheaval and persecution; many millions more have been displaced by famines, floods, earthquakes and droughts. There is little indication that climatic events are becoming either more frequent or more severe, but every indication that disasters are multiplying because of the way in which man is changing the environment. Poverty, environmental degradation because of poor land use and the rapid growth of population all combine to precipitate and worsen natural disasters. The most widespread modern disaster is drought, and the fastest-growing one is flood. Both are largely ecological disasters and they account for some ninety percent of the victims of natural events.

An "unaccompanied child" is one aged under eighteen who has been separated from both parents and has no one with primary responsibility for its care. There have been unaccompanied children in every emergency, and especially in wars. The Armenian massacre of 1915 left thirty thousand children in orphanages in Russian Armenia and a further ten thousand in Greece. The 1919 Russian Revolution and famine saw seven million abandoned children, of whom eight hundred thousand wound up in institutional care. At the end of the Second World War thirteen million children were estimated to have been orphaned or abandoned. In the Second World War in Poland, 1.8 million children under sixteen died; no one knows how many died "unaccompanied."

At the moment, unaccompanied children are to be found in refugee camps throughout Southeast Asia, from Cambodia, Vietnam and Laos; among the famine victims of Ethiopia; among Ethiopian refugees in Sudan; in Lebanon; throughout Central America. In the last few years unaccompanied Haitian, Cuban, Guatemalan and Salvadoran children have sought refuge in the United States and Canada.

Some have been taken in by families. For others, what being unaccompanied means is a search for food, shelter and clothes; or it can mean being passed on from one adult to another; or being put in a detention camp run by the Immigration and Naturalization Service, as happens in the United States with young refugees who cross the borders without papers. For all these children it means that, whatever happens to them, it is not of their own choosing. For people dealing with emergencies, unaccompanied refugee children pose enormous problems. Are their parents still alive? How can they be found? Is there anyone else who is legally responsible?

Many organizations dealing with the welfare of refugees are now becoming increasingly concerned that for too long there has been an

*overemphasis on material help for refugees while far too little atten-
tion is being paid to the stresses they experience. Refugee children are
not only homeless but unable to understand why they have become so.
Though their parents may still be with them, they too may have
become so traumatized by the situation that they are unable to provide an adequate model for the children to imitate as they grow up.
Visitors to the camps on the Thai border, where two hundred and fifty
thousand Cambodians have lived in closed camps since fleeing from
the Vietnamese invasion in 1979, have found children who have never
known life outside and whose understanding of a normal existence is
fashioned by the violence, despair, dependency and apathy that surround them.*

*The long-term effects of early exposure to acute trauma are well
documented. Many refugee children who survived the killing fields in
Cambodia have been exposed to horror equal to that of the Nazi
concentration camps. The indications are that events of this kind
during childhood are liable to lead to breakdown; and even when they
do not, it is possible that refugee children carry the destructive experience of what has happened to them all their lives.*

C.M.

10

Child Exploitation in

the Philippines

Cameron Forbes

On that February morning along Epiphany de Los Santos Avenue, there was a street carnival, a celebration, a dance of delight. Millions congratulated one another. They had faced the tanks; they had formed a massive human moat between the rebels in Camp Crame on one side of the avenue and the loyalist Marines in Camp Aguinaldo on the other. The Catholic Church's Radio Veritas, the voice of the revolution, repeated again and again the news: the Marcoses had gone.

On February 25, 1986, Marcos did indeed go. He left Mala-canang Palace to the ragged from the slums of Tondo. They looked on luxury beyond their dreams; gazed through glass doors at giant gilt Nubian figures holding lamps, glittering chandeliers, a larger-than-life painting of a beautiful woman with flowing hair and robes, a painting of Marcos as a primal Adam figure. They carried away what they could—food, fur-nishings, ferns from the gardens.

Ferdinand Marcos left the Philippines to Corazon Aquino, having already himself carried away a great deal of the wealth of the country. He left her an economy pillaged by his cronies and a land torn by two insurgencies. He left her an army of children—beggars and scavengers, thieves and prostitutes—who were exploited on the streets and in the factories, almost three million of them, out of a population of fifty-six million. They were very much the "children" of Fer-dinand and Imelda Marcos; conceived through greed, venal-ity, corruption, stupidity and arrogance; born into semifeudalism in the country and into mean streets in the towns. Among them were Rosario Baluyot, who is dead now, and Maleni Arguelles, who may be partly living. There was Helen, who still sells her child-woman's body, and there was Adam, bought back now from his pedophile lover.

This army could not be ignored. They were on the street corners, in the parks, sleeping on the pavements, dashing and dodging among the mad Manila traffic. Stationed by their syndicates at traffic lights, they pleaded, with practiced pro-fessionalism, "Give me one peso, I'm hungry." They caught the eye of the new President and on June 3, 1986, Mrs. Aquino issued the thirteenth proclamation of her rule. It said, in part:

> Whereas it is the policy of the state to promote the well-being and total development of Filipino youth and chil-dren, and to protect them from exploitation, abuse, improper influences, hazards and other conditions or cir-

cumstances prejudicial to their physical, mental, emotional, social and moral development;

Whereas recent reports on rampant child abuse and exploitation, especially in Metro Manila and tourist spots throughout the country, have generated the righteous indignation of Philippine society and have inspired greater and coordinated efforts by both government and civic organizations toward a national plan of action integrating all programs and services pertinent to the well-being of children;

Now, therefore, I, Corazon C. Aquino, President of the Philippines, by virtue of the powers vested in me by law, do hereby proclaim the period from June 1986 to May 1987 as the Year of the Protection of Filipino Exploited Children, and hereby create an interagency task force composed of government and nongovernment organizations to prepare a national plan of action and to mobilize resources for implementation of the same.

Rosario Baluyot survived the Year of the Protection of Filipino Exploited Children by only a few days. She died in early June 1987, in the Olongapo General Hospital. A frail twelve-year-old, she had been operated on to remove a foreign body which had caused her severe stomach pains for some time. The foreign body was a blue, one-inch-thick piece of a vibrator which had been festering in her uterus for three months. Rosario had been one of three girls picked up, reportedly by a United States serviceman, in a vacant lot near the main gate of the Subic Bay naval base. The lot, overgrown and rubbish-strewn, is the display area for preteen girls "managed" by a criminal syndicate.

Rosario was one of the estimated three thousand street children in Olongapo, a city of two hundred thousand people about one hundred and eighty miles north of Manila. Before the coming of the Spanish four centuries ago Olongapo was a small fishing community on what was potentially a fine harbor, a fact recognized by Spain. Subic Bay was chosen by royal decree as Spain's main naval base in the Far East. After the United States, in its imperialist mode, had defeated Spain and gained a colony, President Theodore Roosevelt designated Subic Bay and seventy thousand acres of land as a military reserve.

With a series of wars—the Second World War, the Korean War and the Vietnam War—Subic Bay increased in strategic importance; and the Vietnam War, in particular, saw Olongapo blossom as what was politely called "liberty city" for the U.S. Seventh Fleet. Bars, saunas, massage parlors and "short-time" hotels proliferated, and where there was a demand for women there was a supply, mostly from the central Philippine islands of Samar and Leyte. These are probably the poorest regions in a nation where seventy percent of the population live in poverty. The land is infertile, the fish are scarce, so the families export women to the bars and brothels in Manila, Olongapo and tourist centers. Money made from commissions on drinks and from prostitution trickles back to the islands. It often means survival.

The war boom is over in Olongapo but the last survey showed there were five hundred "entertainment centers" with a total of 9,056 registered hostesses and other workers. Another estimated eight thousand prostitutes walk the streets and with them—dodging among the crowd, begging, picking the occasional pocket, selling cigarettes, selling themselves—are about three thousand street children, mostly aged between ten and fourteen. Rosario Baluyot was one of them. Cigarette sellers earn at best twenty pesos (about a dollar) for twelve hours' work and pickpockets average about seventy pesos. Rosario could have earned between fifty and three hundred pesos for two to three hours' short-time service, depending on the market and on the sort of service required. At least twenty percent of this (and, more likely, fifty percent) would have been paid to the pimp. So Rosario may have died for a hundred and fifty pesos.

The only certainty about Rosario was her name; that and the fact that her life was harsh, violent and tragically short. But where did she come from? How was she recruited? (If her pimp knew his business she would have been worth as much as twelve hundred pesos as a virgin on her first night.) But she is dead now and off the streets, while an estimated twenty thousand children still sell themselves in the Philippines.

Most are in Manila, the chaotic capital. They work in tourist belts such as Ermita, and in the grand park, the Luneta, with its stately walks and its statue of José Rizal, the great Filipino hero-martyr. Along Manila's main avenue, Roxas Boulevard, which sweeps along the margin of Manila Bay, past luxury hotels and grandiose monuments to Imelda Marcos's extravagance and delusions of grandeur, is Malate Church. There is a square in front, overlooked by a statue of the Virgin Mother to whose skirts cling bronze children. Below this touching tableau real children await pickups by pedophiles: children like Helen, Chito, Reynaldo and Bong. Helen is thirteen, pretty and a three-year veteran of sexual exploitation. A woman pimp who was a friend of her mother introduced her to a Frenchman. He was so kind, so charming, so patient for many days. Then he had sexual intercourse with her. Helen, who is already an adult sexually, says she wants to be a nurse when she grows up.

Chito is thirteen and Reynaldo is ten. They are the stepsons of a shopkeeper who migrated from the Visayas, the central group in the Philippine archipelago, looking for a better life. He found instead a tiny shanty in a squatter community along the railway tracks in Vito Cruz, a Manila suburb. He found no job but beat the boys if they tried to keep the money they made by begging. So Chito went on the streets, taking Reynaldo with him. They are now on the fringes of drug and sex syndicates.

Bong is fourteen, the youngest child of an elderly laundrywoman whose home is a four-by-five-foot slum shanty made of scrap wood in an area known as Tatalon. He ran away from home when he was ten because of what he calls harsh punishment, dropped out of school and became addicted to gambling, stealing to get money. For Bong the Luneta park became a haven from the filth, the drunkenness and violence of Tatalon, and glue sniffing an escape from the harsh reality of his life. It was in the Luneta that he first sold himself to a man.

To meet the pedophiles, come to Pagsanjan. It is a pleasant drive south from Manila, away from the brown, noxious layer of smog, past Laguna Bay with its fish farms, and Taal volcano, which is one of the smallest volcanoes in the world. Pagsanjan is famous for its falls and infamous for its pedophiles.

One guidebook says that "a trip to Pagsanjan is a must on every Filipino tour itinerary." Indeed it is, for the Magdapio waterfalls are spectacular and the trip to them up the tropical gorge is stunning—if somewhat tiring for the exploited *banqueros* who struggle against the current. What the guidebook does not mention is that other great attraction of Pagsanjan: the children—young boys and girls who are for sale. The youngest, recorded on a hospital treatment sheet, was five years old. Some of these are the children of the *banqueros*, others from the poor coastal villages of Bicol and the Visayas. Buyers should be warned, however, that Pagsanjan is not what it was. For a time it was the pedophile capital of the world.

However, the guidebook does point out that the last section of Francis Ford Coppola's *Apocalypse Now* was filmed at Pagsanjan. The four horsemen of the biblical apocalypse were War, Pestilence, Famine and the pale horseman, Death. In the film Coppola gave his "horseman," the psychotic colonel who loved the smell of napalm in the morning, a gunship to ride and bullets, rockets and Wagner's music to spew over the Vietnamese villages. If people at Pagsanjan are to be believed, a fifth horseman of the apocalypse rode into their town with the film crew: perversion. Some of the crew were pedophiles, it is claimed. They may not have been the first pedophiles to discover Pagsanjan, but they spread the word.

Come to the Pub Magellan. It is only a short walk from the police station. It pretends to be a British pub, but there are no women, none at all. Two guitarists plod their way through Paul Simon's "The Boxer"—"I am just a poor boy . . . Asking only workmen's wages/I come looking for a job but I get no offers/Just a come-on from the whores on Seventh Avenue/I do declare there were times when I was so lonesome I took some comfort there."

At one long table sits a European who is "lonesome" no more. He is surrounded by five Filipinos who look like teenagers. The European is old and fat and he nuzzles one of the Filipinos, who nuzzles him back. For years he was a purser on the Blue Funnel Line and, when he was about to retire, he got lucky. A regular passenger died and left him fifty thousand dollars. At Pagsanjan he has found the perfect place to spend it.

The pub door is pushed open and Barry walks in. He is fat, too, but young, an Australian who weighs about two hundred and fifty pounds. He arranges to take some photographs of children, complains that a boy today tried to overcharge him for a short-time, "after all I've given him." He picks up the menu. The owner is proud of it. He serves good British food; none of your *adobo* and *lechón*. There is steak and kidney pie and apple pie for dessert. For starters there is cock-a-leekie soup. Barry likes the sound of that; he calls it gonorrhea soup (gonorrhea/cock-a-leekie). He laughs, but the pretty boy behind the bar taking the order looks puzzled. "You know about gonorrhea," Barry says, "and syphilis, don't you?"

Couples come in. There is an old man with almost translucent skin, a shuffle, expensive, casually elegant clothes and a cultured French accent. He is escorted by a young Filipino in a T-shirt. Then there is John, from London, with Frankie.

John has been in Pagsanjan for more than four years and he hired Frankie, who was then twelve years old, when he arrived. He says that he hired Frankie to teach him Tagalog, the national Filipino language. John talks about the attractions of Pagsanjan, with a nudge and a wink for me, and with cuffs on the head for Frankie. "He's a good boy." Cuff. "This is the best place in the world to be, if you know what I mean." Cuff.

But it was even better in the old days when there were about two thousand child prostitutes here and it was a buyer's market. Pedophiles flocked to the lodges along the river and took their pick of the boys in the swimming pools, some for "short-time," some to set up house and have relatively long-lasting relationships. And they all fed on the poverty of Pagsanjan, whether by paying three hundred pesos for "short-time" or by regular wages to the boys or by giving gifts to the families of the children or by buying them taxis or even houses. There is much unemployment in Pagsanjan, as well as underemployment. For the grueling trip up the river to the falls, the *banqueros* get thirty-five pesos a day take-home pay, and that probably only twice a week.

Amando did not have a job. His wife was a nurse, but the only work she could get was as a voluntary welfare helper. They have four children. The oldest, Adam, caught the eye of a middle-aged West German. He made Amando a "partner" in a small business. "He courted me to get my son," Amando said. But what did it feel like, to put it brutally, to sell a child? Amando shrugged. "We had no money. And anyway, he didn't try to force the child like some others. Some are sadists." Adam has escaped the physical scarring some of the boys and girls suffer. But mentally? He doesn't want to talk about it.

The West German has gone now and so have the glorious days of Pagsanjan as pedophile capital of the world. Now there are only about two hundred children for sale and about twenty or thirty pedophiles come each week. It is no longer the best place in the world because revulsion, guilt, a church group and the Communist New People's Army (NPA) mobilized the people of Pagsanjan. Children marched through the streets carrying placards reading "Please don't sell us" and a huge sign was erected at the crossroads with the warning "Pedophiles are not welcome in this town." The NPA paid a visit, shot the police chief, a man they claimed was corrupt and an enemy of the people, and read the mayor a list of suggested reforms, including ridding Pagsanjan of pedophiles.

At the same time the Evangelical Church attempted to break poverty's grip on some of the families. Pastor Noel Tolentino, one of the organizers, said: "The people considered prostitution a solution to terrible poverty. It is very hard to eradicate it." The Church has made a modest beginning by funding, through loans, "alternative livelihood projects." It is modest because an appeal overseas, to the home countries of the pedophiles, brought only one response, from the Australian Council of Churches, which sent two hundred thousand pesos. Of that, two thousand pesos went to Amando, who, with Adam and other relatives, now owns a flock of ducks. Asked if they are glad it is over, both Amando and Adam say, simply, "Of course."

But that program reaches only thirty families. The boatmen continue to be exploited and some pedophiles still come to Pagsanjan to look over the boys on offer at the hotel swimming pools and to drink at the Pub Magellan. However, the town has won back some pride and dignity, although Pagsanjan's gain has meant loss elsewhere in the Philippines.

The pedophiles have merely moved their center of operations to Metro Manila or resort islands like Puerto Gallera. They still come from all over the world, indistinguishable from the ordinary tourists. Filipino researcher Susan Fernandez-Magno gives this profile of pedophiles: "The main clientele of child prostitutes are Caucasian tourists, mostly Europeans. They include French, German, Swiss, English and

Dutch. There are also Australians, Americans and Arabs. Recently Filipinos, Chinese and Japanese have increased in numbers. They are mostly male homosexuals, married and middle-aged. They are either owners of multinational business firms selling beauty products, designer clothes, perfumes and jewelry or they are retired clerks or ordinary employees who take vacations here. Among the local clients there are a few big businessmen and many low-income and middle-income homosexuals. Their perversions vary from sadism to voyeurism. Levels of generosity also vary among nationalities."

Fernandez-Magno gives this profile of their victims: "Child prostitutes are male and female children aged mostly seven to fourteen years old who render sexual services to anyone willing and able to pay any amount of money. Recently five-year-olds were found to be already involved in the flesh trade. They come from low-income families whose breadwinners work as laundrywomen, carpenters, factory workers, farmers, dressmakers or prostitutes. Most child prostitutes are simultaneously street vendors who peddle cigarettes, flowers, food or newspapers, or they watch parked cars and shine shoes. Many are stowaways among the migrant child prostitutes. Common causes are poverty, broken family situations, sibling rivalry and authoritarian rearing practices. They usually reside with their peers' families in squatter areas if not with their own.

"Constant exposure to street life has led to the children's recruitment by delinquent gangs in the tourist belt. Membership in these gangs has given them varied skills for survival. Stealing from passersby and tourist-clients is one art they have mastered. Their accounts reveal that in many instances they had to resort to stealing because clients cheated on their payments. When clients are scarce they steal because they need to pay for the next meal. As for child prostitutes who are members of sex rings, stealing is often an additional requirement to rendering sexual services.

"Marijuana smoking, glue sniffing and taking prohibited drugs are other activities child prostitutes indulge in. To them these essentially provide the much-needed endurance and desensitization from the brutalizing and traumatic effects of their job. Particularly among the neophytes in the trade, being high on drugs provides a somewhat anesthetic effect that shields them from the pain inflicted on their frail bodies. For those who have been in the job longer, drugs cause feelings of noninhibition. These enhance the good performances desired by tourist-clients, and thereby make them earn better."

In an assessment of a Joint Project on Street Children, UNICEF says that a strong political will exists in the new government, but goes on to make this pessimistic forecast: "Because street children are the offspring of severe urban poverty and uneven development—conditions which are likely to remain until meaningful structural changes in Philippine society occur—it is very likely that the number of children going on the streets will increase in the next three to five years."

Run by the Department of Social Welfare and Development, the Council of Welfare Agencies and UNICEF, the Joint Project reached and served ten thousand street children in its first stage from 1986 to 1987. Its objectives are: development of alternative educational programs; promotion of appropriate and viable income-generating activities which, at the same time, provide opportunities for street children to earn and learn; sponsoring of alternative play, recreational and cultural activities; organizing street children themselves into community groups; providing counseling for both street children and their families; working toward reintegration of street children into their families and into the normal network of community relationships; and opening possibilities for adoption, foster care, drop-in centers and temporary shelters for children without families.

The Lingap Center *(lingap* means caring) is one of those shelters. It prefaces an outline of its activities with a quote from Camus: "The suffering of children is not in itself what is revolting, but the fact that it is undeserved. If we cannot make a world in which children no longer suffer, at least we can try to reduce the number of suffering children." But the rate of reduction of suffering in the Philippines is painfully slow. The nation has a foreign debt of twenty-six billion dollars and lacks the infrastructure to take advantage of promised aid money.

But one success is a major victory. Bong, the laundrywoman's son from Tatalon, was persuaded by government social workers to go camping on a farm outside Manila. He said he would like to join the Lingap program and while at the center went to a nearby state school. Lingap staff visited his parents and gradually the family was rebuilt. Bong finished his primary schooling with an award as a model pupil and a church-based group has granted him a scholarship to continue his schooling.

Lingap wants to give children temporary shelter, to help them rebuild respect and trust. That will not be easy. Dazzle Rivera, a former head of Lingap, says: "Most young children, those who are below nine years old, do not verbalize that they were sexually abused. We only verify our suspicions after doctors at Lingap confirm that their private parts are swollen or badly lacerated and they have high fever when they are admitted to the center. This is because it is common that children trust the very adults who abuse them: these adults talk to them, give them food and even protect them from being bullied by older street children.

"The majority of the children who have experienced life in the streets perceive policemen to be symbols of oppression, authority and corruption. They are the ones who steal the children's hard-earned money during *bagansiya* [when the police book them for vagrancy]. We have validated case studies of children who have revealed that policemen, with their

names and ranks identified, are actual pimps. How ironic—
the very persons supposed to protect them are the same ones
who actively solicit customers." Ironic and shameful, but not
surprising. Policemen in the Philippines are very poorly
paid. Poverty corrupts, and poverty and corruption are endemic in the police force and in the bureaucracy.

Today there are hopeful signs as far as the war on pedophiles is concerned. In January 1988 President Aquino asked
a family friend, Miriam Defensor Santiago, to take the post of
Commissioner of Immigration and Deportation. Commissioner Santiago had been an independently minded regional
court judge and a lecturer in international law at the University of the Philippines. The Commission has the responsibility of dealing with illegal and undesirable aliens in the Philippines. There are about three hundred thousand of them
and they include drug pushers, gunrunners, gambling and
sex syndicates and, of course, pedophiles. The sums of money
involved in the black economy are huge and the opportunities for graft and bribery great. Commissioner Santiago, with
some understatement, says that when she assumed office the
CID personnel were not very disciplined. Many came to the
office just before noon and left just after lunch; others supple-
mented their low salary by working as "fixers," taking a fee
to help aliens through the bureaucratic maze. As she attempted to clean up the Commission, she also begged for donations, saying that it was very hard to get government
money for the office equipment, vehicles and firearms her
people needed.

Against the odds, Commissioner Santiago has pushed the
CID into decisive action against pedophiles. Two months after she took office, raids were made in Pagsanjan and Puerto
Gallera. In Pagsanjan twenty-two people were taken into custody and in Puerto Gallera nine. Some were charged, some
were encouraged to undertake "self-deportation."

However, while pedophiles may be deterred for a time from visiting Pagsanjan and while they may exercise a little more caution about making pickups in Ermita, the bar-and-brothel district in Manila, the undermanned, underpaid CID will find it difficult to conduct a long-term campaign. Pedophiles will continue to look upon the Philippines as a buyer's market. There has to be a halt to the supply as well as to the demand.

Child prostitution in the Philippines is a matter of national and international shame. It is a stain that is particularly noticeable against the social fabric of the nation, which is family-oriented. Families provide essential support systems among the poor and, among the elite, they are the bases of financial and political power. The Philippines is also a proudly Roman Catholic country, much preoccupied with the trappings of a religion which eighty percent of the population practice. During coup attempts and sieges, chaplains pass through the lines to conduct mass for the rebels. Throughout the year penitents whip themselves bloodily and religious processions wend along country roads. Cory Aquino frequently declares she is President because it is God's will, and the Church leader, Cardinal Jaime Sin, believes that the people's power revolution was won and the dictator toppled because the Philippines alone of the world's nations celebrated the Marian Year, the two-thousandth anniversary of the birth of Christ's mother, in 1985. The cult of the Virgin Mother is extremely strong in the Philippines, but even more venerated is the Christ child, *El Niño:* this in a country where as many as thirty thousand children sell themselves on the street.

Over the years there have been numerous drives against child prostitution. Susan Fernandez-Magno says the lack of success reflects the structural roots of the problem. Fernandez-Magno identifies as the "major push factor" for children to peddle themselves as prostitutes the Marcos regime's emphasis on rapid but peripheral industrialization. The prolifer-

ation of agribusiness firms led to the extensive displacement
of rural families. Breadwinners, being generally unskilled
and uneducated, usually had to do casual work, when they
could find it.

Compounding this was a rural slump because of bad man-
agement by Marcos's cronies and falling world commodity
prices. The cities and towns became magnets for large-scale
urban migration. But most families who sought a better life
found instead squalor in squatter areas: no water, no sanitation, often no work. Some, from pretty but poor islands and
from the central Luzon plains, gravitated to the highest spot
on the bay in the northern suburbs of Manila, the Smoking
Mountain. This is Manila's garbage dump and it is over six
stories high, despite the fire that burns always, deep in the
rotting heart of the mountain. Benjamin Bacaros, the assis-
tant pastor at the Co-Workers' Baptist Church, at the foot of
the mountain, says that the people live only by faith in God.
This is not quite true: they live by the grace of Manila's garbage. Dump trucks roll in and, even as the rubbish falls, people scrabble through it: scraps of fine meals from the fenced
and guarded enclaves of privilege like Forbes Park, tins, bottles, broken toys, hospital drips and tubing. They work, faces
muffled against the acrid smoke, and sell what they scavenge
to middlemen, making possibly fifteen pesos a day. They
build their tiny huts out of tin, plastic and old canvas signs
(like this one: AT THIRD FLOOR, XMAS SALE). For the house-
proud, old bedsprings make a fine fence for those with tiny
yards.

Six-year-old children work beside bent old ladies, because
for the low-income families on the Smoking Mountain and
elsewhere survival is a family affair. Schoolchildren become
child workers, many of them street hawkers. Hawking pays
little, so many street hawkers become easy recruits for child
prostitution rings.

Internal conditions provided the raw material for child
prostitution; the search for a solution to the Philippines' for-

eign exchange problems in the early 1970s, according to Fernandez-Magno, led the government to promote tourism aggressively. While official campaigns stressed beaches, stunning volcanic scenery and colorful folk festivals, travel agents in countries such as Japan were selling packaged sex tourism. Soon, too, the word spread about child prostitutes by word of mouth, letters, photographs and magazines along the international pedophile networks. Heterosexual tourism is a boon to the pedophiles. Along M. H. Del Pilar Street, young mothers beg with their babies outside the bars or lie in shadows on the pavement sleeping, their bodies shielding tiny forms. These were bar girls, now on the streets; their babies will probably grow up to be street children.

It is extremely difficult to prevent pedophiles from entering the Philippines, and there is a serious lack of manpower and motivation in the policing of their activities. Nor does the Philippines have the resources to get the children off the streets.

It is moving to watch the Lingap staff nurse the scarred children; it is a joy to see children at a street school—a basic open-sided shelter, built beside a busy road near the presidential Malacanang Palace—dance at a graduation party, to see years of street wisdom slipping away.

There is Lydia, who is twelve. She wears a pretty dress and clutches a present given her by the teacher. She also has a ten-peso note which she hands to a social worker. This is the "rollback" on a loan which enabled the family to buy a pushcart for vending. Her family does not live far away. We can follow her down a narrow path between high walls and there is a cluster of shanties. They are approached on stepping-stones through stagnant, noxious, smelly, rubbish-strewn water. There is a tap, some distance away, but there are no toilets. People wrap their waste in newspaper and carry it to a bridge over a canal. (Every river, stream and canal in Manila is biologically dead.) Lydia's parents came from the southern Bicol Province to live on the edge of survival in the capital. The vendor cart is a rickety vehicle for their hopes, but it is something, and Lydia, who wants nothing to do with the streets or men, is learning to be a child.

But Lingap, which put Bong on the path out of prostitution, can cope with only a relative handful of cases and there are only a few street schools. The government's strategy of reintegrating street children with their families and of trying to ensure that the families have stable livelihoods is clearly correct. But family impoverishment and child prostitution share the same structural roots.

The 1986 ousting of Ferdinand Marcos is popularly described in the Philippines as a "revolution." People were properly proud of what had happened and there was a lot of bravery—the bravery of ordinary people who flinched from threatened danger, scattered, then forced themselves into position again. But revolution should be a shattering of old molds and structures so that there can be a rebuilding. In the Philippines, however, there was to an extent simply a changing of the elite families. Those who fell out of favor with Ferdinand Marcos and saw their power, influence and affluence diminish have attempted to fill the vacuum left by those favored "crony" families who fled or who have fallen from favor in their turn. Aquino candidates who are dedicated reformers have won important governorship and local government posts, but Aquino coalition power brokers have done deals with members of Marcos's old regime.

Most important, in congressional elections in 1987 seventy percent of the House of Representatives seats went to candidates from landowning families—which does not encourage the belief that there will be meaningful land reform in the Philippines. Poverty and the evils that spring from it, such as child prostitution, are to an extent rooted in the semifeudalism of the rural Philippines.

I saw Maleni Arguelles eight months after the great revolution. She sat in a cot in the malnutrition ward of the hospital in Bacolod, the provincial capital, unsmiling, unblinking, a tiny statue, a haunting, almost ethereal presence. Hunger had eaten her away until skin clung to bone. At three she weighed thirteen pounds when she should have been forty. Perhaps the doctors and nurses managed to nurse her body back to life and health; but what about her mind?

Maleni was one of about two hundred thousand malnourished children in Negros. More than two years after the coming of Cory Aquino there are a hundred and eighty thousand of them, sixty percent of the province's children—and this in a land which, as the Catholic Church's Bishop Antonio Fortich says, is not Africa, is not famine country. "There is food, but no money." Nor, worries Bishop Fortich, is there much sign of land reform.

In the election campaign of 1986 I went to a hacienda under Canlaon volcano owned by an enlightened man. He had loaned land to his workers. They tended their corn and ignored the election. Their leaders, Bobby Tomolin and Rudolfo Villanueva, said: "It is just a drama, a play for us. All elections are. Politicians and promises are nothing to us. Cory Aquino and the opposition cannot help. They cannot help because they come from the highest people. They have guns and goons and riches too. They do not come from the workers."

Cory Aquino's hand-picked choice for governor of Negros, Bitay Lacson, is dedicated, energetic and caring. He has a fifteen-year master plan for the revival of Negros. No one doubts President Aquino's own sincerity. She has said her family's huge (in Filipino terms) holding, the Hacienda Luisita in central Luzon, will be part of a land reform program. But real land reform seems a long way off and fifteen years is time enough for another generation of children to be pushed by poverty into prostitution. The mini-Marshall Plan proposed by U.S. congressman Stephen Solarz to give the

Philippines a billion dollars for five years will help. But the children will still suffer for some time yet. More will be brutalized by prostitution and ravaged by malnutrition; more will be robbed of childhood and of life.

In 1990 child prostitution exists on a large scale in most parts of the world. The various laws and international covenants designed to check it are having very little effect.

The most conservative estimates suggest that many hundreds of thousands of children are involved, that these numbers may be increasing, particularly among boys, and that ever younger children are being used. Some are now as young as five. Child prostitution is not confined, as is sometimes assumed, to Southeast Asia but is common in all countries where other forms of prostitution exist. In the United States alone, more than three hundred thousand boys are believed to be prostitutes and children have been found in brothels in New York, Chicago, New Orleans, Dallas and Los Angeles.

In Asian countries the children who become prostitutes are those from the most destitute urban families and poor rural families. They are lured to the cities by recruiters who promise them work and agree to leave part of any future wages with their families. Once they reach the city, the children are forced into prostitution, most often with tourists. Tourism is the third largest source of GNP in Thailand, and the fourth largest in the Philippines. Prostitution is therefore a major employer of people and has created powerful interest groups. Where it is so well established, child prostitution proves extremely hard to eradicate.

In Western countries child prostitutes tend to be runaways; in Latin America, street children. In both places children turn to prostitution as a way of earning a living.

The sex tourism for which Thailand, the Philippines, South Korea, Indonesia, Taiwan and Sri Lanka are now notorious started in the 1950s and grew out of the recreation centers set up around the military bases during the Korean and Vietnamese wars. When the American soldiers went home, the tourists took their place. Travel agencies in the United States, Japan and Western Europe today offer package tours in which the price of a child prostitute has already been included. These sex tours are advertised in travel guides published by pedophile and homosexual rings, and give advice on how to find a child prostitute and how much to pay him or her. It has been shown that sex tourism of this kind seldom benefits the country in which it happens, in that much of the money earned remains with the travel agent.

The trafficking of children is known to take place from Thailand into Malaysia, from Burma into Thailand, from Nepal into India and from the Philippines and Thailand into Hong Kong, with procurers selling children to brothels and pedophile organizations acquiring children for their members. Child pornography is illegal in all European countries, but that does not stop it being available under the counter and from mail-order firms. It has been estimated that in the United States tens of thousands of children are used in the production of pornography. Child prostitution on such a scale exists not because of any tradition, or because the legislation that could control it is lacking, or because of cruelty or perversion on the part of parents, but as a result of the political and economic changes that followed the Second World War. It appeared in answer to a demand, and that demand keeps it alive today, catered for by people who in the process are making a great deal of money.

C.M.

11

Children with AIDS

in the Bronx, U.S.A.

Sergei Boissier

It is a strange disease: the mother looks at her child and wonders, Who will die first?

As of August 1989 there were 102,621 reported cases of AIDS in the United States. Of those, 1,736 were children under the age of thirteen. It is estimated that the number of children who carry the human immunodeficiency virus responsible for AIDS but who as of yet have not reported any symptoms is three to four times greater. To date, 944 children have died of AIDS.

In New York City one out of every sixty-one children born has been exposed to the virus prenatally. Most of these infants hail from the Bronx, which has the highest drug population in the country. Their mothers are infected with the AIDS virus by using dirty needles to inject heroin or through intercourse with men who are intravenous drug abusers. The rate of in utero transmission from pregnant mother to unborn child is approximately fifty percent.

Some of the infants show no signs of the virus six to eighteen months following birth, but most go on to develop full-blown AIDS. They suffer from a vast array of afflictions: brain diseases and mental retardation, neurological impairments, pneumonia, kidney failure, heart malfunctions . . . Common childhood diseases like chicken pox and measles can kill them. Many never gain the ability to walk or talk, or they lose these skills as the disease progresses. Because of their system's inability to absorb nutrients, many starve to death, their emaciated, bloated bodies wasting away in hospital wards, in many cases surrounded by strangers because their mothers have either abandoned them or died themselves.

The life span of these children averages eighteen months from the onset of the disease. Celeste is one of the "lucky" ones: at eleven, she holds the record for being the longest surviving child with AIDS, having outlived her mother, father and brother, all of whom have died of AIDS. Both she and her brother Eddy were born infected with the virus, the children of two parents addicted to heroin. Celeste is a survivor.

When she is not hospitalized, Celeste lives with her grandmother. Although she has suffered from AIDS since the age of two, it was only two years ago that she discovered the reason for her suffering. She was walking by a newsstand and saw her face on the cover of a national news magazine, with the words "Children with AIDS" written across the top. She did not register surprise, only anger; for years she had been in and out of the hospital, receiving weekly gamma globulin treatments or recovering from the latest bout of illness, but no one had ever told her why.

To Celeste and many other children, Albert Einstein College of Medicine Hospital is almost home. Located in the Bronx, its Comprehensive Family AIDS Center is the foremost center for pediatric AIDS research and treatment in the country. Dr. Arye Rubinstein, the first to identify AIDS in children in 1979, oversees a large team of researchers, and Anita Septimus runs the accompanying social work program. They have enhanced and prolonged the lives of hundreds of children through a combination of aggressive gamma globulin therapy, which helps kill the numerous bacterial infections that affect children with AIDS (as opposed to adults with AIDS, who suffer principally from viral infections), and consistent, compassionate counseling and patient advocacy.

Geographically, the clinic is well placed. The Bronx has the largest number of adults and children with AIDS in the Western Hemisphere, surpassed only by the AIDS epidemic in several central African countries. Unlike their African counterparts, most of the infected children in the Bronx are the products of generations of drug and alcohol abuse. There are exceptions, of course: some children are exposed to the AIDS virus through blood transfusions, others through sexual contact with an infected relative.

Einstein's pediatric AIDS clinic provides the full range of medical services, in addition to extensive counseling, outreach and other social services. One of the most important services it provides is a mothers' group, where HIV-positive natural mothers and their healthy foster counterparts share their frustrations and fears, their anger and hope.

Annie, a frail black woman in her thirties, is a recovering alcoholic and drug addict who has been attending the group since her eighteen-month-old baby died two months earlier.

"I was using a new Tupperware device to cut carrots. I wasn't used to it, and I cut my finger and broke the skin. And I realized, We can't eat this, because it's my blood. And it's not just my blood, it's everyone's blood.

"I am a recovering alcoholic/drug addict and I desire righteousness. The thoughts will come but I don't want to go back to it.

"My heroin habit started when I was sixteen and I started drinking when I was nineteen, after having gotten involved in a sick relationship. I'm from a family of alcoholics, so it was nothing new to them.

"My baby was born July 15. She was a precious baby. I didn't shoot up when I was pregnant with her; I was only sniffing and drinking and sleeping with other guys to pay for the drugs.

"When she was born I took her to the shelter. She was so gorgeous, so pretty. Is this my baby? I couldn't believe it. I wanted to have a happy home for her. Like normal people. Like 'Father Knows Best.' Where people make each other happy.

"The baby got a cough and a cold at six months. They took the baby away from me and gave her to her father's aunt. A case of neglect: I was staying out for two or three days at a time, drinking and drugging. All of my life my feelings didn't mean shit.

"The baby had this annoying cough and they wouldn't take her to the doctor. All through the winter and spring, the cough got worse. I kept thinking, Why isn't this cold going away? In May she started breathing real fast and they took her to the hospital and took some tests and it came out she had PCP *[Pneumocystis carinii]*.

"I felt, God is going to take care of it. I'd been in AA and they taught me I wasn't responsible, so I didn't have guilt. But if I'd been drinking I would have killed myself.

"The baby was in the hospital for a month. I went to see her every day. The pain that she went through, all the sticks in her back . . . but she would turn around and give me a smile. It was amazing. I named her Danies Hope. I was very proud of that name: expectation and desire is the meaning of hope. She was precious. I enjoyed her so much.

"I never did care about myself, so I don't think about being positive. One day at a time. Knowing I don't have to do those things anymore is more important than the disease itself.

"This disease is all from the acts, the lust, the selfishness that is here. It's all in the Bible; God is shaking everybody up. I have a personal relationship with God and I can feel His anger toward people who are doing these things. Some people must die in order for others to live.

"People coming together and helping each other. We were knocked around but now it's good. God is at work and I like it. I would go through it all again to have what I have now.

"I wonder about the abortions I had, but He takes the spirits back no matter what. My cousin has a child, and I read that sometimes God gives the spirit back to another child, so maybe that's her.

"I feel that my baby died so that I could live."

The other mothers in the group listen to Annie with a mixture of pity, admiration and disbelief, thinking that she is perhaps a little crazy; her religious beliefs are too extreme, her positive attitude almost surreal, considering all she has gone through. But she is a survivor, and they listen to her. Many of them are in the initial stages of the disease, and they draw comfort from seeing that a woman can still find joy in her life after having survived a miserable childhood, a drug and alcohol problem, two husbands who beat her, a daughter who died, and AIDS itself, which she has.

Others, mainly the foster mothers, are angry at Annie; they

think it is because of people like her that so many children are dying. But for the most part they keep these feelings to themselves, often burying their anger in laughter and shared jokes, like the one about the man who called the AIDS hot line and asked if it was true he could get AIDS from "annual sex."

Of the children that Anita Septimus counsels at Einstein, the majority are in foster care. The foster mothers are the best caretakers, she says, because they do not have AIDS or the guilt associated with transmitting it to their children. Of the natural mothers, some were infected by their partners, and these are the ones with the most anger, but they usually mobilize well to cope. Others are drug users themselves, and they often abandon their children because they cannot stand the guilt.

According to Anita, "Usually it's the sick child that starts the process of discovering infection. Some of the families got their act together four or five years ago, quit drugs, had kids, and now they are hit by this crisis. They are often so devastated that they resort to drugs again. For them to find a raison d'être with this disease . . . I don't know where they find it."

Apart from the mothers and foster mothers, there is a third category of women, known as "extended family caretakers." These are women like Celeste's grandmother, who has lost a daughter and a grandson to AIDS and struggles against all odds to keep Celeste alive. Apart from Celeste, she has five other children and grandchildren to care for. A few years ago her home burned down, and for eight months the family was homeless, going from one friend's apartment to another. Now they have a home again, and at times the grandmother feels fortunate, even optimistic. After all, her granddaughter has lived with this disease longer than any other child in America.

And yet sometimes she despairs: "I wish AIDS would

come and wipe us all out. I have one blanket for six children and I haven't eaten in two days because I don't even have enough money to buy the children breakfast. I sometimes feel like pushing everyone out of the window, me last."

Another "extended family caretaker" is Juana, who cares for her great-grandson Pablo, aged ten. His father is in jail for killing someone—the only time that Pablo saw him was at his mother's funeral. "Why's Daddy in chains?" he asked Juana.

Pablo's mother was a heroin addict, and she died of AIDS. While she was alive, Pablo was very ill, but once she died he became healthy and has had few problems since. Anita believes that this is because, while his mother was alive, she would inject heroin in front of him. He remembers looking in her purse and discovering all the paraphernalia. If you ask him about his mother, he becomes angry and says, "Please don't mention that lady."

Old, hunched up, withered, Juana is one of the heroines; her life has consisted of caring for three generations of abandoned children.

Juana is Hispanic, as are most of the other families at Einstein, because the Bronx's population is overwhelmingly Latin. Although AIDS is a disease that crosses all social and racial barriers, some consider it a prejudiced disease, as it usually afflicts those against whom society is prejudiced: homosexuals, drug addicts and poor Hispanics and blacks. These groups are not more prone to AIDS genetically but rather societally, because of the conditions in which many are raised: devastated neighborhoods, broken families, poverty, malnutrition . . . These factors sometimes lead to a death-wish mentality in which drugs play a natural role. "The drug personality is self-destructive to begin with," says Anita, "because of the experiences of loss that happened early on in life. This explains the flirting with death. So once AIDS sets in, they almost feel it's what they look for. It's like the unavoidable has happened. They have a sense of doom and fatality." As one mother says, "All my life I've been abused and a drug user. Now they tell me I'm gonna die, and I say, 'So what else is new?' "

Linda's attitude is different. Although she is a former drug addict and alcoholic who now has AIDS, she, too, feels fortunate, because only one of her three children has AIDS.

"I had a rough pregnancy with Sandy; I wasn't gaining weight. Two weeks after she was born she hit 105 fever. I took her to the hospital and they did blood gashes and spinal taps. I stayed in the room for the spinal taps and I should have never done it. She was a little thing and they rolled her up in a little ball and stuck the big needle in like a pencil.

"A social worker told me cold as ice that it was AIDS. It wasn't something I should have heard like that. When I found out that I had AIDS, too, I said to myself, I'm going to stay high till I die. My first reaction was to put a pillow over Sandy's face and blow my brains out. I couldn't face the guilt of having a sick baby and knowing that I had given this to my daughter. But then I realized I'm not God.

"She gets a lot of colds and ear infections and she's a little slow, but to look at her you'd never know. She's a very good baby, always happy, wakes up smiling. . . . A few times we thought we were going to lose her because of the fevers. She's come from death's door to where she is today.

"I've gone through a lot of emotional problems, but now I wake up every day and say, thank God I'm here. I've never enjoyed my kids and my life as much as I do now. There are ups and downs, but it comes with the territory, I guess. I try to make the best of it.

"Every time I get a cold, I wonder if this is it. My main concern is: when I die, are my kids going to be okay? I'm scared of dying. I may not have too much time on this earth, so I have to make the best of it. I still can't believe I have AIDS.

"As time goes by, I write down special things I do with the kids and my feelings. I wrote Sandy a letter explaining why I did what I did, so she'll know exactly how I felt when I did it. That's something special, something they can keep for the rest of their lives. I try to write something down every day.

"Last weekend I had to go to the hospital in the middle of the night, and they put me in this room with danger signs all over the door. I heard one nurse say to another, 'I told you not to go in there—you have two kids!' I ran out into the hall and showed them a picture of my three kids and I said, 'This is what I'm leaving behind. I'm an innocent victim, just like you. I didn't do this to me; my husband did this to me.' "

Many of the group's discussions center around the concept of being a victim, for if a mother accepts her status as a victim she need no longer feel guilty. The guilt comes in many forms: some feel guilty for having taken drugs, either before or during pregnancy, others for having slept with men who were addicts. Still others feel guilty because they cannot care for their children properly; they are either too ill to cope or they lack the financial, emotional or familial resources necessary to handle such a crisis. AIDS most often happens to those least equipped to handle it: impoverished, broken families who have no insurance, no emotional stability, no education, little or no outside support and no motivation to succeed. As Anita says, "In the individual the AIDS virus attacks the immune system, leaving the victim exposed to a variety of opportunistic infections. In the social body the process is reversed: the virus preys on communities whose defenses have already been weakened by homelessness, unemployment, illiteracy, crime, disease, alcohol and drugs."

Not all the mothers are from ravaged inner cities. Mary lives in an affluent town in Fairfield County, Connecticut. Her husband owns a popular restaurant, and so they keep their daughter's condition a secret, because they fear that the restaurant would go out of business were people to find out that Monica has AIDS. Mary and her husband adopted her as an infant, and shortly thereafter she started getting high fevers with alarming frequency. After extensive testing, it was discovered that she had AIDS, at that time a relatively new and unheard-of disease, especially among children. Aged seven, she has survived many bouts of illness and seems to be stable, for now. Her gamma globulin treatment—the primary method of treatment for children with AIDS—is administered through a shunt at the top of her skull, because all the veins in her arms have long since been used up.

"I don't think I would have adopted her if I'd known," says Mary, a practical, friendly woman in her thirties. "Right now she's happy and healthy, but when they first told me she had a year to live, I thought, How am I going to survive this? The answer was, by thinking of the things that would be good in my life once she was gone. I resented the fact that she was still around. I'd mourned enough already. I wanted to go on with my life.

"Now I don't resent her as much. She isn't as confining. She's survived most of the major illnesses associated with this disease: Parkinson's, pneumonia, herpes zoster, chicken pox, big blisters, diarrhea, severe vertigo. . . . She's the big experiment. Now they have a shunt in her skull to feed gamma globulin directly into the brain. I don't know if I'd go any further; there's a limit to what I'll put a child through.

"She's really starting to progress. The doctors are thrilled; she's a 'success story.' But everything's up in the air; they really don't know anything. If we keep her body healthy, there's a good possibility she won't die from neurological problems, but there are so many other possibilities. . . ."

Indeed, it is the vast range of directions that this disease can take that makes the medical process so complicated and questionable. Seeing Monica with a needle and tube coming out of her skull raises the question of whether the process is worth it, since AIDS is considered by most to be one hundred percent fatal. Yes, the doctors have been able to buy time

—often several years—for children like Celeste and Monica, but at what cost?

The answer, for many, is the periods of relative health and joy experienced in between the bouts of illness and the long hospital stays. Grace, for one, gets angry at anyone who questions the validity of trying to keep these children alive. A foster mother who in recent years has cared exclusively for children with AIDS, she currently has two seven-year-old girls who have been with her since infancy.

"When I first got Patricia, the doctor told me she was retarded. She was the first baby I'd ever had that had lumps. I thought she had cancer, because she wasn't growing. I didn't know nothing about AIDS. The only thing I knew was that homosexuals and Haitians got it, and that if you have it, you die.

"When they found out what it was, the agency told me I could give her back! That made me mad—to hell with them.

"Once Patricia started to get better, I said to myself, I wonder if I can bring another AIDS baby home. So that's how Joanna came into my life.

"I've had my frightening moments, but I've been pretty happy. They both look beautiful and that shows the doctors that these kids survive better outside the hospital. No sunshine there, no personal life.

"I call Patricia the little old lady. She thinks she's Diana Ross, but she can't hold a note. She doesn't like to eat much and she has trouble getting up and down stairs. They both care a lot about their appearance, and on Saturdays and Sundays they make me comb their hair special. I feel that's a good thing—caring about how you look. Like a flower.

"I had a third little boy, but I lost him the other day. I cried, but no one can stick him with needles anymore. I told him to look out for my girls up there. That's my way of saying it's all right, but I don't really believe it.

"I pray for a house where I can pay a ninety-nine-year mortgage. I would take them all, but they would have to test positive, because the negative ones have more of a chance to get adopted. I'd be like the old lady who lived in a shoe. . . ."

The question of housing is crucial, for although there are many like Grace—well-intentioned women who would like to care for children with AIDS—few have the resources to do so. Many of the children thus remain in the hospital from birth to death, having never seen the light of day. Others go in and out, depending on their health and the status of their family. If they could talk, and if they knew about the disease, many would be hard pressed to distinguish between the constant physical pain and the various stages of abandonment in which they find themselves. As it is, they are not told anything about AIDS, and so added to the pain and loneliness is a pervasive sense of confusion as to what is happening to them.

"It's a conspiracy of silence," says Anita Septimus, the social worker. "It's a crime not to tell these kids, because on some level they know! We may mask our own truth but children have a sense of truth which is different. I'm convinced they all know what they have, but they also know they have to play the game and stay silent.

"Children who are suffering and dying have a lot to teach adults and this is not happening because of this conspiracy of silence. A lot of them have lost their own parents, but they're not allowed to talk about it. They are dying silently in wards.

"Families and society are engaged in a parallel process of denial. You keep a kid from telling his secret and the kid will become mute. How does it feel to keep a secret like that? It feels like being a Jew during the Holocaust. If we don't get people to accept AIDS and talk about it, we won't be able to do our job properly."

Although a decade has passed since AIDS was first detected, Anita believes that society has made little progress, not only in terms of learning to accept the disease but also in learning how to cope with it. The necessary resources have not been developed: the medical coverage and care, the housing, the education, the understanding. "I was hoping that more people from the general public would join the effort," she says, "but that hasn't happened. My friends still ask me why I'm doing this."

The numbers of children born with AIDS is multiplying at such a rate that any statistic given is soon out of date. "The predictions are horrible," says Anita. "If these numbers are true and people don't change their attitudes, it is going to be a horror story. I am worried that they are going to die in worse poverty than you have ever dreamed of. Unless a vaccine or a cure is found, which I deeply doubt, I see them just getting sicker and poorer, because this disease depletes everything. Have you heard the figures regarding costs? I don't know who is going to take care of that, given our present system."

In the meantime, the children continue to be born with AIDS, and although the lengths of their stories vary, the endings never do. For Anita and others, the challenge is to seek an interpretation that makes sense, that justifies the horror and cruelty of so many young deaths.

"The only way I can feel," says Anita, "is that God has a high plan in mind. We don't understand it now, and we may not understand it in fifteen years, but there has to be a plan.

"With the adults it's horrible, but you tell yourself that at least they've lived their lives. It's terrible for anyone to die young, but at least he's had a life. With the children you can't even say that. It's too sad. The only way I can deal with it is on a deeply mystical level. The biggest changes, the best things that happen to mankind, take place in times of great chaos.

"My sense of justice is really bothered. Anybody who feels that any disease is deserved . . . well, they have a problem. I used to feel a lot of anger but I've moved to a different level of pain. I feel they're in a better world, where they're not suffering. The sadness is there, but the rage is not; I have much more of a sense of acceptance.

"I have a poster at home of a kid who has a look like our kids. They have in their eyes the look of people who have gone through a lifetime. A look of suffering. They've seen and gone through too much. Their eyes are older than their faces. They have beautiful eyes; a beauty that comes from knowing so much. A look from another world.

"I am asked countless times, 'How do you do it?' and I have often wondered how we all do it, since we have been called upon to do a most depressing task—to care for beautiful children who will die ever so quietly on a hospital ward. We are left enraged, tormented, and with that existential sense of the absurdity of life. Why? Why the children?

"One of the kids died this morning. He was going to be put on AZT, and I was telling myself, maybe he's going to be the first success story. They told me he had been sexually abused by his father. He had such a beautiful way of protecting and comforting his desolate mother.

"She buried with her child all the dreams she had had of taking him to the circus, to the zoo, to the beach, to all the beautiful places Adam had planned on seeing with his mom when he got out of the hospital."

Because their numbers are still relatively small, and because they themselves are small—and voiceless—the plight of children with AIDS has yet to reach a wide audience. The public will read with a mixture of fascination and fear the occasional story of a boy in Texas seemingly overcoming the odds by living longer than expected, or of an entire family in Florida thrown out of town because all three children are HIV-positive, but the very appeal of the article lies in its sensationalism, its rarity. Their minds will not accept the prospect of thousands of orphans, abandoned by parents and family, living in overcrowded hospital wards. They cannot envision a city of dying children. That specter is such a contradiction of our image of America—the land of prosperity and opportunity—that we deny its existence.

But the reality of AIDS has a way of outdoing the imagination. It is estimated that by 1991 there could be up to twenty thousand cases of pediatric AIDS in this country. While the adults wonder how these children will be cared for, and in what circumstances they will die, the children suffer in silence and wait: they wait to go home from the hospital, they wait for a mother who will never show up because she is dead, they wait for respite from the unceasing, unrelenting pain, they wait for an explanation, and they wait for death.

Also waiting for death are the street children, the teenagers and preteens who end up on the streets selling their bodies to buy drugs, then doing drugs to be able to cope with having to sell their bodies. These are the children who rarely show up in clinics or hospitals, either because they don't know the clinics exist or because they are scared or they no longer care.

At a forum on street children with AIDS, a social worker describes Johnny, fifteen years old:

"I've watched his sexual practices go from beginning boy-girl first romance to hard-core hustling survival sex. His sexuality: bi, gay, straight, anyone, any time, anywhere. His drugs: crack, alcohol, angel dust. His obsession: death. His means: AIDS.

The number of children with AIDS, until very recently a completely ignored phenomenon, is now known and accepted to be on the rapid increase. Statistics are hard to come by, particularly from those countries where public health programs are blocked by a spirit of denial about homosexuality. Throughout the Catholic Latin American countries and among Hindu, Moslem and Afro-Caribbean communities there are no reliable figures on pediatric AIDS, though the countries known to be worst affected lie in central, eastern and southern Africa and parts of the Caribbean.

By the same token, health officials agree that even in the West people were noticeably slow to observe the spread of the disease to children. It is barely ten years since the first cases were reported from the United States. As of the end of June 1989, according to figures put out by the World Health Organization, 570 cases of pediatric AIDS had been reported in Europe, with the highest numbers in France, Spain and Italy. The true figures are certainly much higher. In the U.S.S.R., where up until 1985 AIDS was still believed to have been created by Western scientists working on germ warfare, there are now said to be over seven hundred adult and child cases. How many are actually children is not known. In 1989, the youngest HIV-positive case was said to be three-year-old Sasha Semin, infected by dirty needles at Volgograd state hospital.

In babies, AIDS is virtually always the result of infection transmitted by the mother during pregnancy. (WHO has said that it believes the risk of transmission by breast feeding to be extremely small.) Infants born to infected women—usually, but perhaps surprisingly not always, unaware of their own infection at the time they became pregnant—have approximately a one in two chance of being HIV-infected. Research carried out in Scotland and elsewhere has shown that it takes fifteen to eighteen months to confirm whether a baby will be able to reject its mother's antibodies. There is some evidence that babies born to otherwise generally healthy women with AIDS will find it easier to do so. However, since there is no cure for AIDS, babies who are infected, and do not fight it off, are usually very small, grow slowly and suffer from chronic diarrhea, a fever and a persistent cough. They have short lives. Most are dead by the age of two.

In older children, a major cause of infection is transfusion with contaminated blood given to treat hemophilia or anemia resulting from malaria or malnutrition. While this danger has passed in Western countries, where blood is now screened, it continues unchecked in many developing countries, as does infection with AIDS by contaminated needles and syringes. The same is true, of course, among teenage drug users everywhere.

In the cities with large numbers of street children, like São Paulo,

Bogotá or Mexico City, the virus has invaded this world of orphans, runaways and abandoned children, spreading particularly fast through the promiscuous homosexual relationships almost universal among the child gangs. Health officials and governments, appalled by what they suspect is happening, are tending to look away, saying that in this, as in all matters relating to street children, nothing can be done. No one knows, in 1990, how many of these children have died, or may be dying, of the disease.

C.M.

Postscript: Celeste died at the end of 1989 as this book was going to press. Dressed in her white Communion dress and surrounded by her favorite stuffed animals, she looked peaceful and relieved in the white casket, despite her bloated face and emaciated body. Celeste was one of the first children to be born with AIDS, and at eleven years old, was one of the longest survivors. But she is only one of many to have lived with AIDS from birth to death. For her grandmother, the ordeal is finally over.

B O O K   M A R K

The text of this book was set in the typeface Janson
and the display was set in Spectra Extra Bold
by Berryville Graphics, Berryville, Virginia.

It was printed on 55lb Glatfelter, an acid-free paper,
and bound by Berryville Graphics, Berryville, Virginia.

Designed by Richard Oriolo

DATE DUE

APR. 1	APR 0 2 '93		

HIGHSMITH 45-220